PRAISE FOR *THE*

"This is a warm, wonderful, inspiring book that entertains and motivates at the same time."
—**Brian Tracy, Motivational Speaker, Entrepreneur and Success Expert, and International Best Selling Author of over 50 Books, including *Eat That Frog!***

"When you have a passion but no formula to follow, *The Barefoot Spirit* will inspire and direct you and your energy. This is a book that shows those with the true entrepreneur's spirit how not to get stuck on the small things and make decisions from the soul. This book is as unpretentious as the wine they produced."
—**Sonya Gavankar, Broadcast Journalist, Face of the Newseum**

"I picked up Michael and Bonnie's book chronicling the Barefoot story with the intention of a quick scan and found myself spending the better part of a Sunday thoroughly enjoying myself reading it cover-to-cover. I believe students will find *The Barefoot Spirit* both a great read and an important lesson in creative problem solving in the face of critical challenges."
—**Pat Dickson, 2013 President, United States Association for Small Business and Entrepreneurship, and Associate Professor, Wake Forest University, North Carolina**

"In 1986, Michael Houlihan and Bonnie Harvey started Barefoot Wine—in their laundry room. Through the years, they managed and marketed it into a product that was eventually sold to E. & J. Gallo. *The Barefoot Spirit* confidently guides any start-up company to success."
—**David Bruce Smith, Publisher and Author of *American Hero: John Marshall, Chief Justice of the United States***

"I thoroughly enjoyed *The Barefoot Spirit*. I will make it required reading because it tells a lovely story, and it embodies so much of the entrepreneurial mindset. I loved the 'voice' of the book and storytelling is such a wonderful way to communicate. I believe students will find it a fun addition to their library and in the process they will learn the most important lessons of entrepreneurship!"

—Rebecca White, Professor, Entrepreneurship, and James W. Walter Distinguished Chair of Entrepreneurship, and Director, Entrepreneurship Center, The University of Tampa, John H. Sykes College of Business, and 2012 President, United States Association for Small Business and Entrepreneurship (USASBE)

"Michael and Bonnie's book is a must-read for anyone looking to start a business that will make it in today's economy. Whether you are starting a company from scratch or investing your money or someone else's, *The Barefoot Spirit* illustrates the hands-on and no-cost best practices that will make your company a success."

—Andrea Keating, Founder, The International Video Crew Staffing Firm

"As an entrepreneur, publicist, and publisher, I found great insight in *The Barefoot Spirit*. Michael Houlihan and Bonnie Harvey's tips on how to survive on less than a shoestring are clever, practical, and, best of all, provide a good giggle to any entrepreneur in panic mode. This book is one that I'm already recommending to my readers, colleagues, and clients in start-up mode—as well as those who are ready to take their business to the next level. Here's to going Barefoot!"

—Hope Katz Gibbs, Publisher of *Be Inkandescent* Magazine

"What I like best about the book is that Houlihan and Harvey lead by example and explain how they took an idea and a little blood, sweat, and wine, and turned it into a multimillion-dollar brand that is now a household name. Talk about a financial gold mine."

—Bryan Beatty, Certified Financial Planner, and a Partner at the Financial Planning Firm, Egan, Berger & Weiner

"Michael and Bonnie took a chance on potentially losing sales when they supported our cause with Barefoot Cellars in the early 1990s. Their co-promotion with the League to Save Lake Tahoe took a strong position on a very controversial issue involving the development of the Lake Tahoe Basin. They helped us get the word out about our cause through wine shops, markets, and restaurants in California."

—Darcie Goodman-Collins, Ph.D., Executive Director, League to Save Lake Tahoe

"Michael and Bonnie started the tradition of Worthy Cause Marketing and for well over a decade used their winery, Barefoot Cellars, to support the Mono Lake Committee's grassroots efforts. Their approach helped spread the word about protection, restoration, and education at Mono Lake—inspiring people to get out and get involved."

—Geoff McQuilkin, Executive Director, Mono Lake Committee

"*The Barefoot Spirit* will appeal to entrepreneurs, business people, non-profit leaders, and anyone who is passionate about activism, unlikely success stories, and—oh yes—wine. In content, message, and even writing style, it's smart, funny, and self-deprecating."

—Michael Tate, Board President, San Francisco Gay Men's Chorus

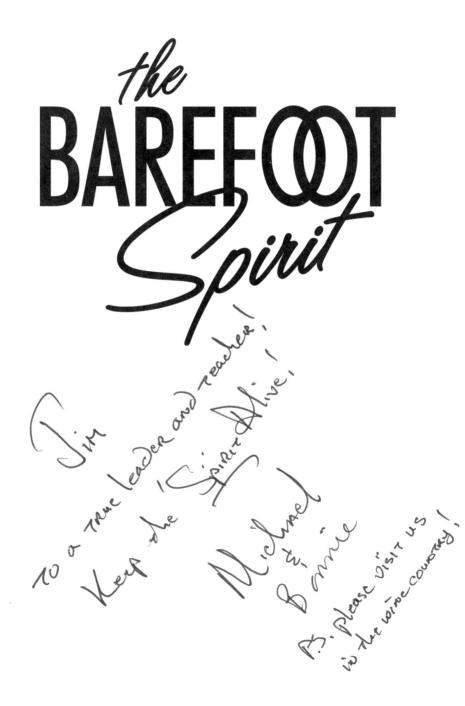

the
BAREF☮︎☮︎T
Spirit

Jim

To a true leader and teacher!

Keep the "Spirit Alive!

Michael
&
Bonnie

B. Please visit us
in the wine country!

the BAREFOOT Spirit

How Hardship, Hustle, and Heart
Built America's #1 Wine Brand

BAREFOOT WINE FOUNDERS

MICHAEL HOULIHAN & BONNIE HARVEY

WITH RICK KUSHMAN

"THE BAREFOOT SPIRIT: How Hardship, Hustle, and Heart Built America's #1 Wine Brand"

Published by Evolve Publishing, Inc.
www.evolvepublishing.com

Cover design by Brand Navigation (*www.brandnavigation.com*) inspired by original cover concept by Thomas Anderson (*www.209designshop.com*)
Cover illustration by Jef Gunion (*www.guniondesign.com*)
Story illustrations by Sidney Marra (*www.whiteboardanimation.com*)
Author photographs by Robert Pierce (*www.rpstudios.com*)
Back cover photograph by Jennifer Wall

978-0-9882245-4-4 paperback
978-0-9882245-5-1 ePUB
978-0-9882245-6-8 ePDF

Printed in the United States of America

10 9 8 7 6 5 4 3 2

This book is dedicated to Randy Arnold who embodies the Barefoot spirit every day of his life—by loving generously, sharing his playful personality, and genuinely caring for people and the environment. We owe him our deepest gratitude for his loyal, wonderful friendship over the decades, during the best of times and the toughest of times. His mission in life is to make the world a better place, and judging by his selfless contributions to all the non-profits he supports professionally and personally, and by all the lives he's touched by simply being Randy, it's completely clear that he has succeeded.

Contents

Acknowledgments

We give our heartfelt thanks to these people for supporting us and nurturing the Barefoot spirit:

Rick Kushman, who took our crazy stories and made them a fun read. We thank him also for his stubborn insistence that the writing style remain easy and conversational, and his unconditional refusal to ever put "to whom" in print.

Karen Kreiger, our publisher, for her ability to keep track of all the loose ends and keep her wits about her when ours went out the window.

Dottie DeHart, our publicist, who kept us in tears of laughter with her humor and her charming North Carolina accent.

All our distributors, for the hard-knocks education they gave us, their appreciation for our hard work and the opportunities they gave us to grow.

All our retail buyers, from the national chains to the mom-and-pops, who believed that a wine with a foot on it would not only sell but would make them a profit.

The hundreds of non-profits and community fundraisers who helped us get the word out about our wine, and who helped us to support our core beliefs through our business.

All the Barefoot Wine lovers who told us what they liked and genuinely appreciated being able to pronounce every word on the label.

And Joe Gallo for his inspiration and friendship through the years.

A Special Shout Out:

To Steve Wallace, The Big Toe, who kept the Barefoot Spirit alive after we relinquished the brand. He became the fearless leader of the Barefooters, and together they grew the brand inspired by Steve's enthusiasm, direction, and faith in the Barefoot spirit.

And, of course, all the Barefooters whose hard work resulted in the phenomenal success of Barefoot Wines, and who crossed the finish line with us:

Barefoot's Sales Team:

Curt Anderson—No. CA Merchandise Manager
Randy Arnold—Director of Brand Development
Phil Aiello—Michigan Sales Manager
Eric Dorton—North Texas Sales Manager
Bill Oakley—So. CA and So. NV Sales Manager
Dan Butkus—NY, NJ, DE, and Philly Sales Manager
Ron Wagner—Northwest Sales Manager
Brian Bostwick—No. CA, No. NV, and HI Sales Manager
Dennis Wheeler—MN, IA, NE, ND, and SD Sales Manager
Scott Markley—IL and WI Sales Manager
Bob Bowditch—Heartland Sales Manager

ACKNOWLEDGMENTS

Steve Wood—Mid-Atlantic Sales Manager
Shelley Saunders—New England Sales Manager
Andrew Cruse—Colorado Sales Manager
Kirk Tomiser—National Training Manager
Craig Johnson—Southwest Sales Manager
Matt Reed—South Texas Sales Manager
Jon Bourdais—Louisiana Sales Manager
Tim Clayton—AL and GA Sales Manager
A.J. Carras—NC, SC, and TN Sales Manager
Andy Broden—Florida Sales Manager
James Solie—No. CA Chain Merchandise Manager

Barefoot's Sales Support Team:

Jennifer Wall—V.P. of Operations and Winemaking
Doug McCorkle—Chief Financial Officer
Martin Jones—Executive V.P., Commercial Director
Aaron Fein—Business Development Director
Gary Arkoff—Account Executive
Deborah Sherman—Logistics and Compliance Manager
Adrienne Barner—Marketing Manager
Jeff Sherman—Sales Support Manager
Dennis Johnson—Wine Club and POS Materials Manager
Katrina Small—Marketing Design Manager
Cain Adams—Merchandising Materials Manager
Charlene Ragatz—Office Manager
Brook Gorham—Materials and Production Planner
Robyn Harris—Accountant
Toni Anderson—Accounting Assistant
Tricia Siegel—Data Analyst
Noel Plumb—Systems Administrator

Introduction

They had a saying at Barefoot that says a lot about the people who created one of America's most recognizable wine brands: You sell more wine wearing a funny hat.

It's simple, true, and something many wineries would never have admitted in the mid-1980s when Michael Houlihan and Bonnie Harvey started Barefoot Cellars and launched the Barefoot Spirit. In the mid-'80s, that idea was nearly revolutionary.

Michael and Bonnie didn't know they were defying convention because they didn't know what the wine industry's conventions were. They started in the laundry room of a rented farmhouse with no money, no wine experience, and no clue about what they were getting into—and that was one key to their success.

The tale of Barefoot Cellars is like no other in wine and it's a landmark in American business. It's a rags-to-riches story in the first degree, a chronicle of how outsiders followed their own path, believed in their ideas and each other, and changed an industry.

Barefoot transformed American wine so completely that it's hard to remember how staid and unimaginative it once was. Before Barefoot, wine marketing and wine labels were as serious as a masters seminar on viticulture. Wine seemed exclusive, unwelcoming, almost foreboding. Barefoot's success brought fun and energy and lightheartedness to wine, and it led the way for animals and art, for bikes, for silly pictures, for embracing everyone. It helped make wine into something that was approachable and egalitarian and thoroughly American.

The Barefoot Spirit is also a close-up of the American entrepreneurial spirit with a West Coast smile, an ode to originality and perseverance, and just as much, one terrific tale.

But this book is more than just the story of Barefoot's unlikely success, it's also a guidebook for any entrepreneur. The against-the-odds triumph of Michael and Bonnie and Barefoot Cellars is a business lesson in creative thinking, optimism, flexibility, using your lack of money and experience, and maybe most of all, in how to learn from the astounding number of mistakes you will make.

This is also a lesson about people. It shows how independent thinkers can succeed, and how listening to everyone—customers, allies, employees, and each other—is the first way to solve problems. Plus, it's a reminder never to be afraid, if the moment is right, to put on a funny hat.

A couple notes about this book: *The Barefoot Spirit* is Michael and Bonnie's story as they and dozens of other people told it to me. But this is not an attempt at pure journalism; it's an act of collaboration, a way for them to tell what they learned and how they learned it.

The conversations among people in the story are, obviously, reconstructed. They came from interviews with as many people as possible. We stand by the gist of them all, but we are not pretending they are accurate word for word. They're in the book so you can understand more about the people who played a role in Barefoot's story.

Finally, I'm doing the writing because, honestly, I've fallen for Michael and Bonnie as businesspeople and just as people. They're creative, quirky, and thoughtful, they stand for something, they love each other, and they listen to everyone. I'm doing the writing because Michael Houlihan, Bonnie Harvey, and the Barefoot Spirit are all worth getting to know.

—Rick Kushman

Many people have been asking us to tell our story because it's such an important chapter in American wine. We chose Rick to write it after we learned the first time we met that he's one of us—a Barefooter at heart. He's a journalist who's covered politics, business, and Hollywood, but for us what matters most is that he's a wine writer who writes and teaches about wine like he actually enjoys it.

He thinks like we do: Wine should be fun, friendly, and interesting, but it shouldn't be scary. We also think the same about business and life. We all believe your values should be apparent in everything you do. So, simply enough, we chose Rick because he, too, has the Barefoot Spirit.

And we agree that Barefoot's story is a significant step in the evolution of wine in America. Our success gave the wine industry and wine drinkers permission to have fun, to be inclusive, and to believe there is not just one way to sell or enjoy wine.

We also want to tell our story because we want to share what we learned. We want entrepreneurs in any industry to know it's not going to be easy, but there is a way to persevere and succeed.

And we want people to know, that even while you're building your business, you can still give back and help the causes you hold dear.

We created—discovered, really—something we called Worthy Cause Marketing, because we had no money for advertising or much of anything at the beginning. So we found a way to support both Barefoot and the people and causes we cared about. We aided hundreds of non-profits with our wine, energy, and time, and their members spread the word about Barefoot. As we grew, we never did advertise, we just supported more worthy causes, and they made Barefoot one of America's most popular brands.

Worthy Cause Marketing was a key piece of Barefoot's success, but there were many other pieces that we discovered, too, through trial and, often, error.

We always tried to be mentors when we were running Barefoot, and now we have the chance to pass along to everyone the lessons that came so hard. There are too many to list, but they include everything from how to survive when you're small and how to turn your debts into assets, to how to grow into a national brand, how to create a company culture that works for you, and how to make your values part of your success. We believe this book can help good people avoid some of the pitfalls and the growing pains we experienced. We learned the hard way; you don't have to.

Within our story are the lessons all entrepreneurs need to survive, to thrive, to be successful, and to give their own brands and companies a spirit of fun, purpose, innovation, and heart. That's the Barefoot Spirit, and we believe it can help anyone with a dream.

—Michael Houlihan and Bonnie Harvey

Chapter One

How Hard Could It Be?

Michael Houlihan drove to the far end of the Piggly Wiggly parking lot in Columbia, South Carolina. That's what he did in every parking lot, and it's what all good salespeople do, park as far away as they can. The spots by the door are for customers. Store managers notice the courtesy.

It was mid-May. The sky loomed thick and close, a dark, steely greenish gray. Michael didn't so much see the clouds as feel them—hot, heavy, and steamy. It was the kind of day that discourages movement. Ah, spring in the American South.

Michael is a tall man, 6-foot-2, a bit gangly, with reddish hair and an air that says he spent some time on a surfboard. He was wearing a dark suit, carrying Barefoot wine samples in a bag over his shoulder, and holding a large, foam-core sign with a 5-foot-tall purple foot. This was not a guy they saw every day at the Piggly Wiggly.

When Michael had driven up, a dark-haired teenager was collecting stray shopping carts and wheeling them back to the store. By the time Michael started lugging his wine and sign across the 30-yard lot, the kid had abandoned his carts and was sprinting for the supermarket door.

"Hey buddy," he said as he flashed past Michael, "you better run."

Say what? Run? Michael looked left and right. All he saw were parked cars. Did he hear the kid right?

Then, *BOOM!* The thunderclap almost knocked him over. Michael felt it in his spine. "Whoa," he thought, "was that it?" He stood there shaking it off. Maybe five seconds later, it began to rain. Not gentle, soothing, wimpy spring rain like he knew in Northern California. This was rain from a fire hose or a falling river. Buckets and buckets in seconds. Drops that felt like walnuts. "Got it," Michael thought.

In seconds, his suit was soaked. His tie was soaked. His shoes and socks and pockets filled with water. He started running for the store.

Then came the wind. Huge, uneven blasts, blowing hard from the left, then hard from the right. Michael's sign turned into a sail. It yanked him west halfway across the parking lot. Then it pulled him east. Then another gust pulled him west again. He was hanging on, figuring if he let go, the sign would land in Georgia. Left, right, lurch, wobble, just don't let go.

Inside the store, people had stopped. No one was checking out or bagging groceries or moving. They were watching this tall, fair-haired California-looking guy in a suit, getting hammered by rain and staggering back and forth, wrestling with a giant purple foot. He disappeared out of view for a moment, then re-appeared and heaved off in the other direction. He was barely making progress toward the door.

"Wet mop up front!"

The whole show took maybe four minutes. Michael tottered into the store, through the automatic doors, and just stood for a second, catching his breath. He was leaking water onto the floor like a broken barrel. He looked up. The whole store, the shoppers, the clerks, the bag boys, the kid who'd been pushing carts stared at him wide-eyed. No one moved. Just people staring.

Michael stared back, dazed and dripping. That was the only sound, the dripping. No cash registers, no rustling, no chatter. Just drip, drip, drip. Above them, out of the ceiling, that supermarket mechanical voice broke in. "Wet mop," it said. "Up front."

A few seconds later, the store manager, a tall man with a Southern gentleman's manner, walked up to Michael.

"Son," he said, "I know you have something to sell me. And I know you want to sell it real bad."

"Yes sir," Michael said. "I do."

Before there were wine labels with dogs and bears and kangaroos, before there were viral campaigns or guerrilla marketing on any scale, before the wine industry had any sense of humor, there was Barefoot.

This is the story of Barefoot's unlikely rise, its against-all-odds survival, and its surprising impact on a wine world that had not yet learned to smile. It is a snapshot of the American spirit California style. It's about following your own path and having faith in your ideas, and about how hard work, creativity, good humor, and concern for people can both create a special kind of business and change the world.

And it's the story of Michael Houlihan and Bonnie Harvey, Michael's business partner and long-time love. They stumbled into the wine business trying to help a friend. They started in a laundry room, with piles of debt and only a hint of what they were in for. But, as their new friend at the Piggly Wiggly could see, they always wanted to sell their wine real bad.

Two decades later, they had created an iconic national brand and a company with a big-hearted, cheerful soul. Along the way, they came to the aid of hundreds of worthy causes across the country, made friends for life in the wine industry, and helped make the world of wine something it rarely had been before—fun.

Their tale is a modern success story, and it's a parable for this new age of the entrepreneur. This book is also an operating manual filled with ideas and guidance for any business— beyond the rather obvious advice to stay out of South Carolina thunderstorms.

Michael and Bonnie started Barefoot Cellars in the mid-1980s, but the name goes back to 1965 and an old plumbing warehouse along the San Francisco Bay.

It began with Davis Bynum, a former newspaper reporter and editor, who started a winery on a busy street in an industrial stretch of Albany, a blue-collar town on the north end of Berkeley. He was, at least metaphorically, about as far from wine country as you could get. This was the '60s, and if the area around him was headed for one kind of revolution, Davis was on the road toward something almost as radical.

There was nothing close to a fine wine industry in California, or America, in 1965. (It wasn't until 1966 that Robert Mondavi built his winery in Napa Valley—and though Mondavi had been in the wine business and in Napa for decades, people called him crazy for constructing a new place.) But Davis loved wine. He had been making it at home for a dozen years and wanted to try the wine business, though he would tell anyone who asked, "Any idiot can start a winery, but you have to be a tireless idiot."

He bought quality grapes from Sonoma County and bottled some quality wines. People who knew him as a home winemaker knew about a slightly less distinguished wine he had made that he playfully called Barefoot Bynum. Those friends may have liked the name more than the actual wine, but they convinced Bynum to make Barefoot Bynum at his new "winery" along with his better offerings.

So Davis resurrected Barefoot Bynum, brewed it up from low-cost grapes, and sold it in gallon jugs. And because Davis was both a guy with a sense of humor and a sense of his market, he called it the "Chateau La Feet of California wine," just to be sure people knew the stuff was not particularly serious.

The problem for Davis—and it was a problem Michael and Bonnie would battle on a much larger scale—was that many of the costs of making, bottling, and shipping wine are the same whether the wine is pricey or not. The taxes, the costs of glass, storage, packing, trucking and more don't change much no matter what's in the bottle, and those fairly fixed costs added up to more than Davis could charge for his jugs.

In 1973, Davis moved to Healdsburg in Sonoma County—genuine, beautiful wine country—where he would become one of the pioneers of the Pinot Noir movement in Northern California and particularly the Russian River area. Meanwhile, his accountant kept reminding him that the purpose of being in business was to earn money, not lose it. So in 1974, he stopped making Barefoot Bynum and the name went dormant.

In the spring of 1985, Bonnie and Michael were living in a small, rented farmhouse on a hillside of the MacMurray Ranch in west

Sonoma County wine country above the beautiful Westside Road. They were just over one hill from Davis Bynum's winery, and Michael knew Davis because he was pals with his son, Hampton, going back to their days together in the East Bay.

But Bonnie and Michael were only vaguely connected to the wine industry and they didn't know much about the stuff inside the bottles. Actually, wine scared Bonnie.

She was like many people, especially in the early 1980s. Wine seemed encased in an impenetrable code and culture, and she was embarrassed to ask about it. She couldn't pronounce most grape names and she figured some snoot would make fun of her if she tried. She loved wine country but didn't like feeling that she needed a master's degree to order wine in some restaurants.

But Bonnie knew business, and her company, In Care Of, organized the offices and dealings of a few people in the wine industry, including her friend, Mark Lyon, an accomplished, unassuming winemaker who is now the head of winemaking at Sebastiani Vineyards. Back then, he was already working at Sebastiani, plus he owned 98 acres of grapes in Sonoma County's Alexander Valley. But in 1985, Mark had a problem.

Although Mark was widely respected as a winemaker who brought an artist's outlook to wine, he was never enthralled with the business side of the industry. That's why he hired Bonnie to handle his office, and how she found that one of his biggest grape-buying customers, a winery in Alexander Valley named Souverain, owed him for his 1984 crop. Souverain was rolling toward bankruptcy and had not paid for about 300 tons of Mark's grapes.

Michael at the time was working around the edges of the wine business, too, consulting on contracts, financing, and negotiations with government agencies, but he didn't know loads more than Bonnie about actual wine.

Still, Bonnie figured Michael could help Mark get at least some of his money back, so in summer 1985 Michael started negotiating with Souverain. Problem was, the winery had been taken over by creditors. The people running the place were mostly trying to salvage some of their own money before the ship sank.

It was a sunny day in July when Michael sat in a big conference room at Souverain talking about their debt to Mark. He was getting nowhere.

It was the kind of conference room you see in lots of wineries, with big windows looking over barrel rooms or winemaking equipment. This one had a view of tanks and a large, white, two-story room. In the middle of the room was a massive, polished metal machine with gears and levers and tracks.

Michael had never seen anything like it. He got up and looked out the window. He'd been getting stumped for a while, so he was vamping a bit to diffuse the tension.

"Excuse me, guys," he said. "What's with the chrome locomotive in the handball court?" Partly, he was making conversation, but Michael was also curious. This thing was huge.

"We call that a clean room," one of the Souverain guys said. "And that's a bottling line."

"A what?"

"A bottling line. It bottles 3,000 cases of wine a day."

Wow, Michael thought. He kept looking out at the winery's interior. He was thinking maybe he could claim something for Mark—cables, hoses, benches, anything to ease the loss.

"What's in those tanks?" he asked.

Funny he should bring that up, the Souverain people said. The tanks held the cabernet sauvignon and sauvignon blanc that had been made from Mark's grapes. There were about 18,000 cases worth of wine sitting there.

Michael kept looking at the winery. The next thing he said came from desperation to recover at least something, but even more, it came from sheer ignorance of the maelstrom he was about to jump into.

"Here's what we'll do," he said. "We'll work your bill off with that wine and some bottling services."

Huh? the Souverain people said.

"We'll take Mark's wine," Michael said. "We'll use your locomotive to bottle it. That'll cover what you owe him."

Michael figured they could bottle and sell the wine and earn Mark a chunk of his lost money. The thing was, in 1985, few California wine people operated like that. There were plenty of wineries with buildings, tanks, and storage rooms that bought wine in bulk and bottled it under their labels. And big places like Souverain rented their facilities and their equipment to winemakers who brought in their own grapes. But instantly becoming a large wine company selling 18,000 cases without any vineyards or buildings or even any land, that didn't happen much.

But the Souverain people said why not. Given their financial mess, they had no guarantee the wine in those tanks would ever get sold. They were happy to have one debt off their books.

Michael was surprised to get anything out of Souverain, so 18,000 cases of wine sounded pretty good. He knew it would take some marketing and some effort, but he figured they could research this, use Mark's experience, and get the wine sold. How hard could it be?

One of the first steps for Michael, Bonnie and Mark was coming up with a name and a label. Bonnie gave them a starting point. It had to be a name she could pronounce. She was not about to be embarrassed ordering her own wine.

Simple as that sounds, it was the kind of outside-the-industry logic that guided Michael and Bonnie through so many decisions. Their complete lack of wine experience often ended up being an asset. Most winery owners don't worry about looking bad in a restaurant, and they can forget lots of their customers do.

What Michael and Bonnie did next was a step that can get overlooked by new businesses: They went out and talked to people. Many start-up teams brainstorm to identify their strengths, weaknesses and challenges. That's Business 101. But that's just the start, because if you're new to an industry, you likely won't know all your strengths, weaknesses and challenges.

It didn't take much for Michael and Bonnie to see they were babes in the wine industry, so they questioned everyone they could find. And not just big names or long-time winery owners—though they did talk to many of those folks—but they picked brains at every level, particularly people on the front lines. That would stay a guiding principle for them. They called it, no disrespect intended, "making friends in low places." Those "friends" were the men and women with clipboards or grease and grape stains on their hands who could describe how things worked, because they were the ones who made them work.

Michael also talked to supermarket managers and wine buyers. They were the people he hoped to sell the wine to, and they were the ones who watched wine sell in their aisles. One of those was Don Brown, the wine buyer for the Lucky supermarket chain in Northern California and something of a legend in the region's commercial wine culture.

Brown was old school before there was old school—gruff, abrupt, sometimes profane, seemingly perpetually irritated. It didn't always win him friends, but it was a style that got people in and out of his office quickly.

It was late summer when Michael went to see Brown in Hayward, across the bay from San Francisco. It was a bit like trying to get an interview with royalty, if the royalty worked in a concrete industrial park with dark halls, the low hum of fluorescent lighting, and cement floors.

Michael signed in, got a visitor's badge, and waited on a small, stiff chair outside Brown's office for what seemed half the afternoon. He sat looking down the long, cement-walled hallways, expecting a forklift to come buzzing through the office space.

When Brown let him in, Michael sat on another hard folding chair in front of Brown's desk. The office was crowded with wine and spirit samples from companies hoping Brown and Lucky would carry their lines. Brown went right into his act.

"Say what you need to say," Brown told Michael, "and get out of here."

"My name's Michael Houlihan and I just closed a deal with a winery to pay off some debt," Michael said. "I'm sitting on thousands of gallons of cabernet and sauvignon blanc. When I bottle it, what should the label look like?"

Brown's grumpiness eased a notch.

"You know, Houlihan, nobody ever asked me that before," Brown said, "so I'm gonna help you." He looked away from Michael as he said that, lest it be interpreted as friendliness.

"Don't make it a hill or a leap or a run or a valley or a creek," Brown said. "I got enough of those. I can't sell more. Don't put a flower on it. And for crissakes, don't make it a chateau."

He was getting a little wound up. Michael figured Brown was seeing the rows and rows of identical-sounding wine brands and thinking about how much trouble he had getting them to move.

"Make the logo the same as the name. It has to be something familiar, something people will recognize and remember. And whatever you do," Brown said and paused for effect, "do it in plain English."

"Got it," Michael said, trying not to get the man any angrier. He hoped Brown would pick up his wine when it was bottled. "Thank you. I appreciate your time."

Michael got up to leave.

"And Houlihan," Brown said as Michael reached the door, "make it visible from four feet away. She has to be able to see it when she's pushing her cart down the aisle. Now get outta here. I got work to do."

All of that was gold, but that last point, the last sentence just before Brown booted Michael into the hall, would become a cornerstone of Michael's and Bonnie's wine business philosophy. They just didn't know it yet.

An equally useful, but far more benign, visit was with Lou Toninato at Souverain. He was the manager of the winery's bottling line, Michael's "chrome locomotive," and Michael and Bonnie both went to see him to learn as much about that monster as they could. While Lou was explaining how the bottling would work, they asked if he had any thoughts on labels.

"I'm no expert," Lou said, "but I have a label room here. Let me show you."

The room was Lou Toninato's library. It had every label from every wine that had been bottled there. Some were from little wineries and winemakers, some were from big boys. There were thousands of labels in small trays that held them like index cards in a library. The trays lined the walls and went nearly floor to ceiling.

"I see which ones get used up the fastest and come back to bottle more," he told Michael and Bonnie. "And I can tell you that most of these only got used once and never came back."

There was a consistency to the failed labels. They were fancy, with curly-cue writing, or ornate lettering, or script that looked like it belonged on the Magna Carta. There were labels that made you squint to read them, and labels that looked like inkblots and abstract paintings. One looked like a carrot stew. Those were the ones Lou never saw twice.

"You have to remember, these are going on a curved piece of glass," Lou said. "You're only going to see about two inches of the thing."

He said the repeat customers had their images centered and visible, not on the top or bottom or in the right-hand corner.

He said when a bottle is filled with red wine, it basically looks black. The labels that stood out were mostly white.

And, Lou said, think about the process of shipping wine.

"OK," Bonnie said and looked at Michael. They had no clue about that process. They nodded anyway.

The bottles come off the line in a hurry, Lou told them, and they get stuffed into boxes with hard cardboard dividers. Then they bang around on handcarts or in trucks. The boxes get tossed into warehouses or shipped to backrooms at stores. When they get displayed, they get yanked out quickly and nearly thrown onto shelves because the clerk has a lot of work to do.

That means lots of labels get scuffed, and when the labels are in color, the scuff shows the white paper underneath. "It looks like damaged goods," Lou said. "No one buys it. When it gets to the front of the shelf in a store, it stops the sale of all the bottles behind it."

Plus, he told them, keep it simple.

"One image, not a bunch of images," Lou said. "Your bottle will be up there with all those other bottles and the section already looks messy and crowded."

Michael and Bonnie stood there and kept nodding. This was so much good information, they didn't know where to start.

"Anyway, that's what I see working," Lou said. "But I'm no expert."

They wanted to hug the guy. He'd given them a master class on wine merchandising and almost apologized for it. And what he said connected to what Don Brown and others were saying. They were starting to get an idea.

Another stop was Petrini's supermarket in San Francisco. It was just Michael again and he went to talk to Art Mueller, the Petrini's wine buyer.

He asked the questions he asked everyone: What do you need? What sells? What don't you have? Where is the gap? We can bottle it any way you want, put any label on it that works for you, he told Art.

They were talking in the wine aisle at the store. Art was a very different guy from Don Brown. He wanted to help, but he was busy. He had shelves to stock and customers to deal with. While Art was trying to answer Michael's questions, a woman walked up pushing a shopping cart. "Hey, sir," she said, "where's the butter?"

Art sent her toward the dairy case. Then a clerk came up with a question, then a shopper couldn't find hot chocolate. A few minutes later, Art finally got to his advice for Michael.

"Here's what you gotta do," he said. "Give me a salt-and-pepper act, make it better than Bob, make it cheaper than Bob, and put it in a pig."

"Got it," Michael said. "Thank you."

Michael walked to his car, unlocked it and sat in the driver's seat. He just sat there a moment.

"What the heck was that?" he said to no one.

The next day Michael called Hampton Bynum, who was working as a winemaker with his father, and asked him to translate.

"Salt and pepper is a way of saying white wine and red wine," Hampton said.

"OK, that makes a little sense," Michael said. "So who's Bob?"

"You don't know Robert Mondavi?" Hampton said.

"'Bob' is Robert Mondavi?" Michael said. "Mr. Napa Valley wine?"

"Mr. American wine," Hampton said. "Don't undersell him."

"I have to be better than Robert Mondavi?" Michael said. His voice had some panic to it.

"And didn't your guy say cheaper, too? I think you have to be better and cheaper than Mondavi," Hampton said. He was trying not to laugh at his friend. "It should be a snap."

"How am I going to do that?" Michael said.

"Make it good. Make it cheap."

"Funny. I'm afraid to ask the last one. What's a pig?"

"That's a magnum," Hampton said. "A 1.5-liter bottle. It's twice the size of a regular bottle. Some people call 'em pigs 'cause they're big and round."

When Michael hung up, he told Bonnie what Hampton said.

"Really?" Bonnie said. "Wine comes in different sized bottles?"

Sometimes, information needs to germinate. And sometimes, the weight of it all will eventually hit a mental button or make an image pop up. The advice from Don Brown, Lou Toninato, Art Mueller, and everyone else had been bouncing around in Michael's head. He was thinking about his San Francisco Bay Area days when he and Hampton would do what they called "product research." Hampton had keys to his dad's Albany winery and they'd sneak some Barefoot Bynum wine before it got bottled. There were days they did "research" for hours. Now, Michael was remembering the old jug bottles with the foot.

They'd need a new label. The old one had the foot on the bottom and it didn't look lively or cheery enough. But it was a good direction. It was a solid image without a hill or a valley or a chateau, and it could be fun. Plus a foot was pretty straightforward.

Michael went to Davis Bynum and worked out a deal. They bought the name and would start up a new brand, and Davis would sell the wine in his Healdsburg tasting room. This was progress, but he and Bonnie needed to figure out the look of the label, something that would be full of life, that would not get scuffed, that would stand out, and that wouldn't tick off Don Brown.

Bonnie and Michael tossed around ideas for weeks, trying to be sure they had their concept right, digesting all the advice and information, analyzing labels they saw on store shelves. One night in October, coming back from a dinner with friends, it was Bonnie's turn to have the weight of all that information suddenly push a button in her mind.

They walked into the kitchen in their little rented farmhouse. It was near midnight. Michael started down the hall, headed for bed. But at that moment in the middle of the night, all those talks, all that info from Don Brown and Lou Toninato and everyone else, all the musing, it all bonded together, became focused and struck Bonnie like a thunderbolt. She had a bright moment of clarity.

"Wait," Bonnie said, "come back here. I've got it."

Michael was exhausted. "Can't we wait until morning," he said. He was close to pleading.

"No, no, no," Bonnie said. "We have to do this now." She was bouncing with energy, almost giggly. Michael looked at her. She didn't get like that often, but when she did, it usually meant something important. He trundled back into the kitchen.

"Go to the chalkboard," Bonnie said. "You're the artist."

Well, sort of. He could at least draw better than Bonnie. They had a small blackboard in the kitchen they used for everything from leaving notes to scribbling stray thoughts.

"I know what the label looks like," Bonnie said. "This is going to be a big success. I can see it stacked in supermarkets. This is going to sell a lot of wine."

Michael picked up the chalk and started to draw.

CONVERSATIONS WITH BONNIE AND MICHAEL

There were so many stories and lessons in the tale of the Barefoot Spirit that we couldn't fit them all into these chapters. So, instead, here's a chance to listen into the conversation as Michael and Bonnie told their story.

Rick: *Did you have any concept of what you were taking on?*

Bonnie: No. None whatsoever. We thought we were going to bottle some wine, sell it, pay Mark back, and have a little left over. We didn't even know enough to be afraid. It was like, Why not?

Michael: We had space in the laundry room because we couldn't afford a washer and dryer. We thought, "Great, we'll use that as an office." If we knew how long it would take, we probably would've said, "Sorry, Mark, looks like you're gonna take the loss."

Rick: *Michael, when you were looking at the silver locomotive at Souverain, what was going through your head?*

Michael: I was looking for comic relief. The tensions were so high, I wasn't getting anywhere, but I had the floor and I wanted to be in charge of the meeting. I just wanted to keep talking.

Bonnie: You were asking them for money and they didn't have any.

Michael: That's what they kept telling me. You get into a corner and you say, "Hey, look, a puppy."

Rick: *Why did you work so hard on the label?*

Michael: We thought, gee, we were lucky to get at least something from those stone faces. So we had the wine and the bottling services. Then it dawned on us, we had to sell the stuff. But we knew opportunity is fleeting and sometimes you have to take the opportunity you get.

Bonnie: We thought Mark would sell it, but we knew we had to come up with the details and business plan. Then it seemed like the obvious next question: What's the label look like?

Rick: *But you didn't start by brainstorming, which is what lots of new businesses do. You started right off talking to people. Why?*

Michael: We approached it like we approached everything else. We looked around for the old guys, the guys with high mileage, who've been doing it for years.

Bonnie: We first asked, who were the people we should talk to? It's the logical next step. If you don't know what you're getting into, ask somebody who's been there.

Michael: And be humble enough to go in with your hat in your hand . . .

Bonnie: . . . and say, "Will you help me, please?"

Chapter Two

Now What?

The story of Michael and Bonnie together—which is also the story of the partnership, energy, and buoyant spirit that would embody one of the nation's most unique brands—starts on May 20, 1983 in a blues bar called Magnolia's.

Magnolia's was on the ground floor of the brick-covered Jacobs Building in Santa Rosa's Old Railroad Square, and Bonnie worked right above it in the offices of a group of lawyers. It was a Friday night, she liked the band, and she'd been there enough to feel comfortable going in alone.

At the start of the evening, though, Bonnie got stuck momentarily just inside the door. She was taking a shot at avoiding the cover charge.

"I'm a single woman," she told the doorman as sweetly as she could. "It's all guys in there. You should be paying me to come in."

Around them, the brass-heavy, bluesy rock from the Mark Naftalin Blues Band was filling the air and rattling the walls. Across the room, Michael was at the bar with his friends, a group that included a musician everyone called Cousin Joe, Hampton Bynum, and Sten Juhl, a guy from Denmark who spoke with a Texas accent and said things like, "Yah sure, y'all."

They were hanging out, watching the room. Michael looked over at the front door. It was open and the doorman was talking to a lithe, dark-haired woman in a sheer, hot-pink dress. She was standing in the opening, with the streetlight behind her. The backlighting created a corona of gleaming yellow light.

"Excuse me, gentleman," Michael told his friends. "I'm in love."

He walked over to Bonnie, who'd won her case with the doorman, and introduced himself. Michael gave her his best blend of chivalry and cool. Bonnie gave back playful and challenging. They bantered and flirted, like so many people in the bar, partly to have fun and partly to learn about each other.

They watched the club scene, joked, occasionally teased to pry loose personal information. They danced a little and talked a lot. Bonnie saw a funny, high-energy, engaging guy who had thoughts on pretty much everything, but she wasn't exactly sold on Michael right off. Michael, on the other hand, fell for Bonnie from the start, and he learned she was quick-witted, confident, and curious about life.

During one break in the music, they wandered outside. Michael was telling a story, and, as he often does, he was getting animated. Bonnie was watching this tall, long-limbed, reddish-haired guy talking loudly, moving around, waving his arms. And Bonnie—who'd never had this happen before and would not again—heard a voice in her head.

"You will be with this man for a very long time," the voice said.

Huh? What? she thought. This guy is yelling and flapping his arms and looks like Big Bird. How long is a very long time? "Voice, come back," she almost said out loud. "Look at him."

And she did. She looked right at him and saw a bright, dynamic, passionate guy. She didn't know why, but right then, everything felt right. Maybe a long time wouldn't be so bad. Maybe that voice knew something.

They closed down the club, then closed a late-night breakfast spot. They were together that night at Bonnie's house and they've been together ever since. Through that weekend, they talked about their peculiar start. Maybe there isn't love at first sight, as the cliché goes, but there really are moments that make you give yourself a chance at love, Michael said.

"You let the other person fumble, be imperfect," he told Bonnie, "because there's something substantive when you're together."

Bonnie thought that, too. She didn't tell Michael he looked like Big Bird when he was telling his story outside Magnolia's. They weren't *that* substantive just yet.

But they did talk about where they'd come from, and where they wanted to go.

Bonnie was born in Portland, Oregon, and grew up around the outskirts of that city. She always liked her business classes, and went to business college after high school. Then, in 1969, she moved to San Francisco.

"My kid brother showed me a magazine of what was happening there," she told Michael. "I was 18. It sounded like the most exciting city in the country."

Bonnie got temp jobs because she didn't want a permanent 9-to-5. She wanted to travel and to experience San Francisco. Those jobs taught her a range of skills that combined with her business training and her innate organized nature. She started managing the records and dealings for clubs, offices, and businesspeople.

In 1982, she moved to Sonoma County about an hour north of San Francisco when an attorney friend—the one with offices above Magnolia's—offered her a job. Bonnie took that part time and continued to run her own business, In Care Of, which organized business and personal offices. Even then, she showed the creativity that would be a Barefoot cornerstone.

To do a little good, and to help spread the word about her business, she donated five free hours of organizing to a charity auction on a local radio station. Then she got the list of bidders who didn't win and called them to sign them up as clients.

Michael grew up in the Oakland hills across the bay from San Francisco. His father had a term as Oakland's mayor. Michael was the product of a Catholic high school that pushed the combination of exactness and creative thinking. He started at the University of California in Berkeley but had a streak of educational wanderlust, so he transferred first to the University of San Francisco, then later to Santa Barbara City College.

"Man, I fell for that town," he told Bonnie.

Santa Barbara was classy, had a cultural backbone, but was still a college town and a beach community. Michael also fell for the beach, learned to surf, and like a lot of college kids, spent a fair amount of time at post-surf bonfires. Those were scenes that would live with him for decades.

But he was young and still restless. He stayed on the coast, but moved to Southern California and finished college at Long Beach State. He worked for the city of Anaheim, then moved back to Oakland after a couple years.

"Southern California wore me out," he told Bonnie. "I loved the beaches, but I'm a Northern California guy. I needed to come home."

In Oakland, he worked on the city's redevelopment, helping people stay in business while they were being moved for city projects. After a couple years, he used his knowledge of government's back alleys and cubbyholes to start a consulting business.

When Michael met Bonnie, he was still living in Berkeley, at least technically. He had a place there and had clients in the Bay Area, but he also had clients in Sonoma County because he loved the North Bay wine country. He spent so much time in Sonoma, he half lived out of his car, bunking with friends on their couches.

"Everything is here," he told Bonnie. "There's the coast, the redwoods, the mountains and rivers, the hiking trails, the vineyards, the parks. And people here appreciate it."

On Sunday of that first weekend, they went for a drive in Michael's green VW Rabbit. They put the top down, and Michael told Bonnie he was taking her on "the most beautiful road in the most beautiful county in America."

So they rambled down Westside Road, which runs from Healdsburg to Guerneville along the Russian River. It was a bright, postcard day, and they passed vineyards draped over rolling hills, went through a redwood forest, crossed a creaky bridge, and saw elegant, century-old farmhouses and green, green valleys.

They stopped at one point, looking at a little white house on a hill sitting by itself in the trees. It was a 1922 cowboy house on land that was part of the Fred MacMurray ranch. "That's exactly the kind of house I want to live in," Michael said.

A year later, it was exactly the house Michael and Bonnie moved into, and a year after that, its laundry room would become Barefoot's first office.

By Monday, they were both back to work, but Michael was coming "home" to Bonnie's house every evening. "You've paid for all our dates," Bonnie said that Monday night, "let me make you dinner."

That night she roasted a chicken. Tuesday, she used the leftovers for chicken a la king. There was enough on Wednesday to fill some wraps with Asian chicken. And on Thursday, she boiled the bones and made chicken soup. Michael was thinking, if she can feed us for four days with a single chicken, this is one resourceful woman.

During that week, they kept talking, about their lives, their pasts, their dreams. And they kept discovering how connected they were. They were both what Michael called serial entrepreneurs. They liked business challenges, were good at solving problems, and had unique views of their businesses.

"When I was in high school," Bonnie told Michael, "I would imagine I was the office manager of a very successful businessman, and he was successful because I organized everything and gave him a firm foundation to succeed.

"I always thought I'd do that for my mate. Get everything organized, give him that foundation, now, go get 'em," she said.

"I always thought I was half a couple," Michael said, "that I'd be in business with the person I loved. I thought, what's the point if you can't share what you do?"

By then, they knew a lot about how each other operated. Bonnie saw how Michael was innovative and energetic, and how he attacked problems from all sides, fixing and finagling everything he could control. Michael learned that Bonnie was clear-eyed and analytical. She could see the holes in plans, or the muddle inside what seemed like solid ideas, and she could see ways to shore up the holes and unscramble the muddle.

"Swashbucklers need someone to come through behind them and correct things," she said.

"I leave a lot to correct," Michael said.

"That would make my job easy," she said.

Michael knew he needed some grounding. He could earn money for himself and his clients, but he wasn't too strong on the keeping track part of his own life. He had, as he told Bonnie, no back-office skills.

As proof, he showed her the crumpled wad of cash he carried around. It was maybe $200, maybe $300. He didn't know the amount. He used it to live.

"You're pretty good with chicken," he told Bonnie, laughing. "So how are you with money?"

"Even better," she said.

Michael gave her the crumpled bills. "Can you keep track of this?" he said softly.

And that was the start—of the commitment, of the enduring love affair, and of the partnership of skills and hearts that would become the Barefoot Spirit.

That October night at the chalkboard in 1985, when Bonnie was hit by the thunderbolt of inspiration about the label, would be a decisive moment for Barefoot, and for American wine branding.

Bonnie could feel the moment, just as she felt the energy and exhilaration. But she also felt some panic.

She knew the idea was good. She also knew you can lose those images that pop into your brain. They're so vivid and defined, then, poof, they're gone, turned into something wispy and vague. She needed to make it solid. She needed Michael to draw it. And she needed this to happen fast.

That's why she was almost vibrating to get it out, and why she hustled a half-asleep Michael to the little green chalkboard in the kitchen.

"I know what the label looks like," Bonnie said. "This is going to be a big success. I can see it stacked in supermarkets. This is going to sell a lot of wine."

Michael picked up the chalk and started to draw.

"Quick, quick," she said. "Draw a foot."

"What kind of foot?" Michael said.

"A nice foot. Just draw it."

Michael sketched a slim right foot along the bottom of the chalkboard.

"No, no, no," Bonnie said. "Stand it up."

He erased it and drew one with the heel at the bottom and the toes straight up.

"Close," she said. "Tilt it to the right."

He erased and drew again.

"No, no, more tilt. Just a little. Make it look like there's some motion. It's like someone is stepping up."

Bonnie's voice was getting louder. She was talking faster, feeling like this was even more urgent. Her panic was growing. They could not lose this idea.

"Is that it?" Michael said. By now the chalkboard had a layer of white dust from all the erased chalk.

"Really close," Bonnie said. "The foot should look like an exclamation point. An italicized exclamation point. And, give it a little more arch."

It got more tilt. It got more arch.

"How's that?" Michael said.

"Now write 'Barefoot,'" Bonnie said.

"I know what the label looks like!"

Michael put down "Barefoot" next to the angled drawing.

"Closer," Bonnie said. "Move it closer. Put the 'T' all the way inside the arch."

Bonnie stopped bouncing and looked at it. The board was nearly white, the air was filled with chalk dust. They stood silently, surrounded by their intensity. Both were taking big breaths. Bonnie's fear had dissipated. They looked at a slim right foot, pointing up at a 2 o'clock angle, acting as an exclamation point for the "Barefoot" written into the arch.

They both thought it was good. But they had no idea that in not much more than a decade, it would become an iconic national label.

"There," she said. "That's what the label looks like. That's going to sell a lot of wine."

The foot sketch made Bonnie and Michael feel like they had a flag to rally around. But they still had much more to learn about the industry, so they kept on doing research and asking questions.

They learned there was less competition in the magnum category, and that buyers like Art Mueller had the most room on their shelves for brands in that big size. They also learned that people didn't buy magnums to try something new—they experiment with smaller bottles—but magnum buyers were loyal customers, and when they bought that big size, they bought into the brand.

And Michael and Bonnie learned that many wineries didn't pay much attention to the wine industry's biggest pool of customers: supermarket shoppers.

Despite all the romance and high-end advertising, the vast majority of people who bought wine didn't go to wine shops, read wine magazines, or even visit wineries very often. The real

American wine buyers—especially in the mid-1980s—were those supermarket customers. And that customer was most often a woman, probably in a hurry and shopping for her family. Often she was on the way home from work before cooking dinner, and she saw wine as a product, a staple, another item on her shopping list like cereal, butter or rice.

And just like with cereal, that wine buyer often stuck with the same brand—unless the taste changed or the price went up. It was easy that way. She could grab the bottle as quickly as everything else she bought, get out of the store, and get home to her family.

Michael and Bonnie were learning all this, in part, because they were new to the wine industry and didn't know its conventions. Being outsiders was, in many ways, a lucky thing for them. They didn't know enough to make assumptions and had to learn the very basics. They asked questions—such as: Who bought the most wine?—that many industry veterans had long stopped asking.

They were also running on the business principles they'd lived by as consultants, and a core tenet was to keep taking inventory. They constantly looked at what they had, what tools they could use, how much more they had to learn.

It's a little ironic for experienced businesspeople, but one of the forces that powered Michael and Bonnie and the Barefoot Spirit was an almost childlike sense of wonder. They didn't mind asking those basic questions—How do you sell this? How does that work? Who buys your wine?—to get the fullest, most fundamental picture.

The answers they were getting were leading Michael and Bonnie to an approach. They told Mark they were going to aim for supermarket customers, that they had a label that wasn't a valley or a chateau, that they were thinking they'd "put it in a pig."

Mark Lyon had spent time in France and thought they were on target. He told them about something the French call vin de pays, or country wine. It wasn't the top-name, premium stuff that

Americans knew, and it wasn't the style lots of American wineries wanted to produce. But it was solid, reliable, everyday dinner wine, and even in France people drank far more vin de pays than they did expensive wine.

"What America needs," Mark told Michael, "is a good $5 bottle of wine. And I know how to make it."

Over the years, Mark Lyon's winemaking has won a number of awards, including the title Winemaker of the Year in 2003 given by Restaurant Wine Magazine. Yet, what he helped start at Barefoot had as much impact on the industry as almost anything else he's done.

Mark understood the Barefoot marketing plan, and he agreed with it. They wanted a wine that would both satisfy people with experienced palates and would appeal to inexpert wine drinkers, like, say, Michael and Bonnie.

Mark explained it to them at his office one day early in the planning stages.

"We want the wine to be varietally correct," Mark said.

"Sure, OK," Michael and Bonnie said. "What does that mean?" they asked.

The fruit would show through in the wines. The cabernet would taste like cabernet. The sauvignon blanc would be ripe and melony, but not sweet. The goal was for the wine to be both delicious and a bit interesting, but most of all approachable.

Mark said that meant making sure there's a bit of acid, enough to give it a little backbone so it wouldn't get cloying. He'd also leave in just a touch of residual sugar—that's the sugar from grapes—that would make it feel rich and full and punch up the taste of the fruit.

"We won't let it get sweet. This will be good stuff and it'll be unique. But we don't want it bone dry because most people won't like that, either," Mark said.

If Bonnie and Michael didn't know much about winemaking, they had started to learn about marketing it. With Mark, they decided the flavor and style they were building needed to be consistent, bottle to bottle and year to year. They'd learned that if supermarket shoppers tried Barefoot and liked it, they'd want the next bottle to taste the same.

Many, many wineries—most American wineries making fine wines—want their wine to show individuality, and to show some sense of the vintage and the place where the grapes grew. That's a piece of wine's magic and an important goal of fine wine. It's something that matters to wine folks choosing between, say, an expensive pinot noir from the Russian River Valley or the Santa Barbara region.

But Barefoot was headed toward the mass market and that has different rules. To sell thousands and thousands of cases of wine, it's certainly important that the wine is good, but it's just as important that it's consistent. One key decision they made was not to put the vintage on the label. That way they could make the flavor steady and dependable, and, as Michael said, they wouldn't have to explain away an off year by saying, well, an elephant got loose in the vineyard that fall.

"If we change the taste and people don't like it just one time," Mark said, "they'll stop drinking it."

"Now all we need," Bonnie said, "is to get people to start drinking it."

It felt like their plans were coming together. Mark would guide the winemaking. Davis Bynum would carry some of the wine in his tasting room. Michael and Bonnie believed they had guidelines to sell to some Northern California supermarkets. And they had a name and the look of a label they liked.

But they didn't have an actual label, and they knew they had as much business doing the technical label design as they did making the wine. That, too, was work for a pro.

That summer in 1985, on a water skiing trip to Lake Shasta with a group of friends, Michael and Bonnie had met Lori LeBoy, a talented graphic designer and artist living in Hollywood. On the trip, all they knew was they liked each other and got along well.

In October, they called Lori. Come meet us in Santa Barbara for Halloween, they told her. We'll have fun and we want to ask you about something. And bring a good costume.

Lori said sure. She figured they'd eventually get around to some kind of business talk, but she knew about Santa Barbara, and she knew Halloween there was legendary.

Lori met Bonnie, Michael and Mark at the Californian Hotel on State Street where they were all staying. She changed into her cat costume, a full-body suit, with brown and white fur and a three-foot long tail.

Mark dressed as a brat. He wore checkered sneakers, red suspenders over a yellow shirt, and a red beanie with a propeller. Bonnie had real braces on her teeth at the time, so she became a kid at bedtime with a nightie and her hair in pigtails, carrying a blanket and a teddy bear.

But Michael was the guy getting the laughs. He was a man in bed—standing straight up with a full bed around him. He had built a frame with lightweight plastic pipe, and Bonnie had sewn blankets, sheets, and a pillow to the frame. Michael also wore PJs, a nightcap, and black eyeshades—with pinholes so he could see.

Out on State Street, the sidewalks were packed. Everyone was in costume. There was a woolly mammoth, women dressed as men, men dressed as women, sailors, French maids, pirates, superheroes, musketeers, and a headless guy carrying his noggin in his hands. Cars cruised the street. There was a massive, happy energy all around them.

It was just coincidence, but the feeling that night, the sense of letting go and embracing the moment, would be a theme in what they talked about the next morning, just as it would be a theme for Barefoot over the years.

When they did meet to talk business, there wasn't much left of the morning. They were four more slightly bedraggled partiers gathering for breakfast at Joe's Café on State Street. Michael and Bonnie told Lori how they were working for Mark and about their plans for Barefoot Cellars. They said Bonnie had a draft of a label they thought would be lively and engaging.

Lori got the idea. Approachable wine, welcoming label. They needed to be conventional enough to be accepted, but fresh enough and fun enough so Barefoot wouldn't look like just another stuffy wine.

"We're walking a tightrope," Michael said. "We're a new look, but we don't want it so new the stores will be afraid to carry it."

Lori said she was in. The four of them got recharged as they talked about their plans. There they were, sitting in a booth in a quirky café, eating breakfast at noon, still a little dazed from the momentous street party, and something became very clear. It was something they understood but never said out loud: this was not going to be a conventional company.

That may have been the first "meeting," but from the day Michael made the deal with Souverain, he and Bonnie had been conducting Barefoot business. While Michael was picking the brains of potential buyers and trying not to annoy the likes of Don Brown or Art Mueller, Bonnie was learning everything she could about bottling and supplies.

She took wine country phone books and called every company that appeared to deal with winery supplies looking for anyone who would talk to her. Most people were too busy, but there was one place, the California Glass Company in Oakland, that kept answering her questions, even when Bonnie, at one point, was calling Ken Camporeale a couple times a day.

Ken was a senior manager there and he told her she'd have to choose among wine bottles that were different shapes and colors and weights. He told her there was something called a capsule that went over the top of the cork. He asked if she had all her licenses.

"I need more than one?" Bonnie said. "Let me get back to you."

Bonnie tracked down licenses. She sorted through the different capsules and corks. She was trying to find the best price and the most reliable suppliers for everything. It was dawning on her that "reliable" could be a relative term.

She told Michael one evening that maybe they should get one supplier who could deliver everything, so they'd only have to worry about one guy showing up instead of herding a pack of them.

"You have someone in mind?" Michael said.

"I have someone who will talk to me," she said. "That's a start."

But before they could make decisions on capsules or bottles, they needed to nail down the label. The label had to work with the bottle shape and the capsule and bottle colors, and it would need a federal OK. (Federal regulations were extraordinarily specific, down to the size of some printing.)

Meanwhile, Lori was working with Bonnie's chalkboard drawing, painstakingly customizing a font letter by letter, creating an original look, including interlocking the "Os" in Barefoot. She made a clean label with a wine-stained, watercolor foot that was cool and playful but still belonged on a good bottle of wine. Lori said it should "look young, be kind of hip, have a sense of levity to it."

She wanted it to be bold enough to stand out, but still have a sense of timelessness and sophistication, because most people still had certain expectations about what a wine should look like. She was designing a label to make a statement without scaring away too many old-school wine retailers and customers.

There was one recurring problem in the drafts she sent Bonnie and Michael: the foot was clunky and short. Bonnie and Lori were talking on the phone about this. Lori was laughing and figured she just needed to find a more slender foot somewhere to get the label right.

"I'll look around," she said.

They hung up and Michael came into the room. Bonnie told him the problem. Then she stopped.

"I know where to find a slender foot," she said. "There's one of those right here at the end of my leg."

She sent Michael off to an art supply store for a large inkpad. She dug out some paper. When he got back, Bonnie took off her right shoe, sat on a kitchen chair, and stepped firmly on the ink then the paper. They went through this maybe a dozen times, like a mini-printing press. They mailed the clearest footprint to Lori with a sticky note that said, "More like this."

Lori called when she got the foot. She had used Bonnie's footprint and created ink and watercolor drawings with greens and yellows for the sauvignon blanc and reds and purples for the cab.

"You know," she told Bonnie, "this is going to work really well."

It was late December in 1985. Michael, Bonnie and Mark Lyon were out to dinner in the town of Sonoma. This was part holiday celebration, part business. They were in a booth at the El Dorado Hotel on the town square.

Michael and Bonnie were filling Mark in on what they were planning for his about-to-be-born wine company. Mark was working on blending the wine. They told him about bottling schedules, the label, the licenses they got in his name.

"We're doing everything the Bay Area chain stores want," Michael said. "We got detailed guidelines from Lucky. Getting the wine into their stores shouldn't be too hard."

They also talked about the expenses, and how the profit margin would be small, so they'd probably need to keep bottling and selling wine the next year or two to cover Mark's debt.

"We're going to get your money back," Bonnie said. "We think this is going to work."

They talked about how they'd scheduled the glass and the corks and everything else so they could start bottling in March. While they talked, Mark got very quiet. He looked less and less comfortable.

Mark Lyon is a very smart man. He's a talented winemaker and a respected grape grower. But his heart was always in the art of wine—in the grapes, the vineyards, the blending and barrels. At the end of the meal, he dropped a bomb on Michael and Bonnie.

He said he didn't want to be a business owner. It seemed more painful to him to try to own the business and market the wine than it did to lose the money. He said he sincerely appreciated all the work they had done for him as consultants and as friends.

"But," Mark said, "I don't want to do it. I can't do it."

Then he sat there quietly. Michael and Bonnie knew Mark well enough not to argue with him. They knew he was sincere and that he had tried. They were thinking Mark was going to take a big loss. And they were thinking about the potential they were tossing away, how even negotiating the deal with Souverain was a small miracle.

But they were friends first, and they tried to comfort Mark. They felt bad and they knew he felt bad. They got in their car and started back toward their homes up north. Michael was driving, Mark was next to him and Bonnie was in back. They were all a little uncomfortable and a little sad. They'd gone four blocks down Spain Street, then another thunderbolt hit Michael. He jammed on the brakes and pulled over.

"Why are we stopping?" Mark said.

"I have an idea," Michael said. He looked back at Bonnie for support. She didn't know his plan, but her look said, "Go for it."

"Instead of us working for you to get this done," Michael said, "you're going to work for us. Instead of it being your company, it's our company. Instead of Souverain owing you money, we'll owe you the money.

"You'll be our winemaker and consultant. We're not going to be able to pay you off right away, because we're going to have to use money from the first sales to get more wine bottled."

Bonnie got the plan right away. "You can sell us your grapes for the next year, and eventually we'll earn back enough to pay you everything."

"Uh, sure," Mark said. "How long do you think it will take?"

"Two, three years," Michael said.

"Four years," Bonnie said. Let's give ourselves a cushion, she thought.

"Right. Four years," Michael said.

"Why not?" Mark said.

They got back on the road and drove into the night. Mark's face was filled with relief. He was positively chatty on the ride back. Now Michael and Bonnie were the quiet ones. They had almost the identical thought: "Uh oh, now what have we gotten ourselves into?"

CONVERSATIONS WITH BONNIE AND MICHAEL

Rick: *Right off, it was clear that you two were both very alike and very different. It made you into a charming match as a couple, but you say it also helped you in your business, right?*

Michael: That's true. I'm front office, Bonnie's back office.

Bonnie: I make sure his shoelaces are tied when he's out there wielding his sword. I'd hate to see him trip on his shoelaces.

Rick: *But it was more than that. You had this synergy—as overused as the word is—between what you both could do.*

Bonnie: I'm a detail person, and Michael's a big picture person. We wouldn't have survived without both of those. Between the two of us, we had most of the bases covered.

Michael: We have different skill sets, but we saw the same goals. We still do, we just get there from different directions.

Bonnie: We respect each other, and each other's talents. We relied on them even more because they were different.

Michael: And we had each other's backs. We took turns encouraging each other when we needed it.

Bonnie: Even when we both needed it, we still took turns.

Rick: *That moment of inspiration in the kitchen when you saw the label and the future of Barefoot. How clear was that?*

Bonnie: It was almost like it was happening right there. I remember pointing to a corner of the kitchen. I could see the stacks in stores.

Rick: *So that was the second time you had a lightning bolt of a thought pop into your head?*

Bonnie: I know, I'm starting to sound like a woo-woo, aren't I? But I only heard a voice once—that was when it said I would be with this man a long time.

The label was more like a moment of clarity. It was the accumulation of everything that everyone had told us. All the puzzle pieces came together in one picture.

Michael: It satisfied everything we heard from everyone we talked to. One of the things we believe is that the elegant solution solves more than one problem. And the label was fun.

Bonnie: That was my requirement. It had to be fun.

Rick: *As the designated artist, Michael, did you know where it was going?*

Michael: Not a clue. I knew it was going to be a foot, because we'd already decided on Barefoot Bynum, but I had no idea how impressive this was going to be.

I was tired. It was late. I wanted to go to bed. I was thinking, "Can we please get this over with?"

Bonnie: You said, "Can't you be inspired in the morning?"

Michael: Yeah, I was going, "Hold that thought for eight hours, please."

Bonnie: But I said, "I can't. I'll lose it. We have to do it now."

Rick: *When Mark told you at dinner he was a winemaker, not a businessman, and he didn't want to do it, what were you thinking?*

Bonnie: We were in shock.

Michael: We were thinking, "Well, that was a lot of work for nothing." It was really quiet after that. We're all chatty people, but it got stone silent.

Bonnie: It was like a challenge. We were very confused and our minds were buzzing. We had those little question marks over our heads. But we hadn't quit. We were both thinking, "Now how do we do this?"

Michael: It was a miracle we got it to that point. We got Souverain to pay us in wine and bottling services. We had a label, federal approval, glass, corks, credit. We just kept thinking, is there a way? Then, driving along, I had that flash.

Bonnie: Mark was wise to say he didn't know anything about the business end. We had so much respect for him as a winemaker.

Michael: When I said, "You're going to work for us," at least we knew that right away we had one of the best winemakers in the state.

Chapter Three

Taking on the Behemoth

It was bottling day. March 27, 1986. Michael and Bonnie were in their kitchen in the morning, a few hours before that giant machine at Souverain was going to fill the first 3,000 cases with cabernet sauvignon.

"This shouldn't be too hard, right?" Michael said to Bonnie. His tone was not confident.

"What could go wrong?" Bonnie said. Same tone.

They'd gone over checklists like they were at NASA mission control. They'd made sure the bottles, the corks, and the capsules had gotten to Souverain, that the labels—front and back—were printed right, and that the boxes had the Barefoot logos, red foot for the cabernet, green foot for the sauvignon blanc.

Today it would be the red ones. Everything had been lined up the day before next to the big bottling line, and now Michael's chrome locomotive was about to go to work.

Michael and Bonnie were as excited as they were nervous. Through nine months of negotiations, research, and market scrutiny, Michael and Bonnie were always hyper-aware they were rookies.

There was, for instance, the way they kept running into the phrase "standard winemaking procedures." They had no idea what that meant, and no one had a definition—no manual, no outline, no simple guidelines—not even the state Alcohol Beverage Control Board representative who told Bonnie they expected the new Barefoot wine to be made using those standard procedures.

Mark Lyon was handling the final blending and winemaking, so it seemed they would avoid any "un-standard" problems, but still. At one point, when Bonnie was making arrangements for that first bottling, one Souverain manager told her not to worry, they, of course, followed standard winemaking procedures.

"Great," Bonnie said. "I've been trying to find out what those are. Can I get a copy?"

"We don't actually have them in print," he said.

So there was Michael later that morning, standing inside Souverain's large, warehouse-like building. He was anxious about his wine and eager for it all to start, almost like a kid about to ride a fire engine.

A major league bottling line like Souverain's is something to see. It's part roller coaster, part gigantic gizmo. It has maybe 150 feet of rubber track the width of a bottle that dips and weaves, climbing small hills, dropping into enclosed sections with different wheels, tubes, and mechanical hands.

That two-story "handball court" Michael had first seen was a clean room for food handling. The line was mostly inside that, staffed by a dozen people making sure nothing fell or missed or got off track. And there were mechanics who kept the machine calibrated to fit each different bottle, label, and wine.

If the bottling line stops, it costs money. Staffers try never to stop it. So the mechanics wore belts that bristled with any tool they might need, and they sprinted around the machine, ducking under arms, jumping over tracks, to fix anything that went haywire, often while the line was running.

Michael had been told all that. Still, he wasn't ready for the speed and intensity. This eight-hour shift would fill, label, and box 18,000 bottles (magnums get packaged in six-bottle cases). That's more than 37 big bottles every minute.

When the line started, the room filled with the roar and the clink, clink of bottles that would be a constant, near-deafening din through the day. Boxes of empty bottles climbed a track, were opened and emptied by the machine, then conveyed to the end of the line. The bottles jostled down tracks and were forced into single file, then got grabbed by a mini Ferris Wheel of mechanical arms that blew in air to clean them. Another wheel dropped a tube into the bottles and filled them with wine. A third wheel lifted the bottles into a narrow cylinder that shoved in corks. Capsules were molded to bottle tops. Labels got slathered with glue and attached front and back. The bottles rolled to the end of the line.

Workers jammed them back into their boxes, then stacked the boxes onto pallets—those square wood platforms that fit prongs from a forklift and are a cornerstone of American commerce—until there were 60 cases on each. That's 360 magnums or more than 140 gallons of wine. A pallet is a lot of wine. Each pallet was shrinkwrapped and moved to a staging area.

Michael was watching this with a bit of awe. Part of him was thinking, "Wine is just another product; these could be shoes or hammers getting stuffed into boxes." He was also nervous. There seemed so much potential for calamity.

Then he saw boxes that weren't fitting the pallets right. Some were collapsing from the weight of boxes on top of them. Others had holes in their sides.

He looked at it for almost 30 seconds. That couldn't be right. What should he do?

"Heeeeey," Michael yelled running toward the box guy. "Heeey, stop!!"

The guy loading boxes looked up, then hit a button. The giant machine slowed and stopped. The quiet was startling, almost unnerving.

Michael was still running to the loading guy, but inside, he was thinking, "Whoa, this thing stops."

The line foreman got to the boxes right after Michael. He was not happy.

"What's the problem?" he said.

"Look at that mess over there," Michael said.

"Yeah," the foreman said. "The boxes probably got hit with a forklift. We'll fix it."

"How do we make sure it doesn't happen again?" Michael said.

"Don't worry," the foreman said. "It'll be fine."

Michael *was* worried. He was new to the wine business and a bottling line, but he had heard that sentence too often over the years. Most times, it wasn't fine.

"No," Michael said. "I want to be sure we don't have any more problems."

"See that big button?" the foreman said. There were half-dollar-sized red buttons all along the machine. "That stops the line. It's easier than yelling."

By the end of the day, after the 3,000 cases were bottled, trucked over winding roads and stored at Davis Bynum's winery,

Michael was back in the country kitchen with Bonnie, telling her how the bottling line had gone.

"Piece of cake," he said.

"Right," Bonnie said. "Really, how'd it go?"

Michael told her about some of the problems, how they got fixed, and how he hit the red button a couple times to stop the monster.

"It stops?" Bonnie said.

He also told her the crew wasn't thrilled to ever stop it, but that once they figured out he was concerned about every little detail, the crew got more concerned too.

That was a business lesson Michael and Bonnie would use over the years. When people have long, tough tasks to handle, they tend to roll through without paying attention to every small detail. It's human nature to take the easy road. But if you're a boss or a client and you ask for high standards, they'll give you high standards. The thing is, usually, you have to ask.

"Well, we've got wine in bottles," Bonnie. "We're a foot closer to getting the money back. Not a mile closer, but we've moved a foot."

"I'll tell you something else," Michael said. "After what I saw today, I have a lot of respect for that chrome locomotive."

Only weeks after that first bottling, with 6,000 cases of Barefoot ready to sell and more ready to be bottled, Michael made his first—and what he assumed would be his most important—sales call.

He was back in Hayward and the industrial park with the dark halls, fluorescent lighting, and cement floors for another audience with Don Brown, the corporate buyer for Lucky Stores. If Lucky carried Barefoot, it might order as many as half of the 18,000 cases that would be bottled by the end of summer. It would be the heart of Barefoot's business. It would save them. Michael and Bonnie thought Lucky could get them out of debt in two or three years almost on its own.

So Michael was sitting on that same folding chair in Brown's office, after the required wait outside.

"Yeah, Houlihan," Brown said, personable as ever. "Whaddaya want?"

Michael put a bottle of Barefoot cabernet and one of sauvignon blanc on Brown's desk.

"We bottled the wine and want you to see it," he said.

Brown picked up the bottle of red and looked it up and down. Then he did the same with the white.

"This is what you asked for," Michael said. "There aren't any leaps or hills or rivers. It's a label she can read from four feet away. The logo is the same as the name. It's in plain English and easy to pronounce. It's a name she'll remember, and a logo she won't forget."

Michael was proud of what they'd done, in the way of a student with a good report card. Barefoot was unique, interesting, and fit everything that Brown and the others said would sell. The wine, he knew, was terrific. The label was friendly and fun. What's not to love, he thought.

Brown kept looking at the bottles. He didn't say anything. The silence was uncomfortable, but Michael sat quietly. Brown looked at the bottles again but said nothing. Michael figured it was just Don Brown being Don Brown. Make everyone sweat.

"So, Don," Michael finally said, "how many truckloads do you want?"

"Are you crazy?"

Brown put the bottle down on his desk and looked at Michael like he was from Mars. Michael couldn't have gotten a worse look from Brown if he had clucked.

"Are you crazy?" Brown said. "I can't buy this. Nobody knows this brand. Nobody's ever seen or heard of Barefoot."

"It's everything you asked for," Michael said.

"Yeah, so what? That doesn't matter," Brown said. "No one's gonna buy something they never heard of. You gotta advertise it. If you're willing to spend $1 million on TV ads, I'll buy it from you."

"We don't have that kind of advertising budget," Michael said. In truth, they had no advertising budget. There wasn't $100 for ads.

"Then you gotta go make a name for yourself," Brown said. "You gotta go sell it to every mom-and-pop store on every corner until everyone knows what Barefoot is."

"That'll take years," Michael said. He felt like he just got hit by a brick.

"Well, Houlihan," Brown said. "You better get started."

About six weeks later, Michael was at a liquor store on Nob Hill in San Francisco, standing in the wine section and talking to the store's owner. He was there with a sales rep from Cavagnaro Distributing Company named Tom, but Michael was doing the talking.

"This is something you're going to want to carry," Michael told the owner. He showed him a bottle of Barefoot.

"Why's that?" the owner said. He'd been running his store for years and he'd taken a lot of sales pitches. His voice and face stayed neutral.

"Lucky doesn't have it," Michael said.

"What do you mean?"

"It's not in the chain stores," Michael said.

"No?" the owner said, mildly curious.

"Nope," Michael said, "not even in Lucky. It would give you something special. And you don't have to charge Lucky prices. Nobody's going to compare because it's unique."

The owner bought 10 cases. Michael and the Cavagnaro rep headed out toward a mom-and-pop store in North Beach.

"You know what," Tom told Michael, "that chain store thing is not a bad way to do this."

"Use whatever you have," Michael said. "Right now, that's what we've got."

"Use whatever you have" became an operating principle for Barefoot. When they finally did get big supermarket chains to carry the wine, they told the mom-and-pops exactly the opposite of what Michael said at the Nob Hill spot.

"It'll show you're just as good as the big boys," Michael would tell a small store owner, "but your customers can stay in the neighborhood to get it."

But that first year—when, as Don Brown said, nobody knew Barefoot—they had to make a big deal out of every possible selling point and use every chance they had to promote.

Their first marketing material, something they handed to store owners and distributors, said their grapes grew next to other grapes that produced an award-winning wine. They said it more elegantly, but that was the crux. Grapes with good neighbors was the best they had.

And unlike some wineries that avoided all marketing on their label in the hope of appearing refined and exclusive, Barefoot sold itself like crazy on the back label. Michael and Bonnie used the largest label that could fit a bottling machine to get more space to pitch to consumers.

In that first year, the complete name of the wine was Barefoot Bynum, in part because Davis Bynum agreed to carry it in his tasting room, but also because it let them leverage some of the Bynum reputation. Hampton Bynum—Michael and Bonnie's longtime friend—was the winemaker for his father, Davis, so they got Hampton to write and sign a note on the back label. Theoretically. Michael and Bonnie, of course, wrote it.

"Barefoot traces its origins to the sixties when Davis Bynum first conceived the idea of producing the 'Chateau La Feet' of house wine," Hampton's message said. "Like the Bordeaux region of France, Sonoma County's moderate climate and rich alluvial soil provide the ideal environment for growing the award-winning grapes used for this premium varietal.

"Continuing the tradition of quality and excellence long associated with my father, I am happy to present this outstanding value. Barefoot is the ideal choice for your personal and entertainment needs. Your guests will be impressed when you put your best foot forward. Let us be your purveyor for fine house wine. Step up to Barefoot!"

So, they gave themselves a tradition, invented the idea of a personal house wine, threw in some foot puns (hundreds more would come), associated themselves with everything from medal-winning wines to Bordeaux, reminded people they were from prime Sonoma County wine country, and used every inch of their connection to the Bynums. Use what you have.

After Don Brown sent him off to sell Barefoot store-by-store in Northern California, Michael did get a couple small grocery groups to carry Barefoot, including Lunardi's, with stores around the Bay Area, and the San Francisco–based Petrini's, which had about a dozen supermarkets.

Petrini's buyer was Art Mueller—the man who told Michael to "put it in a pig"—and he not only came through by stocking Barefoot, he put in a call to Cavagnaro Distributing Company and got Barefoot its first distributor. That's when the real lessons started.

Cavagnaro was based in Vallejo and dealt with stores in San Francisco and the eastern and northern Bay Area. Like most distributors, it handled wine, beer, and spirits. After Mueller's call, Dick Cavagnaro was thoroughly decent to Michael, but he didn't exactly do summersaults to get Barefoot onto store shelves. That was when Michael would learn two stone-cold realities about the wine business.

First, distributors don't build new brands. Not at the size where Barefoot was starting. They can't. They're too busy. Their hands are full with big portfolios and long-time accounts. There's no time—and, frankly, not much incentive—to try to sell something unproven.

And second, that led to a necessity that would define Michael's life for the next decade-plus. It's called a "ride with." The term is often used as a noun—Michael was with Tom on a ride with that day in San Francisco—and it's when a winery person goes on sales calls with a distributor's rep. It is absolutely crucial for a new wine company to spend many, many days on ride withs.

The rides work for distributors who want someone from a winery to lavish attention on store buyers and, hopefully, boost both sales and goodwill. For a winery like Barefoot, those ride withs were crucial because they meant Michael would get to pitch Barefoot to the stores. If he weren't there, the distributor rep would push a brand the store owner already liked. It's so much easier to sell what's already working.

But in the first weeks when Cavagnaro took on Barefoot, he wasn't giving Michael any rides. He said his sales crew was already scheduled to go out with bigger wineries or beer company reps.

So during those first weeks, Michael haunted Cavagnaro's warehouse offices on Fridays. That's because Cavagnaro, like most distributing companies, had sales meetings every Friday to hear pitches from producers—wineries, breweries, and spirit companies—who wanted the sales reps to push their products or take them on rides.

Michael got an initial turn to pitch Barefoot, but for three more Fridays, he just hung out, shook hands, tried to make what friends he could. That friendliness landed him another chance to talk at another Friday meeting a month later.

Michael reminded them that Barefoot was approachable, fun, and different, and it was a good wine for a good price. He said customers who tried it would buy more. While he talked, Michael watched the salespeople, trying to gauge their reaction. There was one guy Michael hadn't seen before.

"What about you?" Michael said to him.

The guy was tall, and had dark hair. He looked to his left, then his right, before he pointed to his chest and raised his eyebrows.

"You're new, right?" Michael said.

"Started yesterday," the guy said.

"Where's your territory?"

"San Francisco. Covered it in my old job."

"Let's go ride through San Francisco," Michael said.

"Uh, sure," the guy said. "Why not?"

They got interrupted by the sales manager, a heavyset, balding man.

"Whoa, whoa, whoa," he said to Michael. "You can't assign your own ride with. You gotta go through me."

"C'mon," Michael said as charmingly as he could. "I need a break, here. I've been trying to get rides for weeks."

The manager looked at him for a moment. He took a breath to show he was exercising enormous patience and mercy. "OK, fine," the manager said. "Ride with Tom. Just make some sales."

On that day in San Francisco, Michael and Tom finished around Nob Hill and headed toward the North Beach and Marina districts of The City. This door-to-door wine selling was still new to Michael, and Tom was filling him in on details. Though he was a rookie at Cavagnaro, Tom had been in the business long enough to know just how painstaking the selling really was.

"You know," he told Michael, "we're going to have to come back and build the display for that guy up on Nob Hill, don't you?"

"Why?"

"If we just deliver him 10 cases, he'll only put out a few bottles," Tom said. "He doesn't have time to build a stack himself. But he'll be happy to have you do it."

"Wonderful," Michael said. "Guess I'll be back next week."

Michael had enough experience with other kinds of sales to grasp that he needed to service the store owners. On the other hand, he was realizing he understood very little about one of the most critical and complex pieces of the wine-selling puzzle: the role of distributors.

As they rolled through The City, Michael picked Tom's brain as much as he could. He told Tom all he really understood was that the relationship between a winery and a distributor was entirely different from what he first assumed.

"You are not," Tom said, "the first guy to say that."

Distributors are a central hub in the wine-selling world. They are, in short, alcohol beverage wholesalers, and they're the middle step of what's called the three-tier system—a tangle of post-Prohibition laws and state-by-state regulations that can make getting wine into stores and into the hands of wine drinkers ridiculously complicated.

In simple terms, the first tier is producers (wineries, breweries, whiskey makers, etc.), the next is distributors, who buy from producers and sell to the third tier, which is the retailers (restaurants, wine shops, liquor stores, and markets large and small).

Most states have what are called "tied house laws," meaning no business on one tier can be "tied" via ownership to a business on another. It was fairly common before Prohibition, for instance, for saloons to be owned by beer companies. The forced separation was a post-Prohibition, anti–organized-crime concept. Whether it works is a debate. What makes it so complicated is that it's a nationwide puzzle that's different in just about every state.

A state like California is a rarity. It allows wineries to sell directly to retailers within the state, tier one straight to tier three. But in most other states, wineries must sell to a distributor first, who then sells to the retailers. And a winery in one state, even if it's

California, is almost never allowed to jump over the middle tier in a different state and sell directly to a retail store there. So Barefoot could sell straight to a Safeway in San Francisco—if Safeway wanted to carry Barefoot, which in the first years it didn't—but Barefoot would need a distributor to sell to a Safeway in Las Vegas.

Barefoot, right at the start, had a distributor in New Jersey, of all places. It was a company called Fedway, and Michael and Bonnie connected to them with help from Davis Bynum. So in that first year, Barefoot was sold throughout Northern California and in New Jersey. Go figure.

As they wove through traffic, Tom was telling Michael there's one universal truth no matter where wine is sold. Wineries, he said, usually misunderstood how to get the most from their distributors. For instance, it was crucial for Michael to be out working the stores.

Lots of producers assume they're done when they land a good distributor, but that's just the start. Even when they have a distributor, winery owners and reps have to go sell their wine. And they have to continually be out establishing themselves and keeping their connections.

"You can't just hand over that responsibility to launch your brand," Tom said. "We do a lot of selling, but I have so many other brands that my buyers already know and want, I can't give Barefoot much attention—except when you're in the car with me."

"Nobody told me that part," Michael said. "I thought I just needed to come out to put a face on Barefoot."

The good news, Tom said, is that if a new brand like Barefoot starts to get some traction, distributors will build on it, because everyone finds time to service accounts that are selling well.

What distributors and their reps offer is their ability to blanket an area. They have enough people to get to most retail outlets. And they deliver the wine. As simple as that sounds, a case of wine weighs 35 to 40 pounds, and there's no way someone like Michael could sell and cart wine to all the stores.

Just as valuable to a winery is that after a distributor buys wine from Barefoot (because they think they can place it), or after Michael gets Barefoot placed in a store himself (to be delivered by the distributor rep), the distributor pays the winery within a month, whether or not they sell it or the store pays for it.

"Without us, you'd have a nightmare trying to get square with all those little accounts," Tom said.

By that point, Tom and Michael were trolling Chestnut Street for a parking spot and headed for a good-sized liquor store in the Marina. Tom was explaining they'd have to give the store owner a couple bottles.

"Aren't free bottles illegal?" Michael said.

"Not samples. They're OK," Tom said. "We can give him one bottle of each varietal."

"Am I going to have to do that a lot?"

"Yeah, probably," Tom said.

"This is going to get expensive," Michael said.

"Yeah, probably," Tom said.

In the store, Michael and the owner talked. Michael gave his not-in-Lucky-Stores pitch, and the owner said, OK, two cases. But he wanted samples, as Tom predicted. Michael handed him a bottle of cab and a bottle of sauv blanc.

The owner didn't seem particularly thrilled about the new wine. But he also seemed like he didn't get thrilled about much. He said he'd see how Barefoot sells.

Back in the car, Michael said he was a little surprised the store owner bought any Barefoot, considering how un-moved he had seemed.

Tom said most small store owners will be like that. Barefoot was new to them, they couldn't afford to take risks, and they'll all be happier when Barefoot makes a name for itself because then they'll have a wine that's popular.

"Will we get a reorder?" Michael said.

"Maybe," Tom said. "I know that guy. The more you stay on him, the more he'll like it. He'll be happy you're paying attention to him. Makes him feel like you're not a risk for him."

"Another person to watch," Michael said. "I'm gonna need five of me."

"Five sounds about right," Tom said. He said getting reorders are also a little more complicated than they seem. Michael thought everything in the wine business was turning out to be more complicated than it seemed.

The thing about reorders, Tom said, was that distributor reps don't have the time, or the incentive, to get them for all their products in all their stores. For the same reason the reps initially sell their proven wines and beers, they make sure to track their most popular products.

Plus a lot of wine companies and other producers pay distributor reps extra commissions—they're called spiffs and they're perfectly legal done right—to move their wines. Products with spiffs get attention from a rep.

"They're a good idea for someone trying to build a brand," Tom said.

"If someone trying to build a brand," Michael said, "had any money for spiffs."

Either way, Michael was going to have to keep tabs on the stores that carried Barefoot and get them to reorder when the wine sold out. Tom said Barefoot looked like it could become a fast seller, and that's good news and bad news, too. The plus side is that it would be selling. The bad news is that, unless Michael got the reorders quickly, that shelf space would go to another wine.

"So if my wine sells well," Michael said, "that's bad for me?"

"It can be."

"What do I do?"

"That's why you gotta go get the reorders yourself," Tom said. "If you bring your rep the reorder, he'll get the commission without doing much work for it. He'll love you. The stores will like you, too, 'cause they'll start to believe you're coming back and they can count on your wine getting delivered."

"I need to go back to every place we've just sold Barefoot?" Michael said. "I need to re-trace my steps to the old places, at the same time I'm trying to get into new ones?"

"That's what I'd do," Tom said, "if there were five of me."

One good thing for Barefoot, Tom said, was that Cavagnaro was a solid company and a good size for Barefoot. They're small enough, he said, that they can't ignore any of their producers so they generally hustle to get reorders.

"So I should stay with small distributors?" Michael said.

"Actually, not always," Tom said. "Some, sure, but the biggies have advantages, too."

Many retailers allocate some shelf space to big distributors, he said. They know those big boys will keep strong products on their shelves. If Barefoot got a big distributor, that could mean some guaranteed prime shelf space, but it could also turn out that the big boy didn't want to use its space for a new brand like Barefoot, so it might not try to sell it at all.

"Man oh man," Michael said.

"Yup," Tom said.

"This is just great," Michael muttered. "Nothing is ever in a straight line, everything is harder and takes more work than it should, everything costs way more than it looks like."

"Welcome to the wine industry," Tom said.

CONVERSATIONS WITH BONNIE AND MICHAEL

Rick: *When you went back to Don Brown to tell him what you'd done with Barefoot, what did you expect him to say?*

Michael: I was so proud of myself. I expected him to buy a couple of truckloads every month.

Bonnie: And to say thank you for doing what he asked for.

Michael: We were thinking, "Here's your dream brand, Don. You said nobody ever asked you what you wanted. Well, here it is."

Bonnie: We did it, Don. Ta-da!

Rick: *Was there a business lesson in his reaction?*

Michael: The takeaway is, you learn what the job is, then you do it. Don wasn't saying no, he was just saying later. He said, prove to me this will move. So, OK, that's what we'll do, even though selling to every corner store in Northern California wasn't our original plan.

Bonnie: That happens to every business. Your plan changes. So you say, now how do we do this?

Michael: At some point when you're an entrepreneur, you're a passenger on your own adventure. You adapt and ask, how do we make this work?

Rick: *You thought you'd sell a big portion of your wine to Lucky and fill in the rest. Instead, you were tossed into the distribution system. It took you years to learn how it worked, but what was the first surprise?*

Michael: I had no idea how much work was involved. I had no idea what I was facing. I began to have a lot of respect for what I had to do.

This distributor rep is reading me the riot act—"If you want to do this, this is what you have to do."—and I'm thinking, "Isn't that your job?" But, he doesn't have time. I was learning how much he has to do, too.

Bonnie: We were the new guys. All his old accounts came first.

Michael: We were realizing everybody wants us to prove it'll sell before they take it on, and that I was the only guy who could do that. I had to sell it. We weren't going to get any help.

Bonnie: We believed it would sell from the beginning, so we started selling. And we had all that debt. That turned out to be a real advantage because we had no choice. We had to go forward.

Rick: *Were you surprised by the first retail buyer reactions?*

Bonnie: Our wine was really non-traditional. Most retail buyers wanted the standard, traditional label.

Michael: They felt safer with the standard style. They were saying, "Oh, you put a foot on it. Maybe you should change it." We said, "Let's just sell to people who like the foot."

Bonnie: The buyers kept saying, they'd never seen anything like this before. We tried to tell them, originality and fun are good ideas. Barefoot could brighten up their wine departments.

Michael: That's when we realized our first job was getting through the gatekeepers. They were used to rejecting anything different. We were new, non-vintage, and we had a foot on the label. We gave them a lot of reasons to say no.

Rick: *Were there any retailers who just got it right away?*

Bonnie: There was one person. Wilfred Wong. He supported Barefoot from the start. He owned the Ashbury Market in the Haight (in San Francisco) and he was trying to do the same thing we were—we were both going after new wine drinkers and trying to make wine approachable.

Michael: At the end of one very frustrating day of rejection, I walked into Wilfred's store and saw the wine section. For a neighborhood grocery store, he had devoted an awful lot of floor space to wine, and he had put lots of energy into describing the wines. He had handwritten notes on the shelves.

I knew I had found an ally, so I showed him the foot.

Bonnie: Wilfred liked it right away. He said it was a really friendly approach.

Michael: He looked at our poster with a beach theme and our sales material and he said, "Perfect. We'll build a stack right here." I was flabbergasted. This was the first real display in San Francisco with our posters and all the point-of-sale material.

Bonnie: I liked all his displays and descriptions in his market. He used plain English. I could pronounce the words. He was our kind of guy.

Michael: Wilfred sold Barefoot for many years. And because of how he was using it, he gave me an idea how to sell to snobby wine shops—tell them they first had to get some customers just to like wine.

Bonnie: It's been great to see him go on to become a major player in the wine industry. He's such an advocate for the average person.

Rick: *The philosophy of the brand was consistent from the start, and it was a guide in tough times. Where did it come from?*

Bonnie: Some of it was going with your gut. Mine said, wine didn't have to be stuffy. You shouldn't need a degree in enology or have to be fluent in French to enjoy a glass of wine.

Michael: That gets into the issue of, what is a brand. It's not just a cute label. It's a movement, a philosophy. That's what we teach people, now.

Bonnie: For us, it was to be approachable, fun and inclusive, and to give people permission to be that way, too.

Michael: That's it. It's what we stand for as people. It's what we're made of.

Rick: *And the mission statement comes out of that?*

Michael: The mission statement—"best wine, best price"—came from a simple concept. We wanted to be wine for the people, for the average person.

Bonnie: My nephew Robert Gilbert lived with us for two years. He called Barefoot non-confounding. That was something original for wine in the '80s. That was what we wanted to be. A lot of it came from Mark Lyon, too.

Michael: Mark said it should be approachable, affordable, and accessible. Bonnie, you were the target audience.

Bonnie: That was me. I was intimidated by wine. I figured there were a lot of people out there like me. I'd go into a store, look at a wine section, and it would look like a pizza. There was too much stuff. I had no idea where to begin, and I was afraid to ask questions because I couldn't pronounce most of it.

Chapter Four

Have You Had Your Brick for the Day?

When Bonnie and Michael started working on Barefoot in 1985, they used their rented house on the MacMurray Ranch as their "command center." They spread sales materials on whatever flat surfaces they could find, but the heart of their operation was a one-room office in what should have been the laundry room.

The laundry room had the best light in the little farmhouse, and they never actually had a washing machine anyway (their most regular laundromat was Mark Lyon's house). They put a couple sawhorses under an old door they found in a nearby barn and made that their desk/conference table/assembly center for sales materials. It sat right under the unused hook-ups for a washer and dryer.

Michael bragged to people that at least their office had a door to the outside. That was important, he said. That's where he and Bonnie went to change their minds.

"It's too small inside," he told anyone who asked why.

By 1987, they moved their office into the attic of the Davis Bynum Winery, which was across one big hill along Westside Road. (The laundry room kept its role as supply center for sales materials.) The winery office was a bit larger, though only a bit. It did give them room to change their minds indoors, but more importantly, it provided space for the couple of support staffers they needed by then. They rarely wrote a memo, though, because everyone already heard and saw what everyone else was doing. Sometimes efficiencies pop up where you least expect them.

The good news for Michael and Bonnie was that they blew through those first 18,000 cases in about six months. They sold to some regional supermarket groups, to small grocery and liquor stores around Northern California, and, of course, to bottle shops and bodegas in New Jersey. Those sales came in big part from hustle, but also from the research Michael and Bonnie had done. Barefoot was unique and approachable, and it had found a niche in the market, albeit a tiny one.

By early 1987, Barefoot was spreading a bit wider in Northern California, and the brand was being handled by a small scattering of distributors, almost all of whom were most enthusiastic about the brand when Michael was riding along, as Tom from Cavagnaro had warned.

Bonnie's duties included tracking accounts and supplies, juggling revenue and debts, and keeping tabs on permits, taxes and all the industry's trap doors. Michael was out every day, either with a distributor rep or on his own, hustling new sales or getting reorders himself and delivering them to distributors. Most evenings he was calling distributor reps, recapping the orders that got placed or going over the reorders he brought them.

And Michael was learning something about selling wine. He got his best response from store owners when he worked with them, and tried to see their concerns and solve their problems. Instead of just boasting that Barefoot was a terrific product, as if he were across a negotiating table from his customers, he found that if he figuratively stood alongside them, saw their businesses and their pressures, he could see how Barefoot would fill a gap or ease a need.

It was the same approach that had led them to the Barefoot brand, label, and attitude. Their research about store shoppers and about the people who bought wine started with the same premise: let's try to see this from the shopper's point of view. In the 21st century, the business term for that is, know your end users.

That's how they came to understand who their target customers were—that person shopping in the store who just wanted a good, reliable, $5 bottle of wine, and who welcomed that friendly foot with the promise of fun, and of California in a bottle.

That's also how they created the concept of a Personal House Wine—an everyday, easy-on-the-wallet, drinkable wine that would appeal to a mass market of regular folks, and be as familiar as anything in their kitchens.

It was an original approach in the category of fine wine. Barefoot wasn't selling its exclusivity or mystery, it sold familiarity, reliability, and approachable quality. The goal was to make the wine a comfortable, welcome friend in America's households, just like a brand of coffee or corn flakes.

Michael and Bonnie's research led them to another piece of the wine-selling puzzle, an idea they called the Velocity Price Point. They found that some things sell way faster at one price than another, and the differences weren't linear. That's why they priced those first Barefoot bottles at $4.99—the sales volume was exponentially better than, say, a $5.99 or $6.99 bottle. It was the difference between staying in business and falling flat.

To get to that Velocity Price Point, they had to work backward to figure the price to charge when the wine left their hands. They couldn't simply pick a price that would cover all their costs and leave a healthy profit, they had to start with the price they wanted Barefoot to sell for on store shelves.

Then they took out the store's cut, then the distributor's cut, the taxes, then landed where they landed. Once they broke it all down, they managed to get most of their wine sold for $4.99, give or take the occasional sale or stubborn store owner. The downside was, their profit margin was razor thin, if there was a profit at all.

Even before the first bottling, their research into costs had shown that they would need to sell more wine than those original 18,000 cases. The profit from those sales wouldn't come close to covering the debt.

But after they worked through that first supply and understood more about the costs of doing business—the corks, bottles, boxes, wine, printing, sales materials, shipping, taxes, samples, commissions, and more—they thought maybe they understated it when they told Mark they'd repay the debt in four years. From what they could see, 40 years might have been a more realistic goal.

In spring 1987, more Barefoot wine was headed for another bottling line. Michael and Bonnie, with Mark as their guide, bought more Sonoma County wine—unbottled and still in tanks—and moved their winemaking and bottling to the little town of Asti a few miles north of Souverain.

They were in the huge facility that once housed Italian Swiss Colony, one of California's cornerstone wineries. Mark helped blend and finish the wine again, and on this day bottling cabernet sauvignon, Bonnie was overseeing the action.

If the wine business still seemed like a spinning monster of an industry to Michael and Bonnie, at least these bottling lines were one piece they grasped—as much as a bottling line would allow. Never get cocky with a big machine. The labeler was temperamental that day and there were some gear problems.

Bonnie hit the stop button more than once. Rick Rizzolo, the bottling line manager, or more often, Mario Dericco, the engineer, hustled over, and Mario would say a polite "I'll get that fixed right away, Miss Bonnie," then scramble off.

By the end of a shift that felt longer than its eight hours, another 1,500 cases of Barefoot Cab were in bottles. Mario and Rick were talking to Bonnie.

"That was a bit of a tough ride," Mario said. He still wore his tool belt. His dark, now-grimy hair was splayed out under his baseball cap.

"We got them bottled," Bonnie said nicely. "I appreciate your effort."

"Thanks," he said. "You good with everything?"

"Pretty much," Bonnie said, "but I have to tell you, there was one problem."

She said it sweetly, like she was asking for a favor that mattered to her. Mario was concerned. Rick moved in to hear, too. This was Barefoot's first time here, and it looked like a company that would be bottling a lot of wine. Rick and Mario wanted to keep her business.

"What can we do?" Rick asked.

"Our bottle says, 'Step up to Barefoot.'" Bonnie said. "We really need to have the toes on all the corks facing up."

Mario looked at her with his mouth open. He was dumbstruck. To bottle those 1,500 cases, the 9,000 corks were poured into bins on top of the machine, where they jiggled around and fell into slots. Then the machine inserted them into the bottles. It was a 50-50 chance what side pointed up. There was no possible way to control the direction of corks bouncing around the bin.

The only thing Mario could think of would be a ridiculous waste of time and money: He'd need extra workers to watch each bottle right as it got a cork, grab the ones with toes down, uncork them, pour the wine out, bring them back to the start of the bottling line and run them through again, hoping they'd get a toes-up cork. If they didn't, they'd have to do it again, and keep doing it until it came in right. Mario didn't know how to begin.

"Uh, well, um," Mario said. He stared at Bonnie like he was trying to decide if she was insanely picky or just insane.

"Uh, you know, we, uh . . ." Mario stammered out as politely as he could manage.

Rick couldn't hold it in. He started laughing. So did Bonnie.

"Mario," Bonnie said, trying to bring him back to life. "I'm just playing. I know there's no way. Gotcha though, huh?"

Yes. Good joke, Mario said. He was still shaking his head a little as they closed up the warehouse.

A couple weeks later, Bonnie was back at the Asti bottling line, this time with sauvignon blanc. The engineer in charge this day was John Ferrera, a guy who was a bit more rough-edged than Mario. It was another long day. When it was done, John was clearly exhausted. He walked over to Bonnie to check in.

"Thanks for all your effort," Bonnie said.

"So we good?" John said.

"Well," Bonnie said. She had gone all innocent and sweet again. "I just have to insist on one thing. We have to have the toes on the corks pointing up."

"Toes up? No way! NO WAY!!!"

John looked at her for a moment. His face got red. Then he launched into a loud explanation of the absolute lunacy of Bonnie's request.

"There are thousands of corks and they're tossed around in the hopper and there's no way, no way, and we'd be grabbing bottles and dumping and re-sterilizing and we'd ruin every cork so we'd need thousands more and, this is the craziest, most ridiculous, do you know how many people we'd need . . ." he blurted.

Bonnie stood there earnestly and listened to everything John said, nodding along with him. She let him finish.

"But John," she said sweetly, like a small girl asking for a cookie, "Mario does it for me."

John couldn't form real words. He stomped off grumbling, probably thinking he was never going to work with this crazy person again. Let Mario do it.

When John was gone from the big bottling room, a couple of women working the line came over to Bonnie. They were giggling. They said she had delivered the joke better the second time, and, besides, John was usually the practical joker, so this was good for him.

Bonnie never knew exactly when John figured it out. Probably when he went to Rick to complain about the nutso lady from Barefoot, she guessed.

A few years later, Michael and Bonnie were at a restaurant in Healdsburg, and they saw John having dinner across the room. John gave Bonnie a thumbs up and mouthed the words, "Toes up."

The good news for Bonnie and Michael in mid-1987 was that Barefoot had found a place in the wine sales pipeline. The mom-and-pop stores and the regional chains were getting sol-id sales from the easy-to-buy, easy-to-drink wine. There was a downside to that, however. Now that Barefoot was in the pipe-line, Michael and Bonnie could never ever let the supply run dry, even for a few days.

If they didn't keep Barefoot on all those shelves, the stores would fill the space with some other wine. Stores don't save shelf space for a new and unproven brand, and once the stores put a new wine where Barefoot had once been, that other brand would probably stay there and Barefoot would lose its foothold.

Meanwhile, Barefoot's distributor reps were overloaded with too many wines—and beers and spirits—to watch the shelves closely. The wines they did focus on were the long-time big sellers. A rep handling hundreds of wines and covering hundreds of stores simply couldn't keep too close an eye on a young, low-priced, fast-mover like Barefoot.

So Michael and Bonnie hired Curt Anderson. He was their first Barefooter. That's what they called him and the scores of people who would come after him over the years, Barefooters. Curt's job was to do what distributors didn't have time to do. He kept the wine on the shelves.

Curt, of course, got almost no budget, because there was no budget for anything, so he hired part-timers, fresh college grads looking to break into the wine business.

Curt's team got long lists of things to check. They would watch the store shelves, get the reorders and bring them to dis-tributors, who certainly had time to deliver wine to stores, because deliveries meant commissions.

They also helped build displays, put up signs, and put down sales materials like shelf notes. They made sure bar codes, price tags, and stickers were in place, and they looked for torn or stained labels. They did everything they could to make Barefoot easy to sell and easy to buy.

Michael and Bonnie considered what they did to be customer service. Curt and his crew—they called the small group Curt's Merchandising Army, irony intended on the "army" part—were serving the stores that carried Barefoot by keeping the displays looking good and by keeping the wine in stock. And they were serving store shoppers who wanted their Barefoot.

When Curt got a display, he never lost it. He maintained more than 75 permanent Barefoot displays in Northern California for more than 10 years. He proved that Barefoot would get a loyal following, if they could just keep it on the shelf.

But, somewhat ironically, Curt's success showed Michael and Bonnie just how expensive it was to grow. Besides all the costs of producing and bottling more wine, Barefoot needed to expand their manpower to sell in new territories, deal with new distributors and buyers, and to cover new stores. If Barefoot was going to expand along the West Coast and across the country, it was going to need a lot more Barefooters.

There were other lessons. Michael and Bonnie had come to understand their profit margin would be vapors for a while, but some costs and challenges seemed to come from nowhere. They were, as Michael said, as predictable as bricks falling out of the sky.

"That's what it's like," Michael told Barefoot staffers. "Every day, bam, smacked in the head by a brick. You think you've got something figured out, then, bam, there's a new brick."

That became their rallying cry: "Have you had your brick for the day?" It was battlefield humor but also a reminder to keep their eyes open, to be prepared, because there was always another surprise brick coming.

There were, for instance, the spiffs—those sales incentives and commissions that Michael had been introduced to so quickly. As Barefoot expanded, there were more and more commissions and incentives to pay at every level.

Or, if a store wanted to put Barefoot on sale, say drop the price to $3.99, usually Barefoot and the distributors ate the cost. Sometimes Barefoot and the distributor would split it, sometimes the distributor would bill it all to Barefoot.

And bigger stores—in the first years, that meant the regional supermarket groups—knew exactly how important they were to Barefoot's survival, so they knew they could ask for ever-larger discounts because Michael and Bonnie couldn't afford to get their wine dropped by those stores.

The term for getting dropped is "DCed"—it means discontinued—and that was Michael's constant nightmare, that Barefoot would get DCed somewhere important, because there's no coming back from that. That was a big reason for the Barefoot-ers. If a wine gets DCed, that means the buyer or manager is done with it, and that wine may never get back into the store or chain, at least not until there's a management change or someone new buying for the department.

Michael and Bonnie learned this by striking out at some stores, or by not getting the reorder fast enough and getting DCed. Or by getting hit with a brick, like the store that discontinued them because Barefoot was selling so fast the wine clerk got tired of con-tinually trekking to the back room to put more bottles on the shelf.

After a few of those, Michael figured it was better not to get picked up by a store in the first place than to get DCed, because at least there was still hope to get in. Michael was still trying to get Don Brown to buy Barefoot for Lucky Stores, but if Barefoot got in, then got DCed by Brown, it would be over. So in one way, things were going perfectly well with Lucky.

On a golden fall day in 1987, a short, dignified man walked into Barefoot's one-room office above Davis Bynum Winery.

He wore a crisp dark suit, and despite his size, he stood tall. He was more friendly than formal, but he got right to it.

"My name is Bob Meyer, and I want to promote your wines," he told Michael.

"We don't have any money for marketing," Michael said. He pointed to the rickety attic office. Bonnie had her desk in the room with Michael. So did Barefoot's secretary, its general manager, and its salesperson. "As you can probably tell, we barely have money for an office."

"Well," Bob said, "then I've come to the right place."

Bob actually called himself "Bob Bob," and so did everyone else. ("Hi," he'd tell the secretary when he called, "this is Bob." "Bob, who?" she'd say. "You know, Bob Bob," he'd say. "Just a moment, Bob Bob," the secretary would say.)

Bob Bob, like everyone coming to the overstuffed office, had to make his pitch in front of the entire staff. It didn't bother him.

"I'm here to give you guys a hand with marketing," he said, "and it's not going to cost you anything."

Bob Bob had a suite at the Super Bowl in San Diego that January. He was hosting a lot of VIPs, including a bunch from Northern California.

"If you give me a couple cases of your wine, I'll make sure it gets poured at the game," Bob Bob said. "And I'll talk it up."

"So what do you want from us?" Michael said.

"Just your wine," Bob Bob said.

Bob Bob showed Michael a hefty list of events he went to every year to pour wine for VIPs and guests, including the Marine Corps Toys for Tots night in San Francisco and the Marin Film Festival. Most were in Northern California, but some were as far away as Fort Lauderdale.

"I do a lot of charities," Bob Bob said. "I'll pour Barefoot at them all, if you want."

Michael wasn't exactly sure how Bob Bob was connected to the charities, but he guessed Bob Bob kept an eye out for new wineries because they were the ones who could use his help. He also guessed that Bob Bob used wine as a kind of barter, which wasn't far from what Barefoot was trying to do.

Michael had been trying to leverage their wine for attention from the start, and this was exactly how it could work. The opportunity with Bob Bob seemed right on target.

"I want to bring them good wine, and something that's new and interesting," Bob Bob said. "People will like Barefoot and they'll like that it's fun. They're going to want to buy it."

Michael said he'd donate two cases for each event. In return, he asked Bob Bob to put up some Barefoot signs and posters, and to hand out a list telling people where Barefoot is available. He also asked for contact names so he could follow up with some of the people, and for Bob Bob to find out where the VIPs bought wine, so Michael could go to those stores and tell them that important people wanted to buy Barefoot there.

"No problem," Bob Bob said. There was amusement in his voice. "You don't mind asking for a lot, do you?"

"And you just walked in and asked for free wine," Michael said smiling.

"Fair enough," Bob Bob said. "I think this is gonna work out with us."

He was right. It was the start of something revolutionary in American wine. Michael, Bonnie and Bob Bob would work together for years, and they're still friends. They were, as Michael told people, kindred spirits, people who used whatever resources they had—and often that was wine—to get things done, to have some impact, to help charities and to help their business.

There was one event, a fundraiser in San Francisco's Chinatown in early 1988 that created another flash of inspiration for Michael and Bonnie. In one way, the Chinatown gathering was like most of Bob Bob's events. It was a fundraiser with some movers and shakers there.

But it was different, too, because of the scale. This wasn't some giant citywide gala, and it sure wasn't the Super Bowl. It was just a party for a neighborhood park. That made it intimate and personal, and it built a bond between Barefoot and the people who were there. The group wasn't particularly large, but the new connection went deep because Barefoot was supporting a park they cared about. That's when the light went on for Michael and Bonnie.

Like most of their creative flashes in Barefoot's young-but-complicated life, it wasn't just one event that hit the switch, it was the weight of everything. Sometimes, you have to hang out with an idea for a while, the way Bonnie had mulled over the concept of the foot and the label. The small Chinatown park was the last piece. It made their concept solid, and it launched Michael and Bonnie toward what would become one of the major, indelible forces of the Barefoot Spirit. They called it Worthy Cause Marketing.

Almost from the start, Michael and Bonnie donated wine to charities. That was one reason they embraced Bob Bob so quickly. And long before they created Barefoot, both of them worked with causes ranging from local parks to environmentalism to civil rights. Worthy Cause Marketing was another step forward. It was a way to support good people and programs, and it was a way to promote Barefoot that felt genuine.

The simple version is they made helping charities their avenue for marketing. And they helped those groups with the only resource they had—wine.

They started looking for events linked to good causes, and particularly causes that were important to them. Michael and Bonnie donated wine, went to the events to talk up Barefoot and add some fun, and they asked a few favors from the charities that cost the groups nothing.

In return for the wine and the fun, organizers thanked Barefoot from the stage so people would know Barefoot was in the house, and they let Michael and Bonnie put up Barefoot signs, hand out explanations of why Barefoot supported those charities, and post lists of stores that carried Barefoot wine.

One key was that Barefoot didn't go to many large, glamorous events. Most, especially at first, were small, community affairs—fundraisers for a park, a local food bank, a struggling AIDS clinic, a theater group, a senior center and more. These were programs perpetually short on funding and attention, and Barefoot helped with a little of both.

Part of the goal was to create goodwill at those events—by bringing playfulness, a sense of humor, and, of course, wine—but Michael and Bonnie wanted to get something else from the events. They wanted market research.

They didn't just talk up their wine, they also listened to the people. They asked about attitudes toward the wine world (most folks were intimidated), toward Barefoot's foot (most people loved it), and toward buying wine (nearly everyone just wanted to find something they liked and could afford).

They also asked people where they bought their wine, and if they had their way, what stores should carry Barefoot. Then, Michael went to those stores, say Steve's Liquors up the street from the senior center, and told Steve he just poured for 250 people, and a lot of them wanted to buy Barefoot at Steve's, if he only carried it. Usually Steve was thrilled to order a couple cases.

Or, a few weeks before an event, particularly small community fundraisers, Michael would go to that Steve's Liquors and tell the store owner he would be pouring at the senior center's fundraiser.

"Would you like to help out?" he would ask the owner.

The guy would say, "Maybe, what's it gonna cost?"

"Not a penny," Michael would tell him. "We'd like to tell people at the fundraiser they can buy more Barefoot here."

Ol' Steve would usually order Barefoot. He was going to get new customers coming in looking for a wine he carries, and he would look like he was part of the fundraiser. It was an easy decision for him.

Barefoot would get much better at Worthy Cause Marketing. And soon they would get someone on board who would supercharge their efforts. But in the first years, when Barefoot needed every friend it could get, their idea was to win plenty of friends just as it was driving more support to needy charities.

This type of marketing was also getting more stores to carry the wine, creating committed Barefoot-drinking customers, and, as Lucky Store's Don Brown had demanded, it was getting people to know Barefoot's name.

When Brown, the buyer for more than 80 California super-markets, sent Michael out to sell store by store—all those independent grocers, liquor stores, and mom-and-pops are called the broad market—their odd relationship didn't end.

Michael would drop in every couple months, sit outside Brown's office on the small, hard chair for a while, then go in, give Brown a progress report on Barefoot and get harrumphed at.

"We're doing well in the broad market," Michael said during one meeting in late-1987. "People are getting to know us."

Michael suspected Brown actually liked him, maybe even respected him, because of his doggedness and optimism. But Brown wasn't about to show it.

"The stores keep reordering and consumers tell us they love the label and the wine," Michael told Brown. "And we have to keep bottling faster and faster."

"Well, Houlihan," Brown said, "keep at it."

It was almost a ritual. Michael would come in, give Brown some numbers, tell him about Barefoot's growth, and Brown would say keep at it.

In summer 1988, Michael was back in Brown's office ready to do the dance again. It started off pretty much as ever.

"Whaddaya want, Houlihan?" Brown said.

"Just wanted to keep you up to date," Michael said. "We're selling even better in the broad market. Every place we put it, it's really well received."

"Whaddaya mean 'well'?"

"I can show you a half-dozen new accounts," Michael said, "and I can show you the growth. Here are the numbers. People really like it."

Brown looked at Michael's stats. Barefoot expected to sell 60,000 cases that year, an increase of more than 70 percent from the 35,000 cases they sold in 1987. They'd started bottling Barefoot Blush that May and it was connecting to the crowds of white zinfandel fans becoming wine drinkers. By then, Barefoot was sold in the more standard 750 ml bottles as well as the 1.5 liter magnums. It was in stores throughout the Bay Area and Northern California, and had begun moving into Southern California and parts of Oregon and Washington. Besides a lineup of smaller supermarket chains, some good-sized restaurant chains also sold Barefoot.

Brown stared at Michael's reports. Maybe he was reading them closely, maybe he was busting Michael's chops again. Then, after two years of shrugs and brush-offs and "get outta here, Houlihan," Brown said something different.

"Yeah, maybe we'll think about putting you in," he said.

Michael just stared for a moment.

"But first you gotta get a chain store manager," Brown said. "I wanna work with someone who knows category management."

Michael knew the term category management. It's something spectacularly out of sync with the romance of wine.

Category management has nothing to do with wine country or vineyards or even wine. It's fundamental retailing, nuts-and-bolts merchandising on a large scale. It applies to wine exactly the same as it does to hammers and napkins and beans.

In short, it means suppliers like Barefoot work with retailers like Lucky to increase profits for the store in that category of product. The theory is, if all wine sales go up, Barefoot sales should go up, too.

The idea changes the relationship between a Barefoot and a Lucky. Instead of haggling over prices and fighting over a finite pool of money, they work together to make the pool larger by increasing sales, profits, rates and more. In essence, that turns each category into a mini-business inside the store.

This was the brick of the day for Michael and Bonnie, the realization that a huge core of their business was merchandising. They were selling wine—and fun and accessibility and the Barefoot Spirit—but so much of what they did to get people to buy it involved hard-boiled, unsentimental, nitty-gritty merchandising.

For Barefoot and Lucky, category management dealt with everything from pricing and discounting, to warehousing, promotions, shipping, labeling, displays, and position on the shelves. It required someone from Barefoot to track sales and keep up the supply in each store and to learn every detail of Lucky's operation, including which Lucky stores ran hot or cold, and the way the seasons, holidays, and consumer moods affected wine sales. The Barefooter would also need to learn the nuances of Lucky's warehouse operation, its trucking patterns, each store's peculiar bottlenecks in shipping and storage, each manager's approach and demands, even the glitches that might come up at the checkout stands. Category management at a big supermarket chain is not for the weak.

When Don Brown brought it up, Michael was still a little stunned that Barefoot might get into Lucky. He just nodded.

"I want to deal with one person," Brown said. "And I don't want it to be you, Houlihan."

"I don't have time," Michael said. "I'm out selling."

"Good," Brown said. "We agree. Go talk to Steve Rinetti. He used to work for me. I can work with the guy."

"So if I hire Steve Rinetti, you're going to put us in your stores?"

"I didn't say that," Brown said. "But you need to talk to Rinetti. If you guys work together, I'll feel better if I decide to put you in."

Michael walked out feeling pretty sure Brown and Lucky would be carrying Barefoot soon. Brown was clear that he wasn't committing to anything, and Michael knew he might decide to wait. But Brown had given away something valuable, and Michael knew how to use it.

Michael had negotiated a lot of deals in his days before Barefoot, and he always told clients the best thing that can happen is when you learn what the other side wants. Then you can make a plan to give it to them and get what you want in return.

Brown wanted Michael to hire Steve Rinetti. Probably they were friends. Also probably, Brown assumed Michael and Bonnie were too new to mass merchandising to grasp the needs of a big chain, but he did trust Steve to handle a fast-moving brand like Barefoot. Whatever Brown's reasons, Michael had a plan to get everyone what they wanted.

Steve Rinetti was a guy in his 70s who had spent 50 years in the beverage industry, much of it in chain stores handling big brands, and he'd worked for Brown for a good stretch. He was happy to talk with Michael.

"We can make Barefoot stand out at Lucky," Steve told Michael. "Your brand has all the right tools."

"That sounds good. We'll hire you," Michael said, "if Don Brown puts us in Lucky."

Steve smiled when he heard that. He got that he was more than a potential chain store manager for Barefoot, he was also a chess piece in Michael's dealings with Brown.

"I'll go talk to Don," he said.

It took a couple weeks, but Steve came back with news. He didn't say how Brown reacted to getting forced into action, but

Michael assumed there was ranting and some swearing involved. Brown hated getting pushed into anything.

"How'd it go?" Michael asked when Steve came back to Barefoot's attic office.

"Don's gonna take it," Steve said.

"Welcome aboard," Michael said.

Steve and Michael talked about the dates and details of Lucky's buy. This was a huge moment for the new wine company. Barefoot was headed for 80-plus Lucky Stores, and Brown planned to run specials and feature it in ads periodically—that's called "putting it on ad."

There was more good news. Lucky was buying Barefoot by the truckload.

A truck can carry 22 pallets of wine—about 1,300 cases. Though some of the big 18-wheelers have room for more, the limit is because wine is heavy stuff, and overweight trucks can damage some bridges or roads.

That, by the way, wasn't something Michael and Bonnie considered for an instant before they started Barefoot—that a truck's load size would be limited by weight and that weight affected shipping patterns through much of American commerce.

For wine producers, the best shipping order they could get was when one buyer took a full truck. That meant the wine would go straight from Barefoot's loading dock to the store's. Drivers didn't have to stop to get more goods to make a full load, and they didn't have to wait outside some warehouse in the midday sun with Barefoot on board and cooking in the heat.

But Lucky's buy wasn't perfect for Barefoot. Brown was getting mixed truckloads. Some of those 1,300-ish cases in each order would be cabernet, some sauvignon blanc, and some the blush. That meant it was likely Brown wouldn't reorder another truckload until Lucky sold through all three wines, so it was possible Lucky could be out of, say, the blush for days or weeks while Brown waited to sell the rest. If Lucky was buying full trucks of each, Brown would probably reorder each varietal separately, and there would be less lag time on any of the varietals.

Still, Michael was thrilled to be getting into Lucky. He and Steve talked about what they could do to get Barefoot noticed among all the brands the chain carried.

"You need a vending machine in Lucky," Steve said.

"I can't put wine in a vending machine," Michael said.

"Not an actual machine," Steve said. "A permanent display."

The idea, he said, was to get Barefoot stacked in the wine aisle, or, even better, out at the end of an aisle or up front, and to use all of Barefoot's colorful posters and stickers and promotional materials to make the display fun and inviting.

"But it is like a vending machine," Steve said. "You gotta keep refilling it. If it runs out, they'll stack something else. You can't let it slip."

This was both an opportunity and a challenge for Barefoot. Steve's "vending machine," and the concept of big displays led Barefoot to create more posters and cheery sales materials displays, and, eventually to "Bigfoot"—that 5-foot-tall foam-core sign that later would drag Michael around in a South Carolina thunderstorm.

But now there was even more ground for Curt Anderson's army to cover. Every store had to be watched constantly. They couldn't run out even in one of the 80-plus stores, because that would get the Barefoot display replaced by something else, and the sudden drop in sales would be a red flag to Brown.

That could start Barefoot down the road to getting discontinued, and getting DCed by a guy like Brown meant they were never, ever getting back in. It would also be a black mark on Barefoot's reputation among chains thinking about putting the wine in. "Out" at Lucky would mean "never in" at a bunch of chains.

Michael was as nervous as he was excited about the Lucky deal. He was not convinced his tiny Barefoot crew had the manpower to handle it, even with an experienced guy like Steve Rinetti involved.

"Are we going to be able to manage this?" Michael asked Steve.

"Maybe," he said.

"Or are we over our heads?" Michael said.

"Maybe."

"Is there any part of this industry where things get easier?" Michael said, mostly just to vent.

"Not that I can think of," Steve said.

Getting into the wine industry for Bonnie and Michael was like getting dropped into the middle of a wild, churning river. There were no safe sides, no calm patches, nothing was predictable. Even when they made progress, rocks and waves seemed to come at them from all angles. All they could do was keep paddling forward.

That's true for most new businesses. There are always hazards, and they seem to come way too fast. What made life more treacherous for Michael and Bonnie was that Barefoot was in uncharted territory for the American wine industry. No one came from outside the wine world and started at a mass-market scale.

At that time, before the nation's wine boom, California was where the vast majority of new wineries were starting, but almost all were born small. The rare exceptions were places like the Robert Mondavi Winery in 1966, but Mondavi grew up in the industry and left his family's winery to start his own. He had connections, experience, and most importantly, money to get the winery rolling.

Virtually everyone else began at a couple thousand, or a couple hundred, cases, and sold from their wineries and tasting rooms and maybe to a few stores and restaurants. If things went well, they grew slowly.

On the other end, there were the giants that formed new, huge wineries using the resources of their current operations. They made hundreds of thousands of cases of wine and used long-standing relationships to sell to supermarket chains around the country. Most of those giants were American, but in the 1970s and '80s, some major European wineries also opened up spin-offs in California as they tried to get a piece of the emerging gold rush in Napa and Sonoma.

In 1987, there were about 700 wineries in California. The giants weren't quite 10 percent of the total owners, but they sold more than 70 percent of the state's wine. Meanwhile, nearly three-quarters of California wineries produced fewer than 20,000 cases a year, and anyone approaching that 20,000 had been around a while.

No winery in decades had launched like Barefoot, an independent company, selling 18,000 cases right off, all of it priced in the affordable range and aimed for the mass market. It's hard to imagine that anyone ever launched on that scale with less money.

So there was no sage to guide Michael and Bonnie and no past examples to track, which was another reason they ran into more than their share of surprises, including one that began happily enough when Barefoot sauvignon blanc won a gold medal in their first major competition—the Sonoma County Harvest Fair—after that first bottling.

Bonnie and Michael were, of course, thrilled. It confirmed they were on the right track. Plus it gave them something more legitimate to brag about in their marketing beyond having award-winning neighbors.

The medal also provided a chance to get some exposure, because fair officials told them all gold medal winners would pour on the Sunday of the fair.

On that Sunday, inside the main hall of the Sonoma County Fairgrounds, Michael and Bonnie started what would become standard procedure for Barefoot at any tasting: they tried to add as much fun and create as much of a party feel as they could.

Barefoot's mission was to be cheerful, but also, Michael and Bonnie thought that other people were like them and weren't at food-and-wine events for an enology seminar. They believed people came for the party.

Michael and Bonnie laughed and kidded with tasters, made their array of foot puns—"This will knock your socks off;" "You'll be head over heels for Barefoot;" "Try some wine with sole"—and generally tried to be energetic and lighthearted. Bonnie brought a pair of joke eyeglasses with a giant nose and Groucho Marx eyebrows.

An hour or so into the afternoon tasting, a man walked toward the Barefoot table. He didn't look like a fairgoer or a winery rep. It wasn't just the sport coat, it was his stiffness and the rather severe look on his face. This man was not looking for a party.

Bonnie saw him and put on her silly glasses. "This guy needs to smile," she said to Michael. Michael didn't hear. He was talking with a couple tasters at the other end of their table.

"I think you have the wrong license," he told Bonnie right off. No "hello," no "how are you today?"

"I'm 21. I'm legal," Bonnie said, still trying to get a smile.

"You can't pour here," he said. His face was still stern.

"We won a gold medal," Bonnie said. "The fair said we had to pour."

"You don't have a license to pour for the public," the man said.

Mr. No-smiles was from the state Department of Alcohol Beverage Control. He said because Barefoot was bottled under another winery's license—first Souverain's then Italian Swiss Colony's—and Michael and Bonnie didn't have a license for a public tasting room, they were only permitted to pour samples for wholesalers and retailers.

"We didn't know," Bonnie said. "The fair said we should pour."

"No matter," he said. "You'll hear from us."

The man wheeled like he was in a parade and walked away. His back was stiff as he moved through the smiling people holding wine glasses and nibbling on food.

Bonnie turned to Michael who had finished with the tasters.

"I think we have a problem," Bonnie said.

"Just one?" Michael said.

"This might be a big one," Bonnie said.

CONVERSATIONS WITH BONNIE AND MICHAEL

Rick: *Where did, "Have you had your brick for the day?" come from?*

Michael: We got it from a couple of Canadian friends who would say it because they knew something unexpected always happens.

They'd get a stuffy British accent and go, "Oh, I say, Rodney, have you had your brick for the day?"

Bonnie: It's a lesson for anyone in business. There's always going to be another surprise brick falling on you. Especially if you're starting a new venture.

Michael: It's like, "Have you had your breakfast?" It says everybody gets one. Everybody in a new business makes assumptions that aren't true, and everybody gets conked with a brick. It's your wake-up call to keep looking for the right way to do something.

Rick: *You invented Worthy Cause Marketing, and it became a foundation of the Barefoot brand. Was there a single idea it came from?*

Michael: It was in Barefoot's DNA. It was who we were as people. And the need to do something like that became clear right at the start, thank you, Don Brown. It was a way we used our values in our business.

Bonnie: We believed if we could get Barefoot to our customers, they would like it. We asked ourselves where can we find the people who would drink Barefoot, and we thought of fundraisers.

Michael: We were already supporting non-profits, so we started thinking, what can we ask from them in return that would help us both? That was the key, it wasn't just charitable giving, we were asking the non-profit members to become Barefoot fans.

Bonnie: We couldn't afford to support every worthy cause, so we supported causes that resonated with us and our basic beliefs.

Michael: We'd get excited about their goals. We're still excited about them.

Rick: *Speaking of excited, that's pretty much exactly the opposite of how a lot of retailers reacted to Barefoot at first. How did the Worthy Cause Marketing change that?*

Michael: The retail buyers would see the foot and say, "That's ridiculous."

Bonnie: We'd get that all the time. They'd say, "Who's going to buy that?"

Michael: We'd say, well, people down the street are having a fundraiser and we're donating the wine. And we're going to tell them they can thank us by coming in here and buying this product from you. So where should we put the stack?

Bonnie: They'd say, "Great idea. Put it right over there."

Rick: *When Don Brown and Lucky agreed to carry Barefoot, that was both good news and more bricks, wasn't it?*

Michael: It was a ton of bricks. First, we realized we had to hire more people to manage Lucky Stores.

Bonnie: So now we're making even less money.

Michael: And Don said Lucky wouldn't advertise it or wouldn't stack it unless we lowered the price to them and put it on special. Our brick for the day was, you dummy, you came in with your lowest price.

Bonnie: That was us. "Here's our best price, Don, we hope you like it." That's the lesson, never start at your lowest price.

Michael: We rescued it a little. We said, at that price, you're going to have to buy more.

Bonnie: There we were again, losing money on every case and making it up in volume.

Rick: *How big a brick was the concept of category management to you?*

Michael: That was a giant wake-up call. Once you get into category management, the romance is gone. You could be selling hammers. It doesn't matter that you have fine wine with a cute foot on it, you're just an item. There's no magic.

Bonnie: We learned it takes a lot more work to sell the product than it does to produce it.

Michael: We also learned he who works the hardest wins. We said, who's doing a good job of it, who should we learn from, and that's when we started paying a lot of attention to Gallo.

Rick: *What was the biggest new challenge in category management?*

Bonnie: We were always planning five, six months out.

Michael: Retailers would ask us, "What about Christmas?" We'd say, "It's only July."

Bonnie: They'd say, "That's right, are you ready?"

Michael: When Christmas happened, it was almost an after-thought. Oh, is it Christmas today? We're working on Easter. Man, I almost forgot how much fun all that was.

Chapter Five

Hit the Enemy Where the Enemy Is Not

It was a sunny spring day in Santa Barbara in 1989. The temperature was in the mid-70s. There was a slight breeze and a small curl on the waves off the coast. Michael was back in his favorite Southern California town.

This day, he wasn't there for a party or beach time. He was riding with a rep from Jordano's, one of the top distributors in that region. Early in the afternoon, they were talking to the owner of a mid-sized market near upper State Street, a stretch just off Highway 101 that has motels and mid-priced restaurants and gets a good number of travelers.

The owner's name was Sammy. Michael liked the guy. He was sarcastic in a friendly way, not particularly pushy, but sharp about his business. The Jordano's rep went outside to make calls on a pay phone, so Michael and Sammy chatted about the area.

"I love this town," Michael said. "There's a spirit here. It's more than just a beach town."

"If you've got a small business like mine," Sammy said, "you want to be in a place like this. It's alive and people are up for all kinds of new things."

"That's what we're looking for," Michael said, "places where people will try something new."

Santa Barbara was an ideal market for Barefoot. The town was made for a wine with a laid-back, lighthearted image and a label that looked like all those footprints on a beach. Plus Barefoot's magnums were convenient for the area's picnic and outdoor-party ethic.

The region fit Barefoot's selling strategy in another way, too: it was a vacation spot.

Santa Barbara, like a lot of towns on California's coast, almost doubled in population on weekends and in the summer, so it was a deceptively fertile selling ground. Barefoot didn't have the muscle yet to duke it out with the big brands in big cities like Los Angeles. It wasn't in enough chains and didn't have the name recognition.

But in a place like Santa Barbara, where there were smaller stores and fewer big names, Barefoot could stand out.

"Everyone's here on vacation, and that's when people will try something new," Michael said. "When they go home, they'll remember us. We'll be that great wine they had on that great trip."

Barefoot's strategy in California at that point was to work the coast, or other vacation regions like the Lake Tahoe basin. They were also getting traction in Oregon and Washington, where sunshine in any form, including from a sunny wine, was always in demand.

For some of the same reasons, Barefoot was selling well in stores and restaurants on military bases around the country. The bases were more willing than big chains to try something new, and they had a straightforward acquisition system. Most of all, the wine and its approach resonated with soldiers stuck on a base somewhere who were happy to find a little taste of California magic.

That beach/vacation/sunshiny sensibility came together in one of the wine company's most memorable brand-building efforts—the Barefoot on the Beach poster.

It looked like a Beach Boys song in picture form. The poster shows a man and woman walking along a soft beach toward an orange and gold sunset. They are barefoot, of course, and are leaving footprints in the sand. All you see of them are long, tan legs. She's holding wine glasses, he's got a bottle of Barefoot, and they are relaxed and in no hurry.

That poster was incredibly popular with stores selling Barefoot everywhere, including Santa Barbara. It was casual, carefree, and romantic—and utterly unique for the wine industry at the time.

So much of American wine selling in the 1980s was built on opposite poles—there were wine coolers on one end and fine wines competing with the Europeans on the other. Even many mass-market wines sold themselves with an air of mystique and seriousness—think Orson Welles and Paul Masson promising, "We will sell no wine before its time."

Barefoot, on the other hand, was serious wine—enough to consistently win medals at major tastings. But it was sold with an approachable smile, a hint of mischievousness, and a ton of California dreaming. That went back to their research. They had learned that most people, including most wine drinkers, didn't want wine to be serious.

"We're selling to everyone," Michael told Sammy, "and the mass market is a democracy. We don't get to tell people what they want, they'll tell us. Our job is to hear them."

"You know who knows that?" Sammy said. "Beer companies. They're the ones who market to everyone and make the world look fun. You're kinda doing beer marketing."

"I take that as a compliment," Michael said.

In 1989, Michael and Bonnie were still dealing with damage from that first Sonoma Harvest Fair when the state Alcohol Beverage Control official told them they couldn't pour wine in public.

Barefoot's license allowed them to blend, bottle, and sell wine as a wholesaler, and to conduct professional tastings for retailers. But they couldn't pour for regular folks. The ABC's reasoning for that sounds like it came straight from Alice in Wonderland.

If a producer had a bricks-and-mortar winery or a tasting room, they could be licensed to pour for the public. They could also be licensed to "extend" the tasting room—that was the regulatory description—to also pour wines at outside events like the Harvest Fair. Barefoot could not get a license for public tastings because, as silly as it sounds, it had no tasting room to extend.

After the fair, Bonnie and Michael met with an ABC official. Their penalty came with two options: pay a $10,000 fine or stop Barefoot operations for 10 business days. At that stage, they would've had trouble paying a $100 fine. They took the time out.

It starts in 30 days, the ABC rep told them. That afternoon Michael was on the phone to his distributors and buyers, asking them to figure out how much wine they'd need the following month.

"If you buy in advance," he told them, "we'll give you a discount."

They mostly avoided serious short-term damage from the ABC penalty, but the long-term impact of not being a fully licensed winery became increasingly annoying. For instance, though Barefoot could still do tastings at charity events (the charities got one-day permits), Michael and Bonnie could only stand at the table—next to it, not behind it. They could talk about Barefoot, but they were not allowed to touch an open wine bottle. Someone from the charity had to pour.

Even worse was the progressively complicated process of paying wine taxes and staying inside the licensing laws. Barefoot was growing. They were adding and changing vendors, and they were producing and bottling wine at more wineries. That was creating a near full-time job for Bonnie just juggling contracts and comparing licenses to remain legit.

Michael and Bonnie had to do something. They started searching for some route that could get Barefoot its own license—its own bond number that would make it a sanctioned winery.

The state ABC said it wasn't possible. No California winery without a building had a full license. The federal Bureau of Alcohol, Tobacco and Firearms said pretty much the same thing.

Bonnie kept looking and kept talking to wineries, suppliers, and lawyers who dealt with tax compliance and wine regulations. She got a few leads, including good recommendations for a woman named Sara Schorske and her Northern California compliance agency.

Schorske said there might be a way, though it hadn't been done in California. It was something called an alternating proprietorship—or alternating premise—license that, in short, meant licensed wineries could share facilities.

Barefoot at the time was using the winemaking and bottling services at Vinwood Cellars in Alexander Valley. Sara said that could qualify. She began trying to work out the details with regulators.

It was not so simple. This involved licenses, taxes and alcohol. All are difficult subjects for regulators. It also wound through both federal and state agencies. That caused more jurisdictional slowdowns.

Sara argued the alternating proprietorship license was a simple and useful concept. Regulators agreed in general, but muddled around on details. Sara has described the ordeal as midwifery.

It took almost two years. In 1991, Barefoot became Bonded Winery No. 5626.

In the years that followed, hundreds and hundreds of wineries in California and across America would get licenses as alternating proprietorships. It's often the first license for people entering the wine industry, because it helps them market and sell before they get their winery built, if they ever do. Hundreds of brands—whether small producers, expensive cult wines, or large mainstream wineries—never build their own facilities and they live by that alternating proprietorship license Barefoot helped pioneer.

For Michael and Bonnie, the license meant they could pour in public after their next gold medal. And their tax-paying process got a little more straightforward. It also meant they had a bunch more forms to fill out.

O ne operating principle of the Barefoot Spirit cuts across any business line. It is, simply enough, "Don't give up. Keep looking for a way." And that principle connected to one of Barefoot's sub-specialties: inventing terms.

When Barefoot became Bonded Winery No. 5626, they still, of course, didn't have an actual winery. Financially, that was a good thing. Contracting and renting cost far less than mortgages and upkeep, not to mention staffing and running a tasting room.

But it could create occasional problems from the vocabulary standpoint.

There was for instance, the issue of how to label some wines. Because they sometimes bought already-made bulk wine, the label couldn't say "produced" by Barefoot.

It was common for, say, a Winery X that used bulk wine made somewhere else to still say on its label, "cellared and bottled" by Winery X, which only meant the winery oversaw the bottling and storage. It didn't address the winemaking. Most wine consumers didn't mind or didn't notice.

The problem for Barefoot was inside the wine world. Buyers for wine stores and supermarkets knew the phrase would often be attached to wine that was inconsistent, or just leftover juice someone was trying to sell off. Many buyers stayed away from one-shot wine producers who might not come back the next year.

Barefoot hadn't built its reputation enough yet. No matter how good the wine was, they didn't want to get painted with that phrase. Michael and Bonnie cast about for something that made Barefoot sound solid and reliable, and that told wine drinkers Barefoot did control its blending.

They came up with "vinted." As in, Vinted by Barefoot Cellars. The Bureau of Alcohol, Tobacco and Firearms was the agency regulating wine labels at the time, and it had no rules about "vinted." Michael and Bonnie thought that might be because no one had used it before, so they gave it a go. They submitted their label with "vinted" for approval to the BATF—and got rejected. The processing agent said it wasn't a phrase already "in the lexicon."

But this wasn't another case of two-year midwifery. Bonnie and Michael had learned the BATF was a big place and if they re-applied, their label was likely to land on a different agent's desk. They tried again four days later.

This time, bingo, it sailed through. Barefoot wine was officially "vinted," just as hundreds of other wines have been since.

Barefoot's inventiveness went beyond language and licenses. There was also a lot of lemonade making, especially in the years when retailers gave the company handfuls of operating lemons because the wine was new and unproven.

One constant challenge, for instance, was that many stores only put Barefoot on the bottom shelf. They saved their prime space for more established brands, and often, more expensive wines. Selling any new product off the bottom shelf, where shoppers rarely notice it, is not easy.

So, as someone at Barefoot said—no one is sure where the motto came from—they "went after the foot traffic." Literally.

They created decals they called Sticky Feet that looked like wine-stained footprints. Michael or Curt or someone working the stores would lay them on store floors down the wine aisle, leaving a trail that stopped right in front of the Barefoot. When stores let them, they would start the footprints at the front door.

And they created a sign that mounted in the store shelf's pricing slot that had a large red foot on it and an arrow pointing to Barefoot bottles. Wherever the Sticky Feet went down, sales went up. The problem was, the shelf signs kept disappearing.

Then the Barefoot folks figured it out. So they designed a special Mylar sign that was strong and flexible, and most importantly, could stand up to getting wacked every night by a mop.

Foot Traffic

Through the first years, Barefoot's survival continued to be a day-to-day war on every front. For instance, by 1989, two of their distributors were bought by larger companies, and when those bigger distributors took over, they already had their hands full with their current lineups of wines and spirits. The result was almost no service for many smaller brands like Barefoot that had belonged to the old distributor.

At those times, it felt like Barefoot was in a freefall. They couldn't get wine into some stores that were long-time Barefoot buyers. And no matter how much stores wanted Barefoot, some eventually gave up and took those other brands instead because it was easier for them.

To avoid the next freefall, Michael and Bonnie learned to keep a close watch not just on reorders and sales, but also on the business of distributors.

In early 1989, a trend among their distributors was hard to ignore. But this was a good trend. One sales team from a Bay Area distributorship was roaring through its territory, selling way more than any other group. In fact, they were selling more than three-quarters of all the Barefoot this mid-size distributor was moving.

They were the North Bay crew, covering from Marin to the California–Oregon border. So on a day in March, Michael called the company and asked to talk to the North Bay manager, just to say thank you. He got connected to Randy Arnold.

"I just called to tell you how much I appreciate the job you're doing with Barefoot," Michael told him. "You're selling a truck-load a month. You're the best team we have working with us."

"Thank you," Randy said. "That's really nice of you to say. But I have to tell you, it's a really easy wine to sell. We love all your point of sale materials, and the stores like the fun look when we stack it. So do their customers."

"Well, we appreciate the effort you're putting in," Michael said.

"It's a great product for us," Randy said. "It reaches the regular person, and the quality's there in the bottle. Wherever we put it, we almost can't keep it in stock, it moves so fast."

Michael and Randy chatted more about selling Barefoot. These were two creative marketers and independent thinkers who saw possibilities beyond the conventional wisdom. They had an instant friendship

"If there's anything I can do to help, let me know," Michael said as they were winding down. "I can send you more stuff or come talk to your team, or anything else you want."

Randy was quiet for a moment.

"There is one thing," he said. "I don't think I'm appreciated much at my company. It would be great if you could tell my boss you're happy with our performance."

"Really?" Michael said. "How could they not appreciate you? You're selling 80 percent of everything they move for us."

"I don't know," Randy said. "Anyway, if you could put in a good word, that would be nice."

A week later, Michael did more than put in a good word, he took Randy's boss to lunch. They were at a steak house on the San Francisco Peninsula, and Michael was singing Randy's praises.

"That man is some kind of salesman," Michael told him. The boss looked bored.

"This guy is making you a ton of money," Michael said.

"Yeah, I dunno," the boss said.

"What do you mean?" Michael said.

"Did you know," the boss said, "that he's gay?"

"So?" Michael said.

"You can't trust them," the guy said.

"What are you talking about?" Michael said.

"They're disloyal. They'll stab you in the back."

Michael was listening to the guy and thinking, what a jerk. He had to stop himself from getting up and leaving. He was also thinking he couldn't wait for the lunch to end to call Randy.

Right after lunch, he went to a pay phone as the boss drove away. He got hold of Randy.

"I just had lunch with your boss," Michael told him. "If you ever get tired of that crap, I will make you my national sales manager tomorrow."

"I really appreciate that," Randy said, "and I appreciate you trying to help. But I've been with this company a long time and I feel a sense of loyalty. Maybe we'll get a management change soon."

That's what Randy said. Loyalty. Michael was torn between noting the irony and wanting to chase down the boss.

"I understand," Michael said. "Listen to me, though. This offer stands, today, tomorrow, whenever. You call if you need to. We'll be there."

Over the next few months, the North Bay territory kept booming for Barefoot. Sales climbed, the team piled on new stores, and the reorders flew in. Michael sent Randy and his crew every new Barefoot flyer and poster they made.

The pattern continued for nearly a year. Then Michael got a call from Randy.

"I quit today," he told Michael. "I just couldn't take it anymore."

"So you're coming to work for us?" Michael said.

"I don't know," Randy said. "I don't know if I still want to work in this industry."

"It's not the industry," Michael said. "Some people are just jerks."

"I know. I'm just worn out."

"Here's what you do," Michael said. "Take a month and relax. Go to Hawaii and get a tan. Call me when you get back. This offer isn't going away."

"OK," Randy said. "Thanks. I'll do that. I don't know if I'll change my mind, but I'll call."

Randy didn't actually go to Hawaii. He worried about the money—he had just quit his job. Instead, he stayed at home in Concord, about 30 miles east of San Francisco, and planted and nursed a vegetable garden. It would be the best, and in truth, only good vegetable garden he would have for years.

A month later, Randy called Michael to tell him what he decided.

"Is that offer still open?" Randy asked.

They met for lunch at John Ash & Co., a restaurant on River Road north of Santa Rosa. Michael felt better about this hire than any person he'd hired before. First off, he just liked the guy. And he knew he was getting a man who was creative and had great integrity. Plus Randy loved Barefoot.

"Where should I sell?" Randy asked.

"Go where you like," Michael said. "That's where you'll do your best."

"What's your marketing budget?" Randy asked.

"Are you kidding?" Michael said. "We don't have one. We haven't got any money." He felt a little guilty. He'd gotten Randy to take the job, then told him he had no budget. Randy didn't look bothered.

"But," Randy said, "you have all that wine. We'll use that."

In 1989, Barefoot sold more than 70,000 cases. That was a sub-stantial amount any way you look at it, more than the sales of the vast majority of the wineries in California, and Barefoot wasn't even a full four years old. It was proof of the appeal of Barefoot, and evidence of Michael and Bonnie's creativity, growing market-ing skills, and simple doggedness.

But they were still fighting their old dilemma: big sales didn't translate into big profits, or really, any profits. Barefoot's mission was to give America a good $5 bottle of wine, and $5 didn't leave much after expenses.

Which meant, more than ever, Bonnie and Michael needed their company to grow. Their tiny profits had to get plowed back into growth. And, once again, growth also meant more costs. They were, as Bonnie called it, surfing a wave of debt and trying not to wipe out.

Bonnie was having a hard time hanging on to bookkeepers, partly because they saw the money issues. One of their first book-keepers gave Bonnie a financial report without the amount they owed Mark Lyon.

"It's so big, you'll never pay it off," the bookkeeper told Bon-nie. "I didn't put it in. It makes you look terrible."

Bonnie knew they owed Mark solidly into six figures. She almost sympathized with the bookkeeper's decision.

Another bookkeeper quit after she saw the numbers. She just picked up her coat and purse and left. Didn't even ask for her check.

"You guys are going bankrupt," she told Bonnie. "You can't afford to pay me."

That race with the wave of debt forced Bonnie to develop a system that managed to both juggle their debts and get Barefoot extended credit.

She started by building the trust of Barefoot's vendors—the people who were owed the money—and by turning them into de facto partners who helped keep the company alive.

A critical step for any new business is to find strategic partners. That's someone who also benefits if you survive and grow. Barefoot's partners weren't just the distributors and stores selling the wine, their suppliers were partners, too. Barefoot was becoming a large volume company—regardless of the profit margin— and the people bottling their wine, printing their labels, selling them corks, boxes, glass, and more all had a stake in Barefoot's performance.

To build their trust, Bonnie never let vendors doubt they'd get paid—even if it was late. She would often tell them, long before a bill was due, that Barefoot would come up short for that payment, but she'd also give them a payment schedule and tell them precisely which incoming check to Barefoot was earmarked for them.

And she and Michael would explain their plans to vendors. They'd detail Barefoot's marketing strategies, show them new posters, tell them growth projections. They wanted their vendors to see that Barefoot had a plan, so they could also see the value to their own businesses when they extended Barefoot's credit.

So Barefoot leveraged their potential growth to, for instance, buy another round of bottles even while they owed for the last batch. It was almost the equivalent of a bank loan. In return, the suppliers got a connection to a growing business, and a trusted partner.

If there was one relationship that kept Barefoot alive, it was the mutually beneficial, highly unbank-like credit extensions from Rick Silvani and his California Glass Company.

Silvani and his people were the ones who first answered Bonnie's questions when she started researching bottles and corks and the like. They did business with Barefoot for years.

And California Glass was one of Barefoot's biggest vendors. After the wine, bottles are the next largest expense for any winery. From Rick's side, those 70,000 cases Barefoot was producing meant he was selling about a half-million bottles a year, with potential for much more.

This also meant Rick was usually the first person Bonnie contacted when there was a money issue, and there were many. Bonnie's constant goal was to keep $1,000 in the checking account, and they wobbled under that line far too often.

In late 1990, Barefoot was facing another tight moment. Bonnie went to the usual well.

"Michael," she said, "go have lunch with Rick."

This occurred with a near-ceremonial regularity over the years. Michael would visit Rick at his office near the Oakland International Airport, take him to lunch at Francesco's, an old-school Italian restaurant nearby, and tell him about Barefoot's progress.

Michael would show Rick new accounts, marketing plans, the sales programs. He would tell him how much more glass he expected Barefoot to need in the next six months.

He'd remind Rick—as subtly as he could—that all those bottles Barefoot was ordering were more valuable to California Glass as future payments than they were just sitting in Rick's warehouse. With Barefoot's account as a receivable, Rick could go to his bank and get more credit if he wanted.

"I'm worth more to you if we grow," Michael would say. "I can pay you what we owe you now, but then we can't grow."

Rick understood the choices. In his ideal world, Barefoot would both grow and pay in full. But what business runs ideally? And Bonnie always gave him a payment plan, Michael always had reliable projections, and Barefoot always performed. He knew Barefoot would keep growing if he helped. He always extended them credit, and Michael and Bonnie were always grateful. Still, Rick would have preferred his ideal world.

After that lunch, Barefoot stayed on course for more than six months, and it felt like they may not have survived without Rick's help. Then Bonnie needed Michael to make the phone call again.

"Hey Rick," he said. "I just wanted to update you. Can I take you to lunch?"

"I dunno," Rick said. Michael thought he heard a sigh. "Last time you bought me lunch, I had indigestion for a week. Can't we just do it over the phone?"

By the early 1990s, Davis Bynum had stopped carrying Barefoot in his tasting room, in part because he wanted to focus on his premium wines. But he told anyone who asked that he was rooting for Michael and Bonnie, and that he admired their indefatigable spirit. He also liked how Barefoot's general cheerfulness and approachability irritated some of the old guard in the industry.

Not long after he stopped carrying Barefoot, Davis was at a dinner sponsored by the Wine Institute, a major trade group for California wine. He was sitting next to Leon Adams, the respected wine historian and author. They talked about the weather, Russian River wines, and Davis' pinot noir.

But Adams had a question for Davis. Adams (who died in 1995) was an old-school-style gentleman. He argued in his writing that wine was a civilizing force. His question didn't sound mean or condescending, but he didn't hide his disapproval.

"Are you still making that wine with the awful foot on the label?" Adams said.

"No," Davis said. "It's been a few years."

"Good," Adams said. "Good to hear."

"These days," Davis said, with a hint of impishness, "Michael Houlihan and Bonnie Harvey are making it. They're doing pretty well, too. I hear they're close to 100,000 cases."

Barefoot had a complicated relationship with parts of the established wine world in its early days. Over the years, they would make great friends in the industry, but at the start, Barefoot's down-to-earth approach and let's-have-fun themes were a departure from the marketing programs much of the fine wine industry had constructed that pushed qualities like exclusivity and refinement.

Michael and Bonnie didn't know they were, in a way, rebels, because they didn't know the conventions of the industry they'd fallen into. That turned out to be a lucky thing for them, because their research and marketing choices weren't affected by that conventional wisdom.

But as they were learning about their business and about their customers' reaction to Barefoot, they had learned not to be pushed off their path. If they needed affirmation that their foot and the simplicity of their brightly colored labels played well with consumers, they found it in places like the large Ojai tasting where Randy poured for Barefoot. The experience was anything but exclusive.

That was when a woman came to the Barefoot table. She was all smiles.

"My favorite used to be the pink one," she said, pointing to the Barefoot Blush label. "Then it was the green, but now I like the red."

Or there was the fundraiser for KQED, the public radio station in San Francisco. More than 50 wineries were pouring, and Barefoot's colorful table drew a constant crowd. One woman in an elegant business suit got to the front of the line, picked up a display bottle and nearly cuddled it.

"I just love your foot," she told Michael. "It's so cute. I'm drinking wine to have a good time, but usually I have to get past the person selling it to me. They make me feel like I'm flunking some test I didn't know about. With you guys, I can just have my good time."

Her sensibilities would be embraced by the wine industry by the end of the 1990s, and Barefoot's continued growth played a part in that. By then, there was a new generation of wine drinkers who bought bottles with bright labels and fun names. And there was a new generation of wine producers in America and around the world marketing fun and approachability, too.

But in the late 1980s and early '90s, Barefoot was in something of a wine wilderness, on its own selling a good time and down-to-earth labels.

In 1991, Randy was in a large Bay Area store, standing in the wine aisle with a folder under his arm, waiting for the department manager. A middle-aged man asked Randy for help. The man wanted to find the wine he had tried on a recent weekend, but he couldn't remember the name.

"What did it look like?" Randy said. "Maybe we can figure it out."

"I just remember it was called Chateau something or other," the man said.

Randy pointed at the shelves jammed with Chateau something-related labels.

"Sorry," he said. "I don't think I can help."

A few minutes later, Randy was still waiting for the manager. Another man asked him for help. Apparently the folder he carried made him look official.

"I had a wine the other night I really loved," the man said. "All I remember was the label had a foot."

"That one," Randy told the man, "we can find."

Michael and Bonnie were a life raft for Randy Arnold, and Randy was terrific as the sales manager for Barefoot, but their alliance grew into so much more. It's hard to imagine a more ideal convergence of three people and a product. They are lifetime friends, sympathetic spirits, and no one is sure who helped who more.

When Randy started with Barefoot in 1990—on April Fool's Day—and Michael said go sell in places you like, Randy knew he was working for the right people. They understood that making him happy with his work would make him a better salesman. They were treating him like an asset, not just another paycheck in the expense column. It was an example of the clichéd-but-always-valid principle: create win-wins for everybody.

And the places Randy liked to go fit Barefoot's mission. He went up the California Coast, following Highway 1 from San Francisco to the Oregon border. He knew that stretch from his old job, and knew the quiet hamlets and small cities along the coast were both vacation spots and deep-rooted fishing and lumber towns. They were also places where Barefoot didn't have to battle bigger brands. It fit one of Randy's operating principles: Hit the enemy where the enemy is not.

Randy Arnold is a special kind of salesman. Beyond his enthusiasm and his knowledge of the market, he worked hard to understand what his customers needed.

He could see that in these towns, the owners of small stores wanted help selling all their products. Randy—like Michael, and eventually the entire Barefoot sales staff—operated as if he were an assistant manager for those stores. He helped with displays, provided sales material, kept a watch on the supply, and generally made doing business with Barefoot an easy thing.

Randy also understood how small personal touches helped business relationships. Often, after he sold a store owner a few cases of Barefoot, Randy would go back to his car and write out a postcard saying, "Thanks for the business. Let us know if we can do anything to help." Maybe 15 minutes after a sale, that postcard would be in the mailbox on the way back to the store owner.

And with Randy running around the California coast, Barefoot's Worthy Cause Marketing hit a new gear. Some of the increase was sheer energy. Randy stepped up the number of charitable events Barefoot contributed to, and he was there at most of them, pouring and putting on a colorful little show.

He considered himself an incrementalist, continually making small changes on a task to perform it better and better. At all those events, he watched people, listened to what they liked, and kept sharpening Barefoot's presentation.

And Randy helped expand the scope of Worthy Cause Marketing with his enthusiasm and his vision of where Barefoot could help and of what causes fit Barefoot's interests and ideals.

There was, for instance, the San Francisco night at the theater in the regal Palace of Fine Arts. Randy brought Michael and Bonnie to a performance by Patrick Makuakane's Nā Lei Hulu I Ka Wēkiu, a Hawaiian dance troupe.

He knew how much Michael and Bonnie loved Hawaii and the culture there, and he'd heard them talk about their fascination with the hula—they thought it was a gorgeous, hypnotic dance, and appreciated that it was rich in the stories and heritage of Hawaii.

During the performance, Randy could tell Michael and Bonnie were spellbound by the show. "Well," he asked them both, "what do you think?"

"They're so graceful," Bonnie said, "and they dance barefoot."

"Absolutely awesome," Michael said. "I love this."

"Glad to hear that," Randy said, "because you've been supporting them for two years."

Randy also helped sharpen the Worthy Cause Marketing approach. He worked with Michael and Bonnie and added a new twist. Instead of telling the owner of, say, ol' Steve's Liquors, that Barefoot was pouring at a charity event nearby and wanted to send customers to Steve, Randy and Michael started going to Steve first to find out what his favorite worthy cause was.

Maybe it was the food bank two blocks down. Barefoot would donate wine to the food bank's next fundraiser, and tell Steve that those people were going to need a place to buy it now. Can we send them here?

This made Steve feel like Barefoot was a partner, helping out a cause that mattered to him and sending him customers.

This is how to merge your business with your values. Barefoot helped a food bank and in the process made friends with the food bank supporters and with Steve. It was, as Michael called it, a way to make capitalism work—for, eventually, hundreds of clinics and charities and causes, and for Barefoot. Their Worthy Cause Marketing *was* their marketing. It made lasting connections and loyal fans—more than they would have with conventional advertising—and it did some good in the world with the one re-source they had, as Randy called it, "all that wine."

Through the years, there were few ideas that Michael and Bon-nie and Barefoot backed more strongly than civil rights, and, in particular, gay rights. In return, there were few causes that earned Barefoot more loyalty from more people. Randy, of course, had a little to do with it.

Early in Randy's career at Barefoot, he came into Michael's office.

"Uh, Michael," Randy said. "I need to ask you something."

"Sure," Michael said. "We still don't have a marketing budget."

"I've heard," Randy said. "So, Michael, you know I'm gay, right?"

"You're kidding me," Michael said.

"Seriously," Randy said, "can I come out?"

"You're not out?" Michael said.

"Yeah, but not as a national sales manager."

"And how is that different?"

"You know, some people won't like it," Randy said.

"So we'll sell wine to the people who do like it," Michael said.

This was a moral stance, but it was good business, too. Randy had long argued that Barefoot could find serious brand loyalty if it worked with marginalized communities, people who would appreciate the attention. That would later include surfers and some environmental groups, but in the early 1990s, gays in America were as marginalized as any group in the country.

And Randy was right about finding brand-loyal customers. Before Randy joined the company, Barefoot supported organizations like the Golden Gate Business Association, a Bay Area gay and lesbian education and business-promotion group that Bob Bob had connected them to. But Randy amped it up.

So Barefoot poured wine at fundraisers for the San Francisco Gay Men's Chorus, for health clinics in predominantly gay neighborhoods, and for AIDS projects from California and Oregon to Colorado and the East Coast.

Supporting the LGBT community was a moral choice, beyond the connection through Randy. Civil rights, and just simple civility, were fundamental beliefs to Michael and Bonnie. (LGBT is a catch-all name for people who are lesbian, gay, bisexual, transgender, or just uncertain about their sexuality.) It was a good move from the business standpoint, too, because many of those folks traveled, spent money on food and wine, or simply appreciated Barefoot's playfulness and break from the old guard.

Supporting gay rights, especially in the early 1990s, just like supporting other civil rights in the 1960s, came with some controversy. But Michael and Bonnie believed the idea of companies shying away from all controversies was a bad approach to living your life, and it was bad business.

"You have to stand for something," Michael told a Bay Area business reporter in 1992 who called to ask about Barefoot's marketing at gay and lesbian events. "And we have a group of reliable customers and enormous potential for growth."

"Aren't you afraid Barefoot will become known as the Gay Wine?" the reporter said.

"I'm afraid it won't," he said.

CONVERSATIONS WITH BONNIE AND MICHAEL

Rick: *If there is anything that distinguished Barefoot, it was the idea that wine could be fun. How did that affect the industry?*

Michael: We wanted to appeal to first-time wine drinkers and beer drinkers. We wanted the taste and package and approach to appeal to them.

Bonnie: We wanted people to have fun even before they opened the bottle.

Michael: In the '80s, wine had such a bad image with so many people. People would say, wine drinkers are all snobby.

Bonnie: We would offer people a taste and they'd say, I don't know much about wine. Why did they need to? That idea came from wine snobs. You never hear somebody say I don't know much about beer.

Michael: That's why Barefoot is an important chapter in the American wine business. It was the first time the wine industry got criticized from within by a product that said, look, you're alienating your customers.

We took a lot of criticism from wine people who didn't agree with us. They thought we were trying to cheapen wine and they thought we were going after their customers. We weren't. We were trying to create new customers for everybody. The wine industry started paying attention because we had good sales. The bottom line is always the bottom line.

Rick: *What other reactions did Barefoot's early success get from the industry?*

Michael: Curt Anderson kept calling us over and over asking for POS (point-of-sale materials like signs that go on store shelves). We didn't know why at first.

Bonnie: We'd say, Curt, that stuff's expensive. Didn't we just send you a big box two weeks ago?

Michael: He'd say, yeah, the "Big Boys" took it all down. We'd say, maybe they just want to find out how often you're in the stores. Just keep showing up and putting it back, and maybe they'll take us seriously and leave us alone.

Rick: *Did that get them to leave you alone? And how long did it take?*

Michael: It took a while, but it did work. Years later, a guy who worked for one of the Big Boys interviewed with us for a job. He said they tried to kill Barefoot for years but we kept coming back. Barefoot got the reputation as "the brand that would not die."

Rick: *Another piece of Barefoot's uniqueness didn't involve wine. It was the way you turned debts into assets by getting vendors to extend your credit. What were you thinking looking at the books in those years?*

Bonnie: I was thinking, the good news is we're growing. But we're going to need a lot more credit. The only place to get it was from our suppliers. Even though I couldn't pay them on time, I needed them to trust me because it would be good for their business, too. That's why I always called way before a bill was due. I'd say, we have a check coming in five weeks and it's earmarked for you, even though I owed it to them a week sooner.

Michael: Nobody ever called Bonnie to say, "you're late." She always called them way before that. It showed them a lot of respect.

Bonnie: Don't avoid them, let them know the situation. It was in their interest that we succeed. I thought of them as allies. I was looking at their business from their side of the desk. It was in our interest that they succeed, too.

Rick: *How dicey did it get?*

Michael: There were times the brand almost didn't survive.

Bonnie: Many, many times, the brand almost didn't survive.

Rick: *You both have a special place in your hearts for Randy Arnold. Tell me more about him.*

Bonnie: Oh, Randy, I can't even think about him without smiling. Randy is the most loving, giving, hardest working person I ever met. The wine industry is blessed that Randy stayed in it.

Michael: He's one of the most innovative marketers I know. This guy is imaginative. He's always looking for new ways to engage the community and to make the world a better place through wine. He sincerely believes in what he does. The guy is selfless, and he's committed to the same kinds of things we are—conservation, health, civil rights. He takes those things personally.

Bonnie: His heart is really in working with non-profits. If it weren't with wine, I'm sure it would be with another product. He loves being of service to others, and it shows in everything he does.

He calls us a couple times a week. We get emails. He sends us a postcard or a gift once or twice a month.

Michael: He's one of our closest friends. We love the guy.

Chapter Six

Mama Mabel, Surfers, and Monks

The rain was coming down solid and straight on this late winter day. Michael was at Ace Hardware in Santa Rosa. His cart had a load of plastic rain gutters and downspouts, and he just needed a couple rolls of duct tape.

Ah, duct tape. The multitalented roll that can fix pretty much anything. When you're a start-up, your entire world seems stitched together with duct tape. In this case though, the tape was more than symbolic. Michael was doing office repairs.

It was 1988—before they hired Randy, before they became Bonded Winery No. 5626—and Barefoot was still in the attic above Davis Bynum Winery. Davis had his own cash-flow issues and didn't spend much on building repairs. So the large, rectangular skylight in the center of the Barefoot office leaked.

In truth, "leaked" wildly understates it. "Poured" is closer. Water seeped down most of the edges, raining on the conference table and desks on storm days. Michael, Bonnie, and the crew had buckets lined up in strategic spots around the room, but they took constant tending and quick repositioning when winds shifted and moved the leak spots.

If anyone had time to think about it, the water problem was something of a metaphor for Barefoot. They were constantly scrambling, constantly adjusting to outside forces, constantly working to keep from getting washed away. But who can stop for irony when it's raining?

Michael hooked up the rain gutters under the skylight, making a rectangle along the outer edges. Then he connected the downspout and sent it out a window. The contraption not only worked, on heavy rain days, it gave the office the background noise of a waterfall. (Unfortunately, when the rain was light, they got a much less endearing drip.)

Barefoot was still in its war to stay solvent—a war it would fight, like many start-ups, for years—and as Bonnie and Michael juggled their finances, they also had to decide regularly if what appeared to be money-making opportunities were real, or whether they would just create new problems.

For instance, they got a stream of brokers looking to send good-sized shipments to Asia, most often to Hong Kong. Usually the brokers came on Saturdays. No one learned why it was Saturdays. Michael and Bonnie figured maybe they went to more established wineries on weekdays, or maybe they thought a Saturday visit would seem unexpected and feel like a windfall.

But most came with problems. Often the brokers wanted huge discounts, or they couldn't promise good shipping conditions. Michael and Bonnie didn't want their wine cooking in the sun for a week on some dock or ship's deck. Barefoot's name would be on it. When people tasted it, they wouldn't know about the week in the sun, they'd think the wine was always bad.

This was a tough call for a new company needing cash, but it's a good lesson. One cash infusion didn't outweigh the potential damage to Barefoot's reputation. Bonnie and Michael, though not always thrilled about their decisions, walked away from any deal they couldn't control. When you're struggling, discipline can be painful.

On one drizzly Saturday, just a few weeks after Michael hooked up his anti-leak system, he was at the office catching up—standard procedure for most Saturdays. He wore jeans and boots and clothes for the rain. The phone rang, and it was a man with a Japanese accent. He represented Kenan Busan (busan translates, more or less, to trading company) and he said his boss, Mr. Matsumoto, wanted to visit.

Sure, Michael said. He expected another fly-by-night broker looking for a discount.

A half-hour later, five Japanese businessmen walked up the stairs and filed in. They were decidedly not fly-by-night. They each carried a briefcase and wore well-cut gray suits, silk ties, slicked hair, and polished shoes. Michael looked at his muddy boots. "Oh well," he thought.

Only one of the men spoke English. He introduced himself as the translator, then introduced Mr. Matsumoto. Mr. Matsumoto bowed. Michael bowed. Mr. Matsumoto handed Michael his business card.

This was an important moment. In Japan, exchanging business cards—they're called meishi—is a ceremony laden with etiquette that can signify the start of a partnership.

Michael knew something about this because his father had worked on projects involving trade with Japan, and Michael had picked up some fundamentals of Japanese business culture.

Mr. Matsumoto handed Michael his card with both hands, a sign of respect. It was turned toward Michael so he could read it. Michael took it with both hands and did not look up. He stared at the card and read it carefully, as if memorizing it. In the U.S., looking too long at a business card can seem like you don't trust someone's credentials. In Japanese business, you study it. But it's an insult to write on it, or to put it right in your pocket, because the card is considered an extension of the person and an announcement of that person's station in the company.

After Michael read the card carefully, he looked up and gave a slight bow, then presented Mr. Matsumoto with his Barefoot card, the one with the foot and the title, "Head Stomper." Mr. Matsumoto looked at it carefully. He did not snicker.

Michael went through the business card rite with each visitor. Then everyone sat at the table. Michael was at one end, Mr. Matsumoto at the other. No one spoke for a moment. The only sound was the drip, the dink, dink, dink of the indoor rain gutters. The businessmen looked up. Their heads all followed the downspout out the window. They looked back at each other, but no one said a word. Michael figured they were too polite to ask, but he was hoping they thought it was part of the American winemaking process.

The interpreter sat next to Mr. Matsumoto, who would speak in Japanese, but directly to Michael. Then the interpreter would get up, go to Michael and talk quietly in his ear. Michael would answer in English straight at Mr. Matsumoto, and the interpreter would hustle back to talk in his boss's ear. This was a tiny room. The shuttle diplomacy was beyond unnecessary, but tradition is tradition.

"Before we begin," the translator told Michael, "Mr. Matsumoto wants to make something perfectly clear." He opened a briefcase and carefully placed a document in front of Michael. It was from Bank of America, 555 California St., San Francisco, and it said $45,000 had been placed into an account from Kenan Busan for Barefoot Cellars. It didn't say for what.

That told Michael two things. These guys were serious, and the meeting was about how much the $45,000 would buy. He was also pretty sure these weren't people who would leave a shipment of wine sitting on a dock for a week.

"There are lines that haven't been filled in," Michael said to get things started.

"Yes," the interpreter said. "We will talk about that."

They went back and forth a while. This was potentially huge for Barefoot. A serious cash buyer meant no risk, no waiting to get paid, and major help digging out of their hole. Plus Mr. Matsumoto implied this wouldn't be a one-time buy.

There was a caution flag for Michael, too. Multiple buys meant he had to be careful not to give up too much to get the deal, because whatever they agreed on—if they did agree—probably wouldn't change for future shipments.

So they haggled over how many cases the $45,000 would buy, what wines—cabernet or sauvignon blanc or both—would be in the deal, and all the smaller details.

Things started to get a little edgy. Often, when a negotiation starts to stall, Japanese businessmen set it aside for a moment and talk about something else.

"Mr. Houlihan-san," the interpreter said, "Mr. Matsumoto wants to know why you have only two Barefoots?" He meant, why just the two varietals?

Michael got a playful look. He smiled straight at Mr. Matsumoto. Then Michael put his left foot, boot and all, on the table, followed by his right foot. Michael gave Mr. Matsumoto a palms-up shrug that said, "This is all I've got."

The room went still. Mr. Matsumoto started laughing. He had a hearty, slap-the-table laugh, and his team laughed with him.

Whatever tension had been in the room was gone. Mr. Matsumoto slowed his laugh, then it kicked in again.

He brought his interpreter to his end of the table and spoke to him. The interpreter came back to Michael.

"Mr. Matsumoto respectfully asks," the translator said, "if you could print the back labels in Japanese." That was it. There was going to be a deal, now they were just working out the fine points.

Michael figured he'd stay with what seemed to be working. He had a Barefoot cork in his pocket. He took it out and put it in the interpreter's hand, then folded the man's other hand over it so the cork was covered.

"Tell Mr. Matsumoto," Michael said, "the cork's already printed in Japanese."

The translator went down to his boss, told him what Michael said, then showed him the cork. All that was on it was the foot.

Mr. Matsumoto cracked up again. He passed the cork around to his team. They all laughed, too.

Mr. Matsumoto and Kenan Busan eventually bought 20,000 cases of Barefoot. The shipments started in 1989 and would continue until 1992 when the Japanese importers found a better price from a larger company.

That deal was more than a near-miracle for the struggling Barefoot, it was also an affirmation for Michael and Bonnie that they'd chosen a path that was resonating. It was a reminder to trust their plan and what they had learned.

And it confirmed to them that the Barefoot Spirit—that making their wine fun and accessible, that simply being approachable and fun themselves—resonated, too.

Michael's feet-on-the-table move could have been a deal-breaking moment of rudeness. But Mr. Matsumoto, a serious man

"The cork is already in Japanese."

from a serious business culture, appreciated the laugh. The cheerful California wine was something he could sell back home, but he also chose to do business with Barefoot because of the cheerful spirit.

The Kenan Busan deal came with an unhappy surprise. There never seemed to be good developments without some downside or hidden cost. In this case, it involved the size of Japanese homes.

Michael and Bonnie expected to ship magnums, the 1.5 liter bottles, because those were still mostly what Barefoot produced. The thing was, Japan is a big nation on small islands. Homes and furnishings there, including the refrigerators, are smaller than in America. Japanese fridges didn't have room for magnums.

So Barefoot had to quickly ramp up its 750 ml bottlings—the more common, standard-sized wine bottles. It was worth it for the deal, but it was still another layer of logistics and a hit to the profit margin.

There was another catch to shipping 20,000 cases to Japan. They didn't scan. That's an industry term meaning the sales can be seen and registered by the American groups tracking statistics on wine sales. The Kenan Busan sales didn't scan, so those cases were not included in any sales reports on the wine industry.

And Barefoot needed every case they sold to scan because big sales numbers on major industry reports would help convince stores and distributors that Barefoot was for real. The wine world, like most industries, looked for reliable producers. Don Brown at Lucky had sent Michael out to prove he was reliable. Other chains and other buyers were just like Brown.

The reason was simple: they had no business interest in helping Barefoot get established. They didn't want to spend money, use time, or take on the risk of anyone's start-up phase. They waited for sales numbers and other types of proof that Barefoot was substantive and would be around a while.

So, as Barefoot was finding its feet and trying to convince the industry it really was substantive, Bonnie and Michael looked for kindred spirits—people, groups, and companies more or less traveling the same path as Barefoot, with the same attitudes and approach to business, and in a similar, less-than-fully-established, stage of growth. Those emerging companies, like Barefoot, were also looking for partners to help them grow.

Michael and Bonnie's alliance with Rick Silvani at California Glass was one example. Barefoot's Worthy Cause Marketing was a pile of examples. Kenan Busan was in that category. And, at one point, they thought they found a new strategic ally in Denmark.

This one came about with the help of Christian Thomsen, a big, blue-eyed man with dual Danish and American citizenship. Chris was Barefoot's controller and he was the guy who put the company on solid, professional accounting footing in the early 1990s. He was also the guy who suggested taking a shot selling wine to FDB, an emerging Danish supermarket co-op.

FDB ran hundreds of stores called SuperBrugsen outlets. This was Scandinavia, and Barefoot's enduring "California in a Bottle" theme seemed like a slam dunk for a part of Europe where people are socially open minded, and where the winters are long, dark, and cold.

FDB had an office in Menlo Park, in the Bay Area's Silicon Valley, with a buyer looking for California products—cheese, nuts, Pacific salmon, whatever—that would resonate in Denmark. When the buyer saw the Barefoot label and the posters with the beach, the tan legs, and the sunset, she was thrilled.

Chris handled the negotiations, which were mostly in Danish. The buyer said she saw the foot as an international symbol, a representation of the roots of winemaking. Plus a foot is fun, Chris said.

FDB ordered about 24,000 cases, then taught Barefoot that Scandinavian store managers can be just as hard-headed as anyone anywhere.

Michael and FDB's California buyer wanted to send Danish store managers all of Barefoot's posters along with a letter explaining that they should sell Barefoot as a delivery of California sunshine and as a fine wine. The letter also said, be sure to let customers know that Barefoot had both a happy-go-lucky soul and a list of medals for its quality. In short, it was not a novelty item.

But the letter got tangled in FDB's chain of command. It might have been a territorial dispute, it might have been stubbornness up the line, it might have been some internal Machiavellian move for power. Whatever the reason, the letter never made it to the Denmark stores and few FDB managers put any effort into selling the wine. Many never even put Barefoot on their shelves. Sales were grim and eventually FDB cut the order short.

FDB still gave Barefoot a welcome, if one-shot, influx of money, but it was an example of how tough business can be when you work with companies that have a mindset different from yours.

About the same time, though, Michael and Bonnie were making a new business connection, and this outfit was very much in sync with Barefoot. The company also had a playful outlook, a nimble resourcefulness, and an irreverent spirit. It was called Trader Joe's.

The year was 1989. A broker in Southern California told Michael about this rising new company that seemed a little crazy, but in a good way, just like Barefoot. Go talk to them, the broker said.

Trader Joe's started in Pasadena in 1967 with a South Seas motif and the notion that its buyers were traveling the world, finding distant treasures and exotic products to bring back home. By 1989, Trader Joe's had about 30 outlets, mostly in Southern California, and when Michael walked into the Pasadena store, he could see this connection was going to work out.

There were sailing knick-knacks and nets all over the walls. Employees wore Hawaiian shirts and called managers "captain" and clerks "mates." They had products with names like "Kiwi-from-Paradise Juice" and a large wine department that had almost no big-name brands. Most of all, the place was fun.

"We think the entertainment part is just as important as the retail part," Tim Bekins, the Trader Joe's buyer, told Michael. "It brings people in."

"Funny to hear you say that," Michael said. "In our business plan, we call it retail entertainment."

Although Trader Joe's had been around more than two decades by then, the supermarket industry still had doubts about the company. Trader Joe's was so different. They sold things like imported cheeses, unusual spices, smoked meats and fish—staples of today's foodie culture that seemed downright strange a couple decades ago—and they sold it with a smile. Long-time supermarket pros didn't know what to make of the approach. Michael loved it. He thought that Trader Joe's knew their customers, and that the place was perfect for Barefoot. Tim thought the fit was a bull's-eye, too. And he thought the timing couldn't be better.

Trader Joe's customers were moving from beer and wine coolers to actual wine, and Tim believed Barefoot's label, profile, and playfulness were ideal for that shift. Trader Joe's customers were mainstream, middle-class people who were intimidated by hard-to-pronounce wines. Tim said Barefoot would give them a chance to try a premium wine that didn't scare anyone.

"The juice in the bottle over delivers for the price," he said.

"Well, yeah, that's what we think," Michael said.

They talked like two music fans who realized they both loved early Beatles. As odd as this would seem in just a few years, Barefoot and Trader Joe's were outsiders in their industries, and Michael and Tim were both pretty thrilled to have found another company on the same wavelength.

It was a relationship that would last for years as both companies grew into nationwide brands and kept their founding spirits. By the early 2000s, Trader Joe's would be buying 100,000 cases from Barefoot annually. On the downside, industry watchers didn't see those sales because they didn't scan, either.

On a hot afternoon in late 1992, Michael was driving around San Clemente, a small city on Southern California's coast. He was a little lost. He was looking for an office he thought would be near the beach.

But the address took him through some very un-beach-like commercial streets in the middle of town, and when he found the office, it was a tiny storefront in a busy street-side strip mall.

Michael was wearing a suit, his standard uniform on a business call. He went in the front door, but still wasn't sure he was in the right place. The group he was looking for was getting a formidable reputation.

This room was maybe 12 by 15 feet. A guy with medium-long, sun-bleached hair sat behind a battered, crowded desk. He was in his late 20s or early 30s, and looked fit and tan. He wore bright shorts, huarache sandals, and a faded T-shirt. A surfboard hung on a wall rack behind him.

"Is this the Surfrider Foundation?" Michael asked

The guy smiled. "You found it," he said. "International headquarters."

Michael immediately liked the unassuming guy. Michael also liked the unfussy room filled with papers, files, and surf gear. He introduced himself and said he had been learning about Surfrider.

"We want to help," Michael said.

Michael showed him a bottle of Barefoot and the Surfrider laughed. "Very cool," he said. "Love the foot. It's like Hang Ten or something."

They talked a bit. Michael explained Barefoot's approach to wine and its connection with the beach. The Surfrider told Michael about the foundation's latest project, the Blue Water Task Force.

"What can we do?" Michael said.

"We don't have much money," the man said.

"Neither do we," Michael said. "But we have wine."

Michael heard about Surfrider through a Southern California distributor rep, who said the group was a natural fit for Barefoot. He said Surfrider was interested in the same things as Michael and Bonnie—clean water, safe beaches, open spaces, and the environment. Plus Michael used to surf.

The Surfrider Foundation started in 1984 trying to protect a prized surf break at Malibu. They spread through Southern California, working to preserve beaches, keep the ocean clean, and protect beach access, and they grew to include programs that taught people about the coast and the environment.

They were, mostly, grown-up surfers—lawyers, business-people, wage earners, doctors, teachers, folks who had jobs and families and still surfed and loved the beach. Every day they surfed, they saw the threats to the water, the coast, and the people who lived and visited there.

Their latest front in 1992, the Blue Water Task Force, was a ground-breaking idea designed by chemists, engineers, and oceanographers. It was part Neighborhood Watch for the ocean and part giant chemistry project. Surfrider gave little kits to surfers all along California's coast that could help diagnose exactly what was in the water and where.

The kits were the size of a pack of cigarettes. A surfer would open the top, slide out a little Petri dish, dip it in the water, seal it up, write the location on it, then drop it into a mailbox with pre-paid postage. It went to a Surfrider lab that would test the sample. They were creating maps of California's coastline, piecing together the details of what spots were clean and what spots were not.

Surfrider came up with this plan because lots of surfers and lifeguards, and lots of kids just hanging at beaches, were getting rashes or infections or serious illnesses when they spent long days in the ocean, especially along some of Southern California's most popular beaches.

The Blue Water Task Force quickly developed both cred-ibility and some political muscle, because environmental officials couldn't ignore the hard data from the kits, and because their own tests confirmed the results.

And when Surfrider found dirty beaches, a lot of those spots would get closed down. That meant businesses along those stretches, the hotels, restaurants and more, had serious incen-tives to either clean up their acts if they were responsible, or to pressure whoever was polluting—which included municipal sew-age operations—to fix the problem.

When he learned the details of the Blue Water Task Force, Michael wanted Barefoot to help. But donating wine was only one piece. They needed to get more people to use the kits, and to raise money to pay for them and the lab work.

"We'll give you wine for your fundraisers," Michael told the guy at "international HQ." He was thinking out loud. "And how about this? We'll put neck talkers on our bottles. We've got Barefoot spread all over Southern California, and most of it is in beach towns."

"What's a neck talker?" the guy said.

Neck talkers are common in supermarket aisles. They're the small tags that hang off bottle necks and usually say something like "$2 off cheese with this purchase." Michael's version would say "Hang Ten for Clean Water" and would ask people to send $10 to Surfrider to help pay for the tests.

"Our typical buyer is a mom out shopping," Michael said. "She's got kids getting all those ear infections you were talking about. Maybe we can get her to send a check."

In June 1993, the Surfrider Foundation issued a press release announcing the partnership. "Barefoot Cellars, long-time advocate and supporter of environmental causes, has put its 'foot down' on the side of clean coastal waters," it said.

"These surfers are responsible professionals and are the real guardians of our coast," Michael said in the release. "Their intimate relationship with our coastal waters has made them painfully aware of the pollution that threatens us all."

The neck talkers came out on August 1, 1993. They were surfboard shaped and the circle around the bottle neck was a cartoon surfer dude dangling his toes off the front of the board. They asked people to send $10 to the Surfrider Blue Water Task Force and promised that Barefoot would contribute $1 for every $10 sent in. It was the start of one of the most enduring, and most visible, worthy-cause relationships in American wine.

Barefoot would hang the neck talkers on thousands and thousands of bottles of wine, and raise thousands of dollars for Surfrider. The Blue Water Task Force would test water all along the California coast, and in coming years, its chapters spread the tests throughout the country, from Hawaii to the Eastern Seaboard and the Great Lakes to the Gulf Coast. They would force clean-ups along some world-famous beaches like Santa Monica, San Onofre, Santa Cruz and more. And they would create a perma-nent, nationwide, citizen-powered water-testing program.

Barefoot got questioned at first for the campaign, mostly by analysts who said you should never ask for money on your product. But Michael and Bonnie believed in the Surfrider Foundation. And they believed lots of people who drank Barefoot wanted to protect the coast, too. Barefoot was a major help kick-starting the Blue Water Task Force, and it never stopped supporting the Surfrider cause.

By the late 1990s, when Barefoot had become a national brand, and Surfrider had spread around America, Michael was back at a chapter meeting in Orange County to say hello to some old friends. Surfrider meetings have a touch of happy zealotry to them. People stand up, introduce themselves, and say what kind of surfboard they use, like, "Hi, my name is Sally Smith, I ride a 10-foot O'Neill." When it was Michael's turn, he didn't want to misrepresent. These were die-hards, serious surfers. He hadn't been on a board in years.

"Hi," he said. "My name is Michael Houlihan. I ride a 750 Barefoot."

He got cheers.

Barefoot's early support of Surfrider was one of the most prominent examples of a core principle of the Barefoot Spirit: Bet on people who are doing the right thing.

It's both a moral stand and a good business choice to put your resources into a cause you believe in, even if the cause isn't completely popular—yet. A start-up business and a start-up cause make good partners.

Bonnie and Michael believed that businesses should take a stand on things that matter to them, which does not exactly sync with a long-held idea that businesses are best off when they avoid controversy. Bonnie and Michael saw it differently. From a pure business standpoint, they were a start-up, but staying quiet and under the radar would get them nowhere. And they might as well make noise for causes they believed in.

From a personal standpoint, they wanted to make a difference or leave something good in the places they walked, and they believed any business they owned had the same obligation.

And sometimes, taking a stand means trusting the people who work for you. That's where Barefoot landed in early 1997. It started with a call from Randy Arnold to Michael.

"How do you feel about Tahoe?" Randy asked him.

"I love it," Michael said. "It's beautiful. It's a special place. Why?"

"You know there's algae growing in the lake and it's starting to get really serious," Randy said.

"Yeah, I know," Michael said. "Maybe we should try to help."

"Glad to hear you say that," Randy said.

Randy had connected Barefoot to a campaign called Keep Tahoe Blue. He was arranging for neck talkers on Barefoot displays around Northern California and Nevada and was preparing to donate wine to fundraisers.

"You know that's pretty controversial," Michael said. "There are a lot of people who don't want to slow development up there."

"I know," Randy said. "But it's the right thing to do."

"Yeah," Michael said. "It is."

Keep Tahoe Blue was both a campaign and the trademark of a group called the League to Save Lake Tahoe. Even then, it had already been on a decades-old crusade to protect Lake Tahoe, its high Sierra watershed, the air in the Tahoe basin, and the quality of life around one of the most beautiful places in America. It started as a coalition of environmental groups, and by the 1990s it had stopped the sewage flow into the lake, reduced development in the region, and limited the size of the roads and the number of casinos in the basin.

But in the mid-90s, the fight got bitter. Some groups and companies—builders, casinos, ski areas, restaurant chains and more—worried that curtailed growth or tough environmental control would damage their businesses. There was anger and fear on both sides.

In 1997, Barefoot was still pushing to get into vacation spots, and Tahoe was a hugely popular destination for much of the West in winter and summer. Yet, despite warnings to skirt the bitter political fight, Barefoot stepped in. They put on the neck talkers, put up signs and displays, did what they could to make their case.

There was a quick reaction. Chain stores around California told them they wouldn't display Barefoot with the Tahoe neck talkers because they were too controversial. Some stores and restaurants at Tahoe said if Barefoot kept supporting Keep Tahoe Blue, they would stop carrying Barefoot in the basin and in other locations, too. Other stores and restaurants in Tahoe just dropped them.

In June and July, when the region was crowded with visitors and Barefoot was usually everywhere, its sales in the Tahoe basin slowed to a trickle.

That changed on July 27. For a while, the folks at Keep Tahoe Blue had been working quietly to bring President Bill Clinton to Tahoe, and on July 27 he came to Incline Village on the lake's North Shore for what he called the Lake Tahoe Presidential Forum. He got leaders on both sides of the fight to start talking. More powerfully, he told them that Lake Tahoe was both a singularly beautiful place and the singular reason any business was alive there. They would only stay alive, he said, if the lake survived—and the lake's health was iffy. If Tahoe turned green, there would be no real estate business, no restaurant industry, and almost no traffic to casinos.

Clinton signed an executive order creating a single partnership among the agencies governing Tahoe's health to ease the bureaucracy on both environmental groups and businesses. And he got the business leaders and environmentalists to work on plans together.

It was like a light switch went on. It wasn't a battle anymore, it was a community cause. Dark blue "Keep Tahoe Blue" stickers popped up on cars, trucks, and SUVs from Reno to Sacramento, San Francisco, and Los Angeles. Keep Tahoe Blue became a rallying cry for how to be both pro-environment and pro-business. Environmental groups and business leaders working together helped corral hundreds of millions of dollars from state and federal agencies to repair the health of Lake Tahoe. The Keep Tahoe Blue theme never left the fabric of life in the region.

As for Barefoot, stores immediately stopped complaining, the chains around California allowed the neck talkers, and within weeks of Clinton's forum, stores in the Tahoe area reordered and restocked Barefoot, Keep Tahoe Blue tags and all. Sales in the basin climbed back to the normal level and kept climbing, and sales around California got a nice bump, too.

It was a quiet Monday morning in 1993. The phone rang in Barefoot's office. The secretary told Michael it was a lawyer from New York.

Michael is not the world's most serious man. He picked up the phone and answered the way he usually did.

"Hello," he said, "this is the Head Stomper."

The lawyer ignored it. "I represent the Baron Eric de Roths-child," he said.

Michael was thinking, you just can't make lawyers laugh. "What can I do for the Baron today?" he said.

Baron Eric de Rothschild is a towering figure in the wine world. He owned, and still owns, Chateau Lafite Rothschild, one of the most celebrated and expensive wineries on the planet. It's in Bordeaux, France, its reputation is centuries old, and its wines can sell for hundreds, or thousands, of dollars.

Barefoot, of course, was a wee bit different. In 1993, its wine sold for $4.99 a bottle, though often it was on sale for a dollar less. And there was that foot on the label.

"The Baron takes umbrage," the lawyer told Michael, "with your use of the term 'the Chateau La Feet' of California wine. He feels it will cause confusion in the marketplace. He has retained our firm to take all the legal steps necessary to compel you to cease and desist."

Barefoot had been using that little wordplay since its start. It was Davis Bynum who began the joke. Now, here was a powerful bastion of Old World wine, maybe *the* bastion, threatening to sue Barefoot for, in short, having a sense of humor.

And Michael could not have been more thrilled. That's because he and Bonnie and the Barefoot team had been working toward this moment for more than two years.

This was, remember, a wine company with no budget for ads or PR, so they scrambled continually to generate any kind of Barefoot publicity. The idea for this play dawned on them after Michael's frustrating sales visit to a snooty New York wine shop where the owner bragged about how much Chateau Lafite he sold.

"You know what we need?" Michael told Bonnie when he got home. "We need to get Chateau Lafite to sue us."

Well, as long as Lafite didn't actually sue. They wanted the threat, something to get enough attention to show how different Barefoot was from wineries that used words like "umbrage." And they thought that if the Baron or Lafite lawyers got wind of Barefoot's "La Feet" slogan, that might push the button.

So in mid-1991, Barefoot started giving its "Chateau La Feet" T-shirts to friends and business allies heading to Europe or international wine festivals. When brokers wanted Barefoot wines for trade shows like Vinexpo in France or the London International Wine Fair, Michael and Bonnie made sure they also took stacks of the shirts, and that they put them on anything that moved.

Finally, the Barefooters think, a young Rothschild relative saw the slogan at a wine marketing seminar Michael gave at the University of California, Davis. Maybe she even wore a T-shirt back to the Chateau.

But if Michael wasn't sure what exactly prompted the lawyer's call, he did understand this would only work if he got something solid to show to newspapers before he gave in to Lafite's demands.

"Really?" Michael said. "The Baron takes umbrage? I'm sorry to hear that. But you're going to have to threaten me in writing. Can you write that down and fax it to me?"

Fine, the lawyer said. He'd send it by the end of Tuesday.

Tuesday morning, Michael and most of the Barefoot office staff paced hopefully around the fax machine. A little after 10:30 a.m., the phone rang and the fax started beeping. It was a threat from something in Paris called the Societe Civile de Chateau Lafite-Rothschild. Even the stuffy name was perfect for this story.

Michael re-sent the fax to Dan Berger, a respected Los Angeles Times wine writer. Michael had gotten to know him a bit because Dan had been generally appreciative of Barefoot. He wrote about it the next day.

The Lafite vs. La Feet story went national on Thanksgiving week after a wire service picked up Berger's piece. It was ideal for newsrooms trying to fill a quiet holiday weekend.

The story of the powerful Baron threatening plucky little Barefoot "to avoid confusion in the marketplace" showed up in places ranging from the Chicago Tribune, the Orlando Sentinel, and the Independent of London to CBS radio, the Osgood File, and Paul Harvey's "The Rest of the Story." It eventually, and improbably, made the Weekly World News, that goofy tabloid that ran stories of aliens hanging out with American presidents. (The item ran near a story of a multi-headed cow.)

The first media call came in at Michael and Bonnie's house at 6 a.m. on Thanksgiving morning. Michael spent the weekend giving phone interviews and answering reporter after reporter.

"I agree with the Baron," Michael told them, "if people confuse our wine, which costs $4.99, with his, which costs $100, we'll be ruined."

"These guys have to be kidding," Houlihan told other reporters. "Our bottle has a big purple foot. Theirs has lots of fancy European writing, most of which you can't pronounce."

Michael said he would change the slogan to "Chateau La Foot." "We have a foot on our label," he told the San Francisco Chronicle. "We're always going to be Chateau la Something-of-the-Lower Leg."

The news stories worked out so well they could have been written by Barefoot's PR people, if they'd had PR people. The stories said Chateau Lafite embodied what scared people about wine. They were unbending, exclusive, humorless. But Barefoot, the stories said, was the opposite—friendly, innovative, playful. And they laughed. Nobody in polite wine society laughed.

The Barefoot crew didn't let it end there. They clipped and copied the columns and stories for Barefoot's sales team to hand to every mom-and-pop and wine shop owner, every supermarket manager and wine clerk, to tell them that carrying Barefoot made *them* look good. Now Safeway or Bill's Bottle Shop was siding with the little guy, the Americans with a sense of humor who were getting bullied by French fuddy-duddies.

There was an immediate and sustained spike in Barefoot sales, and the echoes lasted for years. Nearly a decade later, Michael and the salespeople would still hear wine buyers or store managers asking, "Wasn't there some baron or duke in Europe trying to shut you guys down?"

Michael and Bonnie were driving up the hill toward their little ranch house on a warm summer evening after work. They were both in business suits, both tired, both anxious about the challenges facing their company.

Normally, these two are talkers. They're thoughtful people who digest what they see and hear, think about it, and talk it over with each other. But this day, they were both exhausted and quiet.

When they got near their house, they saw something strange. There were moving waves of rich brown flowing around the front of it and rolling down the gentle hill below.

Bonnie and Michael reached their gate and saw the brown swaths were long, loose robes worn by a half-dozen young, shaven-headed men who skipped and danced around the yard and hillside, then broke into spins while they held their robes out like capes.

Michael and Bonnie looked at each other, mouths open. They looked back at their house. The robes and bald young men were still twirling about in the end-of-day sunshine.

"Whaaa?" Michael said.

"Monks," Bonnie said. "We've got monks."

"How do we get rid of them?" Michael said.

They parked in their driveway and walked toward the house. Most of the monks were teenagers, but there was one older monk standing on the porch. The young monks reeled themselves in and headed for the porch, but they didn't go to the older monk. When Bonnie and Michael reached the porch, the monks were all standing around Mabel.

"Hey," Mabel said. She smiled like a little kid. "These are my new friends. Aren't they sweet?"

If there was one person who embodied the Barefoot Spirit— the optimism, kindness, creativity, never-give-up attitude, and the cheerful, all-embracing heart—it was Bonnie's mom, Mabel Hurd.

And if there was one human who naturally attracted like-minded, gentle-spirited souls, and who connected the people around her into one complementary community, it was Mabel. She was a quiet force of nature, tall, high-shouldered, and seemingly interested in everyone. People reflexively called her mom or grandma, without knowing that everyone else called her that, too.

Mabel had been a Rosie-the-Riveter welder during World War II, helping build liberty ships in the Portland shipyards. In late 1987, Mabel was living in Sandy, Oregon, in the foothills of Mt. Hood, growing and selling organic blueberries. She had also developed emphysema. That's when Bonnie and Michael called her.

They told Mabel to come live with them in Sonoma County. It was just as green, the weather was so much kinder, and, besides, they said, they needed her help.

That was what Mabel needed to hear. She lived to be useful. In the near decade she lived with Bonnie and Michael in the farm-house on MacMurray Ranch, she was everything from domestic help to office staff to, most of all, guardian of the sunny spirit.

Her health improved steadily in Sonoma County, and her emphysema became almost a non-issue after about a year or so. And if her move to dry weather and life with Bonnie and Michael saved her, she saved them, too.

One of the first things Mabel did was plant a 20-by-80-foot gar-den filled with vegetables and herbs. In the early 1990s, she began calling it Michael's Sanity Garden, because Barefoot was spreading far beyond Northern California and, she said, if Michael was on the road throughout the West Coast trying to sell wine, "he should know good things were growing back home." She also figured that, no matter what happened, the garden meant at least they'd have food.

Mabel also canned fruits, did laundry, cooked meals, baked cakes and pies, even made ketchup for Bonnie and Michael. She helped organize Barefoot's point-of-sale materials, rolled posters, folded T-shirts.

And she was Barefoot's PR "machine" in the first years, clipping newspaper and magazine stories where Barefoot was mentioned—like the Chateau La Feet episode—copying them and then highlighting the Barefoot references by hand so Michael and Randy and Barefoot salespeople could give them to distributors and store buyers.

As Barefoot grew, that PR machine included "Footnotes," a one-page handout listing medals Barefoot had won, raves from critics, press mentions and anything else to nourish the idea that Barefoot was hot. Eventually, they had paid staffers put Footnotes together, but Mabel handled all that for years.

Just as much, Mabel gave Michael and Bonnie an outsider's perspective on the wine world, even beyond their own outsider-ness.

Michael came back exhausted from a sales trip to Southern California in late 1993. He told Mabel it was a disaster because the stores were stocking up for Christmas and New Year's.

"We sell wine," Michael said. "Everyone's buying Champagne."

"That's easy," Mabel said. "Why don't you have a Champagne?"

"I can barely sell wine," Michael said. But he thought, you know, why don't we? "What would I call it, anyway?"

Mabel barely paused. "Well, I'd call it Barefoot Bubbly," she said.

It took a few years. Barefoot's sparkling wine didn't hit the market until 1997. A year later, Michael and Bonnie toasted Mabel for her 80th birthday with a wine named Barefoot Bubbly.

Mabel was something valuable even beyond that presence that was so full of life. She was a flesh-and-blood business lesson: Don't just look in conventional places for help, and take the help wherever you find it. Good ideas can come from anyone, and people running a business—but particularly a start-up—need to keep their eyes, and their minds, open so they won't miss that useful-but-unconventional idea, and so they won't dismiss it. Just as much, strategic partners can come from anywhere, too.

Bonnie and Michael turned to Mabel because she was family and because they knew she could help with day-to-day chores. They didn't plan that she would name products and bolster their PR efforts, and they had forgotten how much she would lift their spirits. Sometimes a start-up business, or any business running at full speed, can overlook resources in arm's reach, even if that "resource" turns out to be your mom or, well, monks.

The monks started coming around after Mabel made friends with a young Thai woman named Dao. Dao brought them to visit that first day because she thought they'd like the farmhouse. She was certain they'd like Mabel.

Dao formally introduced Michael and Bonnie to the monks that day. Their leader, who they would come to call Old Monk, was the only one besides Dao who spoke any English, and he was hit-and-miss. He thanked them for letting the monks visit Mabel.

They came back regularly for years to visit Mabel. They spent most of their time outdoors, hanging out in the vegetable garden and around the flowers. The monks were in the garden one afternoon when Michael and Bonnie came home. Mabel had been weeding, and the monks seemed to be just watching her and pulling a weed here and there. But there was no discard pile.

"Where'd the weeds go?" Bonnie asked Old Monk.

"They were young and sprouting and full of life," Old Monk said. "We ate them."

And sometimes the monks did more than munch weeds. When Barefoot went to big tastings and events, Michael and Bonnie usually brought piles of those "Chateau La Feet/La Foot" T-shirts. There was a day when three boxes got delivered on a Thursday evening and all of them—more than 400 shirts—needed to be folded for a weekend event. Folding the shirts was slow going because it was tedious to get the angled foot to show just right.

Michael and Bonnie left the huge pile with Mabel in the morning and asked awkwardly if she would fold whatever shirts she could get to. They said they'd help her finish that night.

When they got home and walked in the house, they heard a sing-song chanting coming from the merchandise center (aka the laundry room). Bonnie and Michael turned the corner and saw Mabel and Dao and the monks all folding shirts. The monks were singing happily.

Mabel gave them a sheepish grin. "I figured out how to get them all done," she said.

At first, the monks would only visit with Dao. But within weeks, they started driving to the house themselves, just showing up with no warning. They'd walk up, bow, and say hello. One Christmas morning in the early '90s, Old Monk came to visit by himself.

He knew it was a holiday for Mabel and Bonnie and Michael, so he came just to be respectful. When he was leaving, Bonnie walked him to his car.

"We're happy you come to visit," Bonnie said. "You're always welcome. But why do you come? What brings you here?"

Old Monk smiled.

"Because of Mabel," he said. "We like to be near her life force."

By the early 1990s, Barefoot Cellars was starting to feel more permanent to Bonnie and Michael. Not necessarily solvent—they still put every dollar back into growing—but it appeared they might actually be around a while.

Besides the hard work and constant adapting to circumstances, there had been some luck, too, what they called their miracle of the month—like the Kenan Busan deal and the Danish adventure—but they could also see they were getting real traction.

They'd seen the appeal of their wine and their tone. The Trader Joe's alliance showed they weren't alone in thinking America wanted a good $5 bottle of wine. Barefoot was attracting larger and better distributors. People at tastings and charity events told them they liked the wine and the foot.

In 1993, Barefoot hit a milestone: It topped 100,000 cases sold, with 102,000. "I figured if I kept telling people we were at 100,000 long enough," Michael said at the time, "it would eventually be true." In 1994, they hit 120,000 cases.

They were established throughout the West Coast, in chains like Lucky, Safeway, Thrifty, Costco, and Raley's in California and into Oregon and Washington. In the Pacific Northwest they added chains like the Fred Meyer supermarkets. Randy had spent almost a year in Southern California at one point with marching orders not to get more than a mile from the ocean, and Barefoot's beach cachet was strong.

Barefoot was also winning medals for its wines and getting praise from wine critics. They added chardonnay to their lineup in 1992 and bottled it in both the 750 ml and 1.5 liter sizes. (They considered the conventional 750 ml bottle to be the "trial size" and the magnums to be the "loyalty size.")

And Barefoot introduced American wine's first Spanish-language shelf talkers. Those are the sales notes on store shelves and these said, "El Vino Para Todas Las Comidas." The Wine For All Your Meals.

And yet. All the success and growth came with more surprises and more costs, just as the early growth had. Every new territory meant they needed yet more Barefooters to work sales and watch the reorders and displays. There wasn't any great economy of scale on winemaking or shipping costs. Every move seemed to bring new fees and taxes. Their profit margin remained wispy. Growing was critical. It was also expensive.

When they launched Barefoot, Bonnie and Michael thought they would be in it for four years. That was their guess on paying off the debt to Mark Lyon and building Barefoot enough to make it an attractive acquisition for another winery. Eight years later, they were laughing at those naïve estimates. They could see this would be a long haul, and in '94 they'd come to understand they had no idea what the length of that haul would be.

By the early 1990s, the Bynum name had not been on the bottle for years, and Barefoot had also moved from Davis Bynum Winery to a business park in Santa Rosa, but Michael and Bonnie were still friends with Davis and Hampton.

On a mild, late winter day in 1994, Michael went to visit Davis and wound up standing in the parking lot with him, watching a repair crew high up on the roof hammering away.

"Why didn't you fix the roof when we were there?" Michael said.

"It wasn't worth it," Davis said.

"So why now?"

"I have to. The leaks are coming into the tasting room," Davis said. "I don't have you guys up there anymore to move the buckets around."

CONVERSATIONS WITH BONNIE AND MICHAEL

Rick: *Tell me more about that tiny, leaky office at Davis Bynum's winery.*

Bonnie: It was one large room, about 600 square feet or something. We had three people in the field and three of us in the office, and it was stuffed.

Michael: When we went to four in the office, it started to get crazy. Everybody had to sit down for the door to open. If someone was standing, it would hit them. When we got a knock on the door, everybody sat down.

Bonnie: We were audited for California sales tax once. It was summer when the auditor came. There was literally no room in the office for another body, so we put him out in the hall.

Michael: We put him in a utility closet, remember?

Bonnie: Oh, that's right. We put up a card table and a folding chair. It was about 105 degrees in there.

Michael: There was no window, no AC.

Bonnie: It had one bare light bulb. It was a multi-year audit. That audit was over in two days.

Michael: We felt bad for him. We tried to give him a bottle of wine but he couldn't accept it.

Rick: *Of all the worthy causes, the Surfrider Foundation seems to be the most perfect for Barefoot.*

Bonnie: It seemed so natural.

Michael: Bonnie had always been a stickler for clean beaches. Ever since I met her, she's been picking up garbage wherever she goes, especially on the beach. When we heard they were actually testing the ocean for swimmers' safety, we thought, geez, these are our kind of people. These guys are the guardians of the beach. How can we help?

Bonnie: It was a match for our lifestyle and for the Barefoot Spirit.

Michael: It really set the tone for a lot of our Worthy Cause Marketing. It showed us how much a business could help a non-profit and, in return, how much we could create goodwill toward the brand.

Rick: *How important was Mabel to your lives?*

Bonnie: She supported us in so many ways. Mabel had the Barefoot Spirit way before the Barefoot Spirit was ever dreamed of.

Michael: She kept us going. Sometimes, we'd come home and she'd have made us a pie.

Bonnie: Yes, she did. When things got rough, she'd bake a pie. How sweet was that?

Michael: She was our private rooting section. She was like a coach. We'd say, we have all this work to do, and she'd say, well, you'd better get started. And she was willing to pitch in, do hard, physical work.

Bonnie: She worked hard her whole life.

Michael: We asked her to come to live with us because she had emphysema. A year later, I came home one day and Mabel's running a big rototiller, one of those two-handled things that's like holding onto a bucking bronco. She was putting in a vegetable garden for us.

Rick: *Other people saw something special in her, too. I mean, besides the monks.*

Michael: Yes, they did. And she was great at reading people. We didn't listen to her all the time, but she was always right. Every time we didn't listen to her, we regretted it.

Bonnie: If you're a phony, you didn't get past Mabel. When we were considering hiring people, we'd run some of them by her— we'd bring them over to the house—and sometimes she'd say, don't hire them. We'd say, but they're perfect for the job. A year later, they'd be gone.

Michael: She just had an aura about her.

Bonnie: Almost everybody who knew her would eventually call her mom.

Chapter Seven

The "Romance" of the Wine Business

Jennifer Wall walked around the Barefoot offices in Santa Rosa on a Saturday in early September 1995, chatting with Bonnie and Michael. She was wearing jeans, a T-shirt, and tennis shoes. Michael and Bonnie had ridden bikes to the office and they were in casual Saturday clothes, too.

Jen was a winemaker, but in 1995 she was working on the production side of the food world at Calistoga Mineral Water. Michael had called Jen and asked her to drop in that Saturday.

Jen didn't know them, but she knew about Barefoot. A couple years back she had worked at Vinwood Cellars, the winery where Barefoot was bottled in the early 1990s. She thought maybe Michael and Bonnie wanted help with a production issue.

As she waited for him to bring it up, they strolled into one of the offices.

"This is where you'll be working," Michael said.

"Oh," Jen thought to herself. "This is an interview. I should have dressed better."

They went into the conference room. Michael started mapping out the salary structure and Barefoot's income stream. Jen saw pretty quickly that she was talking to a pro of a salesman. Michael charmingly assumed the close, and went right into the pay and company structure without asking whether Jen would take the job. She appreciated the technique.

"What happened to your old winemaker?" she asked.

The early 1990s had a couple rough weather years for California wine grapes, particularly for northern California and white wines. The grape supply was feeble, and big volume wineries like Barefoot, which would produce 156,000 cases in 1995, were scrambling.

During the summer, despite it all, Bonnie and Michael managed to squeeze out time to hike in one of their favorite places on Earth, the wild, spectacular Kalalau Valley on the northwest coast of Kauai. When they got home, all that nature-induced calm disappeared in one "poof." Barefoot sales had screeched to a stop. They asked their staff if something happened.

Turned out, their winemaker had enacted his plan for handling the wine shortage.

"He said we should stop selling," staffers told Bonnie and Michael.

"Stop selling?" Bonnie almost sputtered.

"Are you kidding me?" Michael said.

This was a growing, fast-moving company still surfing just ahead of that monster wave of debt. They were struggling to keep stores stocked and happy, and any hiccup in the supply line could be devastating.

Michael and Bonnie looked at each other.

"New winemaker," Bonnie said.

So they started the hunt. They called their old friend Mark Lyon at Sebastiani Vineyards and asked if he knew of anyone he trusted who was looking for a job.

"We had a woman come in a couple weeks ago," Mark said. "She was really good—creative, analytical, and she just understood things. I thought we should hire her but the board thought she was too assertive."

"I'm not sure that's possible," Michael said. "We need to get her over here."

That's how Jen landed at Barefoot that Saturday. Michael called, just said they wanted to talk with her, and now Jen was getting asked about dealing with a statewide wine shortage.

"Somewhere in the world," she said, "there's too much wine. We'll find it."

They talked about a plan to maintain the supply of chardonnay, which was the immediate concern, and to keep the flavor consistent, the quality up, and the price down. When any brand, whether it's cereal, hot dogs, or wine, suddenly gets a price hike, even if it's small, shoppers try something else.

Jennifer Wall had been a biology major at the University of California, Santa Cruz, aiming for med school. Her father was a food-manufacturing executive, so she knew a bit about that industry. Her parents moved to Sonoma when she was still in college, and after she graduated from Santa Cruz she moved north to join them.

Her science background got her a job as an assistant at Vinwood Cellars in Alexander Valley in 1991, and she fell in love with winemaking working for renowned winemaker Kerry Damskey.

She learned the wine business there, then learned the juggling act of production at Calistoga Mineral Water, which had more than 60 different products. Now, sitting in Barefoot's offices, she was brainstorming an inventive blend of winemaking and production to keep Barefoot alive.

Jen knew that Chile had a white wine glut and their grape prices were low. She said they could buy and crush the grapes in Chile, but not ferment them into wine there. Instead, they could ship the grape juice to California and make the wine in Sonoma County, which would save money and help with quality control.

"Have you done something like this before?" Bonnie said.

"Never," Jen said. "But I'll make it work."

To understand her plan, it helps to remember that yeast eat the sugar in the juice from crushed grapes and create alcohol as a by-product. Yeast are not hard to find. They live just about anywhere there is moisture, but most wineries get rid of the native yeasts and use their own.

It also helps to know about SO_2 (sulfur dioxide). The wine industry would not survive without it. It's a purifier and stabilizer used for a range of chores, from fighting mold in the vineyards to killing bacteria to controlling the fermentation of the grapes.

Wineries also use it to get rid of those native yeasts when they want to use their own strain, which can affect everything from fermentation speed to the taste or feel of the wine.

What made Jen's plan different was that she would use enough SO_2 to keep the grape juice from fermenting in Chile or on its ride from South America, and to keep any bacteria from weaseling in.

When the juice got to California, Jen would run it through something called spinning cones—a relatively new tool in winemaking, though food companies had used some version for years. The cones, in essence, increase the speed of evaporation and separate the components of a liquid like grape juice or wine.

Jen would spin out all the SO_2, and once again she'd have the starter juice from the crushed grapes. Then she would add yeast and ferment it, just like any other wine.

Jen went to work for Barefoot on September 18. To make sure her plan would work correctly, she experimented with apple juice, which was decidedly cheaper to play with than fine wine grapes.

Then, in early March 1996, she went to the Maule Valley in Chile, bought chardonnay grapes, crushed them, put the juice into massive flexible pouches that filled their 20-foot shipping containers, trucked the containers more than 200 miles on steep, winding mountain roads to Valparaiso on the coast, loaded the containers with the pouches into the hold of a cargo ship, shipped 40,000 gallons of grape juice 6,000 miles to the port of Oakland, off-loaded the containers, put them onto trucks, and had them driven north to winemaking facilities in St. Helena in Napa Valley. Then, Jen removed the SO_2, started fermentation, and made wine to match Barefoot's chardonnay profile. Nothing to it.

Jennifer Wall would become a foundation of Barefoot's expansion into a national brand and her working relationship with Bonnie and Michael would last a decade. Their friendship is ongoing. And like Mabel Hurd and Randy Arnold and so many others, Jen didn't just fit the Barefoot Spirit, she helped expand it.

A part of that spirit is about believing in your ideas with passion, drive, and humility—the humility to take chances, to be wrong and fix your mistakes, and to let someone else have the right answer if it works for your business.

That connects to the idea of having confidence there's an answer out there for every problem. That's why you keep looking for it, keep managing every factor you can control, and simply enough, keep believing there is a way.

And Jen was a gold-plated problem solver. By the time she joined Barefoot, Michael and Bonnie were expanding to sell nationwide. Jen's production background, combined with her blend of nimble winemaking, creative thinking, and analytical skills, helped ramp up Barefoot's volume for national sales.

A big part of going national was Barefoot's production program they called Just in Time Wine. Michael and Bonnie came up with the idea to ease their always-stressed cash flow. Jen figured out how to manage it.

The plan was to bottle Barefoot just before it was shipped, rather than to have thousands of cases sitting in warehouses waiting for orders and racking up storage costs. In short, they didn't want to make or bottle wine until they knew it would be paid for and shipped quickly.

Barefoot produced wine through four routes: (1) it bought bulk wine in tanks, like Mark's original cab and sauv blanc, (2) it bought juice from grapes before it was fermented, then Jen made it into wine, (3) it bought grapes and Jen had them crushed and made into wine, and, (4) it contracted with wineries to make wine to Barefoot's specs. Jen made sure everything fit Barefoot's costs, flavor, style, and timing.

The Just in Time program meant she had to pay constant attention to every route. She tasted almost daily to decide which bulk wines, juice, or grapes to buy. If she got behind, there'd be no catching up and there'd be a gap in the supply.

The sales team kept her supplied with trends and figures about everything from seasonal ebbs and flows in the market to growth projections to discussions with a new supermarket chain.

Jen developed detailed calculations to plan wine production and bottlings that she called the Never Run Out Formula. It was based on the sales team's info and her own sense of the industry, the grape supply, the seasons, and even the accuracy of previous projections.

This idea of complete, 360-degree info sharing about sales, winemaking, and everything else was surprisingly unusual. But it was a crucial part of Barefoot's survival and growth.

So many companies operate like paramilitary organizations with a need-to-know chain of command. Their counterproductive goal is to tell their own employees as little as possible, only what managers think their people need for their day-to-day tasks—often without grasping what workers really do need to know to do their jobs well.

Michael and Bonnie figured everyone needed to know everything. That kept their people invested in Barefoot. It helped with problem solving, because everyone could see the challenges and sometimes a solution for one unit would come from another unit. And Just in Time Wine would not have worked without that full disclosure.

As Barefoot started to grow nationally, the company was evolving to operate on a larger stage. They were getting new distributors, expanding the sales team, creating an agile production plan.

Then, once again, they ran into the wine business. In this case, it was the astoundingly erratic collection of rules and regulations governing how to sell wine in America.

Michael was in New Jersey, working his way along the southern end of New York Bay. He was riding with Stephen Della Vecchia, a rep for Fedway, Barefoot's long-time distributor in the

Garden State. Michael and Stevie D, as everyone in the industry called him, had become friends over the years.

Stevie was explaining that it's legal in New Jersey to give the shop owner an incentive to carry a wine. That's a no-no in California and many other states, but Retail Incentive Programs—called RIPs—were fine in New Jersey, if you do them correctly.

The first natural thought, then, would be to offer the store owner a straightforward discount, like a dollar off per case. But that's illegal, Stevie D said. New Jersey considered that paying for store space.

"So how do I do this?" Michael said.

"That's always the question, isn't it?" Stevie D said. "What you can do is, you give him an American Express gift certificate."

"That's funny," Michael said. "No, really, how do I give the guy a RIP?"

"Seriously. An American Express gift certificate. He spends it like cash. Not one from Visa, and not MasterCard. Just AmEx."

New Jersey's liquor laws—who can sell, how they can sell, how a winery like Barefoot must deal with stores and distributors and anyone who might touch a bottle of wine—range from mildly arbitrary to flat-out bizarre. And in that way, New Jersey is very, very normal, because there is no normal. There are no standardized rules, no nationwide guidelines or regulations about anything involving alcohol sales.

Every state has a different system. It's like going to Europe. You need to learn a different language for each country. In wine sales, you need to learn the regulatory language and how to survive it in each state. Salespeople call that Compliance. Compliance is a nightmare.

For instance, here were a few of the rules Barefoot, and any wine producer, had to deal with in the mid-1990s:

- New Jersey, besides the American Express thing, was what's called a One Man, One License State. So was New York. That means a person or a company was only allowed one retail liquor license. So, in two of America's biggest wine markets, no chain stores sold wine. You couldn't get a Safeway or a Kroger to spread your brand. You had to go store-by-store, block-by-block, the way Michael did when Barefoot started.

- New York was also a Bottle Shop State. That meant if you sold beer, wine, or spirits, you couldn't sell food—no chips, no cheese puffs, no M&Ms, not even peanuts or pretzels. No snacks, period.

- Massachusetts was a One Man, Three License State. That was only a little better than New Jersey.

- Washington state allowed chain stores. Supermarkets could sell your wine. But it was a Posting State. That meant if you wanted to drop or raise the price of Barefoot, you had to notify liquor authorities one month beforehand, so all your competitors would know what you're doing.

- Idaho allowed chain store sales, and it was also a Posting State like Washington. Sort of. To drop the price, you had to announce it one month prior. But to raise the price, you had to give *four* months notice.

- In Ohio, you couldn't give a store a discount for buying in volume. That's called a Case One State. The 100th case costs the same as the first case.

- Michigan was a Bottle One State. You couldn't even give a discount for buying by the case. That created near-chaos for Barefoot and any winery because many stores only ordered a couple bottles at a time.

- Georgia allowed supermarket wine sales. It wasn't a One Man, One License State, or a Posting State, or a Case One or Bottle One State. Should've been a dream to operate in. Except, it was a Franchise State. They're also called Married States, because you can't fire your distributor. Once you signed with a distributing company, there was no separation, and that distributor had you exclusively. Your options were to buy your way to freedom— which was not cheap—or to leave the state for three years, then come back and get someone new.

- Connecticut was also a Franchise State, but you could get a second marriage, as long as you didn't divorce the first distributor. And if you made any lower-price deals with the second spouse, the first one got the lower price, too.

- Pennsylvania was a Government State. The only places selling wine, beer, or spirits were the state Liquor Control Board stores. And if Barefoot wanted to put the wine on sale, the state never shared the cost the way a chain might. So if Barefoot Cab was going from $5.99 to $4.99 for a June special, Barefoot had to charge the state $1 less per bottle so the buck would come entirely out of Barefoot's wallet.

- Oregon had state stores selling spirits, but beer and wine could be sold in supermarkets.

- Half of Mississippi's counties were dry—and many of those counties made it illegal to even drive through them with alcohol in the car.

It goes on in endless, headache-inducing combinations and tweaks. Some states added blue laws that restricted alcohol sales on Sundays, or dry counties, dry cities, or crazy quilts of wet/dry/lord-knows-what regulations across states like Texas. Learning Compliance for the entire U.S. was like studying for a bar exam.

And then there were rules governing tastings. This was a big deal for Barefoot. The wine was still an unknown in much of the U.S. in the mid-1990s, and its sunshiny-fun sensibility was still very different for wine, so many people wanted to taste it first. But that wasn't always easy.

More than 20 states simply banned all wine tastings in retail stores, and loads of states that did allow tastings tacked on some thoroughly-odd caveats. Such as:

- Connecticut allowed one-ounce tastes between noon and 8 p.m. No more than four bottles could be open at the same time.

- Oregon allowed tastings, but only with wines grown and bottled in Oregon.

- Michigan tastings were legal only with wines not yet sold in that store.

- Minnesota was the opposite. The wine had to be sold—and in stock—at the store.

- In New Mexico, Barefoot could run a store tasting, but Michael could not bring the wine. He had to buy it from that store, and retail was two or three times more expensive than if he'd taken it from Barefoot's stock.

- In Wyoming, a tasting had to be conducted by a broker, not a Barefoot employee, and the broker had to live in Wyoming.

The best, though, was Maryland. Barefoot could conduct a store tasting—but only if the public didn't know about it ahead of time. Barefoot or the store could not advertise it, not even with a poster. It was supposed to be spontaneous, as if Michael wandered in and said, "Hey, as long as I'm here, anyone want to taste some wine?"

Compliance is a massive issue for any wine company going national. The slapdash nature of the rules, the helter-skelter demands, the sheer number of variations, make doing business across the country so much more complicated than just gearing up to be large.

The reason for this mess? Thank you, Prohibition. All those seemingly random laws are its aftereffects. The reasons make only a little more sense than some of the laws.

When the 21st Amendment allowed America to drink again in 1933, there were still some voices arguing for Prohibition, because some people never give up on a bad idea. To appease the teetotalers, the amendment gave most of the alcohol regulation to the states—making control more local.

One big concern for those locals was the way organized crime had thrived during Prohibition, and each state, city, and police force devised their own scheme to stop the mob. Not many of the rules worked, but they did give America a spectacularly haphazard system.

And talk about an exercise in problem solving for an expanding winery. Barefoot had to play the wine-selling game 50 different ways. They had to find people who knew the rules and quirks of each state—often laws in one state looked like a neighbor's, except there was almost always some peculiar tweak—then build an internal system that tracked both the regulations and what sales strategies worked where.

Barefoot's approach and pricing scheme had to be different in almost every state—sometimes in every county within a state. That's why the question, "How do we do this?" became as much a part of Michael's traveling gear as his suitcase.

Barefoot expanded into Nevada in the mid-90s, and it seemed like the move would not be terribly complex. Nevada's licensing appeared similar to California's, plus Safeway already carried Barefoot in Southern California, and it had authorized about two dozen Safeways in Nevada, mostly around Las Vegas, to carry the wine.

When a chain "authorizes" stores to carry something, that doesn't mean every store actually *will* carry it, it just means they can. If the store manager wants to. Often the manager needs to be sold on the product.

Michael was riding with a distributor rep from Wirtz Beverage Nevada, a big, wavy-haired guy named Anthony. Wirtz was based in Chicago and Anthony had a touch of both Chicago's swagger and its "Ds"—"Da Bears, Da Bulls," that sort of thing. It made Michael think Anthony probably fit into Las Vegas just fine.

Michael and Anthony were sitting in the car outside a large Safeway in the Las Vegas suburbs talking strategy. It was Nevada-desert hot. The AC was going, but it only helped a little.

They wanted the store managers to make good-sized orders, at least 10 cases, because Barefoot was selling fast and because big orders usually meant the store had to store the wine on the floor—which meant a big display.

Michael said Barefoot had success in California giving stores a free case for every 10 they bought. Anthony shook his head.

"We can't do that," he said.

The alarm went off in Michael's head. Of course, this wasn't going to be simple.

"Why not?" he said. "This is Vegas. I thought we could do anything."

"You can't give away alcohol in Nevada," Anthony said.

"Seriously?" Michael said. "You have legalized gambling. You have legalized prostitution. For crying out loud, I can walk down the strip with a drink in my hand. But I can't give some guy a free case?"

"Nope," Anthony said. "No free booze."

Michael sat there for a moment. He was thinking.

"OK, then," Michael said more calmly. "How do I do this?"

"Well, if you wanna do that," Anthony said, "we usually give him 11 for the price of 10."

"There you go," Michael said.

It was a warm, late summer day in Sacramento. Bonnie and Michael were at the races. They sat in a VIP box at Cal Expo, home of the California State Fair, and they were on something of a hot streak.

They didn't know much about horse racing, but the State Fair races had been paying off for them, and that was because, like with so much involving the ponies, they had gotten a good tip.

A few years earlier, Barefoot won its first gold medal at the state fair wine competition, and Michael and Bonnie—with their non-existent advertising budget—looked around for ways to let people know.

Their friend, G.M. "Pooch" Pucilowski, the chief state fair wine judge, suggested they sponsor a horse race at the fair. The price: Almost nothing. Barefoot just had to donate a case of wine to the owner of the winning horse. In return, Barefoot got its name in the program and up on the track's big board in front of about 35,000 people. They even got to name their race.

It became a tradition for Barefoot. Win a medal, sponsor a state fair race—and call it things like the Barefoot Run or the Barefoot Shuffle. It always seemed to get them a nice bit of publicity, and the bonus was Bonnie and Michael got the fun of a day at the races in seats just above the winner's circle.

This warm day, as they waited for the Barefoot race, they saw the Northern California buyer from a good-sized supermarket chain down on the rail near the finish line. Bonnie told Michael to go invite him to sit in their VIP box.

"I like it right here," the buyer told Michael when he got to track level. "I wanna see their noses."

The man was clearly a racing fan. So Michael just chit-chatted. He mentioned that the Barefoot race was coming up.

"I saw it's the sixth," the buyer said. "Who do you have?"

Michael said he wasn't much of a betting man, but Bonnie always wagered on Barefoot's race.

"Who's she have?" the buyer asked. The man had an odd intensity to his questions. He took the racing game seriously. Michael tried to stay in the casual-fun realm.

"She's got a pretty wacky system," he said. "She only bets on horses or jockeys who have something to do with feet in their name. It's worked every year. Last year, she won with a horse named Fancy Dancer or something. This year she's betting on Shabby Shoes."

The buyer looked down at his racing form, then at Michael for a moment. Michael couldn't tell if he was considering Bonnie's system or was appalled by what he considered an amateurish approach to horse racing.

"Alright," the buyer said. "I'm putting my money on Shabby Shoes. If he wins, you get an ad and displays in all our stores. If he loses, you're DCed."

Michael went back to the VIP box and told Bonnie what happened.

"Is he serious?" Bonnie said.

"I don't know," Michael said, "but that nag better win."

The sixth race started well enough. Shabby Shoes broke from the gate and tucked into the first turn right behind a pair of leading horses. On the backstretch, he lost a little ground. Michael and Bonnie were clenching their hands. Through the last turn, Shabby Shoes stopped losing ground, then moved into third a couple lengths back from the leaders. They went into the stretch and he inched closer. The two leaders were pounding the turf almost in unison, nose to nose. Shabby Shoes was coming, but there wasn't much ground left. Then he was a length back, then half a length. All three surged at the finish. It looked dead even. It was a photo finish.

"Oh geez," Bonnie said. She and Michael had been screaming for their horse. Now they both stood quietly. It seemed like an hour before the mechanical voice came out of the sound system.

"Ladies and gentleman," it said, "the winner is . . . Shabby Shoes."

Bonnie and Michael jumped up and down and let out some hoots. They looked down at the buyer still on the rail near the finish. He hadn't moved.

Only a few weeks later, the supermarket chain put Barefoot wine in an ad, and gave them display space in a lineup of stores. Michael and Bonnie were, of course, thrilled. But it also sent a shiver through them both. They wondered what would have happened if Shabby Shoes' charge up the home stretch had been a half step slower.

Getting Barefoot into supermarket chains was the obvious-but-often-confounding key to becoming a national brand. Seemingly every step came with some Catch 22. For instance, many chains wouldn't carry Barefoot, or any brand, until it became a national top 100 seller in its category (like wine, soup, cereal, etc.), but no product can crack the top 100 without being in the chains.

Or: The big chain in, say, Florida wouldn't carry Barefoot until the big distributor there handled them; the big distributor in Florida wouldn't handle Barefoot until the big chain carried it.

But the quest with any chain began with something that was often way harder than it sounds—getting an appointment with the wine buyer. Sometimes Michael or other Barefoot salespeople would wait weeks, or even months, to get an appointment with a buyer. Then the appointment would get cancelled and they'd wait more weeks.

When they got in, they had to convince the buyer that Barefoot would sell, that it would fill a need, and that their company was solid and would be in business when—or if—the buyer wanted more.

Michael learned how hard that could be right at the start dealing with Don Brown and Lucky Stores. It never got easier.

Michael worked for four years to get one midsize chain in Southern California to take Barefoot seriously. He started in the early '90s, when Barefoot was selling well in another set of markets owned by the chain's parent company. Michael visited the chain's corporate offices in the San Fernando Valley regularly enough that at least the buyer gave him appointments.

Michael would come in and talk about how fast Barefoot was selling, particularly in those affiliated markets. The buyer would nod and say he still wasn't sure. At the next meeting, Michael would promise the buyer the same kind of results Barefoot got in those other markets, and the buyer would say he wanted to be sure the numbers wouldn't drop.

"I want to study it more," he'd say.

On a Friday morning in spring 1994, Michael went back to the chain's headquarters. Barefoot was still doing well in the affiliated stores, it was winning medals, getting press, and it was spreading along the Southern California coast.

"We're going to put you in," the buyer said. "We're going to supply all our stores out of our warehouse. We'll have a purchase order out on Monday."

That was great news for a lot of reasons. Finally, the chain would carry Barefoot, plus the affiliated markets would be increasing their buy. The frosting on this cake was that it was going through the company warehouse. That meant one delivery spot, no going market by market.

Michael called Bonnie and told her the news and that he was coming home.

"They've put you off so often," Bonnie told him, "maybe you should stay there until Monday and pick up the order yourself."

Good idea, Michael said. He called the chain's office and made a Monday afternoon appointment.

On Monday afternoon, nobody in the chain headquarters could find the purchase order. They sent Michael into the wine buyer's office, but the man he'd been dealing with for four years wasn't there. It was a new guy.

Michael introduced himself and said he was just picking up a purchase order for Barefoot.

"Sorry," the new guy said. "I don't have an order for Barefoot."

"I was promised an order today," Michael said. "We're delivering to the warehouse."

"The other guy's gone. Friday was his last day."

"So we're still going in, right?" Michael said. "I can wait 'til tomorrow or whenever you process it."

"I'm making the decisions now," the new buyer said. "We're not putting you in. You gotta start all over with me."

"We justified it over four years. You have all the numbers," Michael said.

"I'm in charge now," the buyer said. "You have to justify it to me. Go do a study."

It took two more years of reports and visits to the corporate offices. Barefoot finally went into the chain in 1996.

This kind of back-and-forth was unusual, but only a little. Every big chain or major store had tests and demands, because no retailer wanted to risk doing business with a wine that might not sell or a company that might not survive.

That explained—sort of—those Catch 22s. And what Barefoot faced was complicated and plenty annoying, but it's the kind of problem young businesses face in any industry. Proving yourself, assuring everyone that your business is sturdy and reliable is always tough early on, and each industry has its own tests and demands.

Barefoot's approach was a combination of hustle and solid research: they took inventory on what tools they had, got a read on what the chains wanted, and looked around to see what tactics worked for other wine companies. Then they followed their plan with a balance of conviction and adaptability.

They also used a bit of risk taking to deal with that chicken-or-egg problem when distributors and chains each wanted the other to take Barefoot first.

It started with Michael or another national salesperson going to, say, the buyer for Kroger in Michigan, and asking, "Who's your favorite distributor? If you were going to put us in, who would you want our distributor to be?"

The Kroger's buyer might say Acme Beverage Company out of Ann Arbor.

Then the Barefooter would go over to Acme Beverage and say, "Kroger says you're their favorite distributor, and they'd love it if you took us on. Let's work out the pricing so we can make a presentation to them."

Barefoot was betting Acme would think Barefoot was a shoe-in and would, of course, be happy to have another brand in Kroger. And they bet that Kroger would be happy to see Barefoot with Acme and would put them in—and no one would ask, or care, who committed to the arrangement first.

There was a risk to this tactic. Everyone needed to stay happy. If Kroger decided not to put in Barefoot even with Acme on board, Acme would drop them. And if Acme backed out, Barefoot would stand no chance with Kroger, in Michigan and maybe anywhere.

So they paid close attention to what it would take to sway both chain buyers and distributors. And they got help making their case from what was still a surprisingly rare source of information for the wine industry in the mid-1990s—the public.

One advantage Michael and Bonnie had when they started Barefoot was the seeming disadvantage that they knew almost nothing about the wine industry. When you're a start-up, and you know your industry, the reflex is to do what's been working for everyone else.

Sometimes, that's the way to go. But, if you're new and small and look like everyone else, how do you stand out?

Barefoot's look, style, and approach were new, in part because Bonnie and Michael didn't know what worked for everyone else, but also because their research led them away from conventional wisdom.

Barefoot never lost that drive to do research and to listen to what regular, wine-drinking, non-industry people thought. For most wineries, one place to get public feedback is in your tasting room. But that wouldn't work for Barefoot, since it didn't have one.

So Michael, Bonnie, and their team talked to everyone they could at tastings and fairs and charitable events. And they used an 800 number.

It's inconceivable in this 21st century wired era of technology and blogs and social media that any winery, or almost any business, would not have an 800 number. But in the late 1980s and early '90s when Barefoot hooked up the number because it seemed like a good idea, no one at Barefoot, and no one they knew in the industry, had ever seen it before. In the first years, the 800 number was on the label. By the early 1990s, it moved to the cork.

Michael and Bonnie did get some warnings from friends and, of course, from lawyers, who said the number would make Barefoot a target to get sued by anyone who spilled wine on their couch. Michael and Bonnie thought the info they'd get was worth the risk. Besides, it wasn't like Barefoot's name wasn't already on every bottle. (They did expect the occasional goofy call from late-night parties.)

By 1995, Barefoot was getting 50 to 60 calls a week. By the new century, that number would more than double. The calls came from people saying they drank Barefoot regularly, or they liked the foot, or they found it on vacation and wanted to know where to buy it in Oregon or South Carolina or Wisconsin. Some calls were complaints, and that info could be even more useful. But most were from people asking the same thing, "Where can I find more Barefoot?"

The 800 number was an early version of social media. It gave the Barefoot team a way to talk with customers, answer questions, connect with them in real time. It also gave them a chance to turn people with complaints into fans.

When the 800 number went on the cork, the guy who handled those calls was Randy Arnold. He turned the fan building into an art form. If someone complained about, say, a bad cork, Randy would send out a replacement bottle (if it was legal where they lived). At a minimum, he'd get them a T-shirt.

If there was a Barefooter in the area, and state laws allowed it, Randy would send the Barefooter to the house to make the delivery. "Hi, I'm from Barefoot, I heard you got a bad cork," the Barefooter would say. The people at the door would have their jaws hanging open. "Here's another bottle, and here are a couple T-shirts. Have a nice evening."

Some of the calls were so good Randy would play them on the answering machine at Barefoot's office.

"My lovely wife and I are enjoying a nice glass of your cab," one guy said into the phone one night. "We're both barefoot. Not only that, we're both naked. Later, I'm going to drink some wine from her shoe."

When he could, Randy called back quickly, though he generally steered clear of people drinking from their shoes. He picked up a message one Friday evening from a party in Chicago. The callers said they loved the wine and made everyone take their shoes off before they phoned. Randy called back.

"Hi," Randy said when a man answered. "My name is Randy. I'm from Barefoot wine."

The guy on the phone started woo-hooing. He called out to people at his party, "Everyone, quiet. Hey, QUIIIEET! The Barefoot Guy's on the phone."

"The Barefoot Guy." How good was that? A salesman returning a phone call got turned into a superhero. It also got him the permanent nickname, The Barefoot Guy.

"I just called to say I'm glad to hear you're having a good time," Randy said. "Thanks for drinking Barefoot."

"Hey everyone," the party man yelled to his friends. "He said, 'Thanks for drinking Barefoot.'"

People at that Chicago party started cheering. Randy could hear the whoops and the yays. "We love Barefoot," people yelled. "This wine is great." "We love your foot."

That doesn't sound particularly ground-breaking in this current hyper-connected world when making personal connections is a mainstream business tactic. But it was new then, and it came from thinking the way any business needs to think—Barefoot wanted to connect in a human way with their customers.

There was another class of critical info they got from the 800 number that they called "supportive complaints," like calls from shoppers saying their stores ran out of Barefoot. Randy returned those quickly to get details, then he'd call Barefoot's distributor in the region.

"The Johnny's Market on Main Street sold through," Randy would tell a distributor rep. "Could you go get a reorder?"

"How do you know?" the rep would ask.

"We have people," Randy would say.

The rep would reorder quickly, and start keeping an eye on Johnny's because Barefoot, apparently, had troops out there checking for empty shelves the way the giant wine companies did. Michael or Randy never saw the need to tell reps that their "people" were customers getting the phone number off a cork.

Barefoot also used some supportive complaints to show chains there was genuine, pent-up demand for the wine. They'd catalog the "We-can't-get-Barefoot-here" calls,—including names, addresses and phone numbers—and bundle them for one region, say Gainesville, Florida. They'd include similar requests from Worthy Cause Marketing events in the area, like a Florida River-Watch fundraiser, and then bring them all to the Florida buyer for the Publix supermarket chain and say, "These people are asking for you to carry Barefoot."

Sometimes that display of genuine demand, coupled with the meetings and sales studies, was the last push to get a buyer to say Barefoot is authorized. That, however, was when the heavy lifting started.

Michael was on the phone with their Barefooter in Florida, and he was flabbergasted.

"Really?" Michael said.

"Really," his Barefooter said.

"We failed because a shopping cart knocked the tag off?" Michael said.

"Yeah, or something did," the Barefooter said. "And in store 53, we never even got in. We couldn't get past the back door."

In the mid-to-late 1990s, Barefoot was selling nearly 200,000 cases a year and getting more and more authorizations from chains. But they were rarely simple and clean. Most were authorizations for a test of Barefoot's performance. And there were many things that could go wrong in a test.

The tests could last from 30 to 180 days. If a buyer gave Barefoot 30 days, it meant he expected them to fail and, probably, was just trying to get those pesky Barefoot salespeople to go away.

Usually, though, tests went three to six months, and the buyer would authorize it in maybe 20 stores, which sounds like a lot, except a chain like Publix, for instance, had more than 1,000 stores, with 700-plus just in Florida.

A chain that size had different caliber stores—maybe three levels of sales volumes—and Barefoot's difficulties could start with getting authorized for low-volume, C-level performers, where any new product would struggle.

Even if Barefoot got test-authorized for 20 A-level stores, they still had to convince each manager to take Barefoot in.

The clock started ticking the day the wine got authorized, but weeks could pass before any stores even agreed to sell Barefoot. Then every step on the road of getting bottles from Barefoot to the retailer, then to the customers, then recorded as a sale was a war against Murphy's Law.

The danger started in a simple place: the bar code. It's called a Universal Product Code, or UPC code. (A UPC is what makes each varietal of Barefoot a SKU—a Stock Keeping Unit.) Those bar codes translate very long numbers into digital info. Every scanner and every label had to get programmed with every number exactly correct. Considering how many thousands of products there are in those enormous stores—how many thousands and thousands of bar codes—and considering the potential for simple human error to get one digit wrong here and there, it's a wonder any product passes any early test.

Here are all the things that had to go right for Barefoot to get a sale:

The wine would get delivered to the store's loading dock. If things went well, Barefoot's distributor rep brought the right size and varietals. That did not always happen. Sometimes, for instance, the rep brought chardonnay and zinfandel, but the test was for chard and *white* zin.

But if the right wines and bottles reached the loading dock door, that's where the UPC code got its first scan. This scan only worked if:

- The corporate buyer sent the authorizing orders to the store manager.

- The manager saw them and didn't get waylaid by one of the hundreds of other chores needing attention in a supermarket.

- The manager forwarded the orders to the department manager and loading dock crew.

- The department or loading dock manager had someone program the UPC codes into the dock's door scanner.

- The code got plugged in with all the numbers right.

On good days, the door scan worked. Barefoot got in the store. Next task: Get the wine from the back room onto the floor.

It sounds simple enough. The store or department manager just tells a clerk to put Barefoot somewhere where store customers can buy it. Except, if no one planned for it, the cases sat in the back room. (The Barefoot team, at those times, said their wine was getting some back room aging.)

Then came the question of exactly where it went on the floor. If a new wine is going to sell at all, it needs a decent display. The display is everything.

The worst placement was a single row on a shelf in some odd section, maybe set up by region or price. Shoppers rarely knew to look there. Only a little better was a single row in the varietal, one row of Barefoot Chardonnay among all the other chardonnays, facing customers who may never have seen the wine before. That didn't get much action.

A few rows together helped some. The next step up was what's called a Brand Set, when all of Barefoot's wines—the cabernet, sauv blanc, chard, etc.—were sitting together. That got noticed, made the wine look popular, and was easy for returning customers to find. Barefoot had an advantage with its magnums, because many stores always set mags together by brand.

Another good placing was only for whites or blush wines. That was a spot in the beverage refrigerator—stores call it the cold box. Chilled whites outsell the warm ones by miles.

It got even better with a stack, which is some kind of display out on the floor. That started with a Side Stack—cases stacked against the wine shelf with a big sign. Then came an Island, which was a stack people could walk around out in the middle of the aisle. The prime wine section space was an End Aisle. That's a stack or Island at the front of the wine aisle, even before you get into it.

Best of all was a stack or Island outside the wine aisle, maybe by the meat counter, or, if they struck gold, near the checkout stand. Shoppers didn't have to go near the wine aisle. That fit Barefoot's target customer, the person in a hurry, shopping for her family, looking for her everyday products.

And how did they get good displays? It always depended on the manager. Sometimes Barefooters convinced managers the wine was well-priced and would move quickly, so they needed a big supply stacked on the floor. Sometimes managers gave Barefoot good placements because its colors and cheeriness brightened the store. And where it was legal, Barefooters would add things like beach chairs and umbrellas to the display and, of course, come build the stack.

So let's say Barefoot scanned correctly on the dock, got through the back door, got out of the back room and into a decent display. And let's say a customer found it, put a bottle in her cart, and went to the register. Then the checkout clerk rang it up, and, bingo, there's one sale for Barefoot. Unless the scanner at the register was programmed wrong.

And when the front scanner was off, who would know? The entire supply of Barefoot might sell and go out the door, but if the scan was off by one digit, none of it would register. When the chain buyers checked in on results, they'd see zero Barefoot sales.

But if everything went right and the sales of the first supply get recorded, then it was time to reorder. The bad news part about being a fast seller is you need to get reordered quickly.

The thing was, no alarm went off that said, "Time to Reorder Barefoot." Often, if a Barefooter or distributor rep didn't check, no one at the store would notice. Wine clerks would, however, give the empty shelf space to another brand.

If a Barefooter did get the store to reorder, it was time for one more adventure with the scanner—the code tag on the shelf. Same old tightrope, plus there was the added risk a shopping cart or a hand truck or just a kid playing around had damaged the tag or knocked it off.

But on those good days, everything worked: The orders moved through the company; people in the store communicated; the loading dock, checkout, and shelf scans were perfect; the wine got a good display; the reorder got handled; the overworked distributor rep had time to deliver it; and the order was correct. If all that happened—and the wine was selling fast enough—Barefoot would pass the test. In one store.

Take all those potential calamities and multiply by 20. If Barefoot navigated them all, store by store by store, the buyer would be satisfied and the chain would put Barefoot in for real.

Then the playing field—calamities and all—expanded instantly. Now there were mess-ups lurking in 200 stores, or 500 stores. Buyers still watched the numbers, especially on a new product. It was as if the test never ended, because even just a few months in, the buyer could discontinue the wine. Remember, getting DCed meant Barefoot might have to wait years before it got another shot with that chain, if it ever did.

And the Barefoot crew learned that the most common time to lose a new account was, well, right away. Right at the start, during a test or right after, because no one, not the store manager, the distributor rep, or the clerk stacking bottles, was used to the new product.

Barefoot had its share of chain store disasters in those first years of going national. From 1996 through about '98, their expansion was stop-and-go, because it took almost three years to fully grasp all the nuances of the tests and the chains. But they finally did get some control by doing what worked for them before: They organized.

They made lists of potential hazards and solutions, chain by chain, store by store. The lists got longer as they got more experience, and as they experienced more problems. Their solutions included sending Barefooters to follow wine into a new store to make sure the orders got processed. They helped clerks build displays where it was legal, and they took a bottle to the register to be sure the bar code scanned.

Going national and getting carried by companies with hundreds of stores across the vast American landscape also meant they had to hire a lot more Barefooters, more people to do what Curt Anderson's Merchandising Army had done years before. Except, instead of a dozen part-timers, now they needed a real army.

On a blustery day in spring 1995, Michael fell in love with the city of Madison, Wisconsin. Madison, like so many college towns, had a bustle to it, an eclectic cultural scene, a worldly outlook, and a thirst for almost anything new, including new foods and wines. Barefoot did well in places like Madison.

Michael was headed for a store he would fall in love with, too, a place called Brennan's!—emphasis on the exclamation point.

Michael met the owner, Skip Brennan, at a trade show earlier that year. They hit it off and talked about sales, about trying to be interesting, and about how much work it takes to stand out, especially when you're new. Skip described his stores with enthusiasm.

"It's the Fourth of July, Michael, the Fourth of July," he said. "Things are happening everywhere. We've got music in one spot, we've got colors and samples and action all over the place. It's exciting." Skip could have used an exclamation point at the end of his name, too.

Skip Brennan was a kindred spirit, and Michael and Bonnie were still looking for those and for strategic allies who approached businesses the way Barefoot did. They weren't sure if Barefoot could afford to expand into Wisconsin. It was a state with big chain supermarkets. But Skip and Brennan's! looked like they might open the door.

So there was Michael in Madison on that blustery spring day. When he got to Brennan's!, the store was holding a cheese tasting. More than a dozen people stood in line to sample three-, four-, five-, and six-year-old yellow cheddars. Cheese is a big deal in Wisconsin, and a huge deal in Brennan's!.

The place was like a Trader Joe's crossed with a farmer's market. Skip had music playing. He had food from around the world, a big fruit section, a big vegetable section, and a massive cheese department complete with a cheese sommelier. He also had a very large and colorful wine section. Barefoot would fit perfectly into this amusement park of a store.

"How long would it take us to get up to 500 cases a month throughout Wisconsin?" Michael asked Skip when they were sitting in his office.

"Probably two years," Skip said. "You'd have to get into a lot of chains and they're gonna want you to advertise."

"How much would it cost us?" Michael said.

"More than you have," Skip said.

Michael's solution was to offer Barefoot to Skip and his five outlets exclusively in the state. He could say that no one else had it, not other stores or the chains. Skip would have to buy by the truckload, which would make the deal more efficient for Barefoot, but the only other thing Michael asked was that Skip promote it well.

Skip said he'd promote Barefoot like crazy. And he'd conduct tastings, and have Michael and other Barefooters in to pour.

"I'll put you right next to the cheese," Skip said.

Skip Brennan did indeed go crazy for Barefoot. He bought newspaper ads and radio spots, and put up a bright wall of Barefoot and its posters. He held tastings with Michael and Randy—right next to the cheese sommelier. There were winter days when the temperature reached maybe 5 degrees, or maybe it soared to around 8, but scores of people tromped through the ice and snow and mingled around the Barefoot and the cheese. It wasn't long before Brennan's! was selling more than 2,000 cases a month.

The success with Brennan's! was a lesson in how to manage the unmanageable. On the surface, it sounded like a bad idea: give one store with five outlets exclusive rights in a state with more than 5 million people. But if Barefoot had taken the standard expansion route in Wisconsin, it would have been hugely expensive and, probably, less successful for years. The start-up and maintenance costs with Brennan's! were tiny, and the sales were terrific—much better than if they'd gone into the chains.

Plus Skip Brennan was a great fit with Barefoot. He was another example of an unconventional strategic partner who would work with Michael and Bonnie for years.

He would also provide a template for Barefoot to move into other hard-to-navigate regions. Like Texas. Managing new wine sales in Texas was only marginally less difficult than managing wine sales on Mars.

Texas had dry counties next to counties with government-run alcohol sales next to open counties that had dry cities. Every county, every town seemed to have different regulations, and they were 100 percent arbitrary. Not to mention Texas is huge. There are vast stretches of nothing between cities and towns.

So Barefoot went the Brennan's! route. They gave an exclusive deal to Kel Becker and his stores named Pinkie's. This was another energetic operation—almost enough to have rated an exclamation point—with a handful of liquor stores and markets, mostly in West Texas around oil towns like Lubbock, Amarillo, and Midland. Pinkie's Barefoot sales also stayed solid for years.

Those kinds of deals did more than solve some problems. They also created relationships—both business and personal. Michael and Bonnie regularly hosted Skip Brennan and his staff for dinners at their home when Skip brought his crew to California. That's part of the Barefoot Spirit, too: Be in business with people you like. Plus, in the case of Brennan's!, there was a bonus for Michael and Randy and a few others—they learned a lot about cheese.

Dealing with quirky stores like Pinkie's and Brennan's!, just like selling to the assorted mom-and-pops around the country, was a reminder there are countless ways to do business and to sell wine. Barefoot, Brennan's!, Pinkie's, and Trader Joe's were unique in their industries. Every business has to adopt its own style and techniques that work best for its product, size, and place. You do what works.

And, sometimes, what works can be surprising.

On that ride through New Jersey with Stephen Della Vecchia, Michael was having a day of discovery. He and Stevie D found one of the oddest—yet effective—sales approaches of their careers.

It was in Atlantic Highlands, a dug-in seaside town where some stores still seemed to be living in 1950. Michael and Stevie D pulled into the parking lot of a Buy-Rite, and they could see from their car that this was a different kind of store.

The windows were covered with butcher paper signs that said "$3.99" and "$4.99" in six-foot-tall numbers. The "$3s" and "$4s" were the size of a man, the "99s" were just a bit smaller. The signs didn't say what cost $3.99, they only had the prices.

Inside, the store was neat and busy, but it had a discount house look, as if everything was a bargain. The only shelves were along the walls. The aisles were created by lines of products selling from boxes, like they just came off the truck. There were wine shelves stocked with bottles, but the section was mostly cases cut open. And there were signs everywhere with large prices and nothing else.

The owner was a guy named Abe. He was somewhere in his 60s with a craggy face, rumpled clothes, and the posture of a question mark. He had a cigarette in one hand, another burning in an ashtray, and he looked like Central Casting's version of a long-time Jersey Shore shopkeeper.

He sat at the front of the store, watching his territory on something that looked like a pulpit a few feet above the floor. The checkout counter was at chest height for shoppers so Abe could ring them up without leaving his roost.

When Abe talked, he was almost as loud as his signs, waving his arms and spouting words in a high-volume, whiskey voice.

When he stopped to talk with Michael and Stevie D, he still stayed on his perch. Michael had to hand his business card up to Abe.

But as gruff as he was, Abe liked talking about his store.

"I have to ask," Michael said after they'd chatted a bit, "what's with the '$3.99' in the window?"

Abe looked at Michael's business card again.

"Michael, right? Well, Michael, you gotta qualify the customer," Abe said. "They see that price, they get a warm feeling. They know they can afford something in the store."

"But it doesn't say what's $3.99," Michael said.

"Doesn't need to," Abe said. "Look around. Whaddaya see? Those are big prices. Not high prices, big prices. Makes customers feel good, makes 'em think everything is on sale."

"That works?" Michael said.

"See that wine there," Abe said. He pointed with his lit cigarette. "Last week, it was selling for $5.99, but I had a small sign. This week, it's got a big sign, and it's $8.99, and you know what? I'm selling twice as much."

"Wow," Michael said.

"Wow," Stevie D said.

"You know who figured this out a long time ago?" Abe said. "The beer guys. They've been doin' this for years. You ever see a small beer ad? They don't work. Big prices. They work."

As Barefoot grew in the middle 1990s, every new state or chain or Buy-Rite hammered home the same lesson. There was no single method for selling Barefoot, which meant they needed to

"Not high prices, BIG prices!"

keep reorganizing their operations, so they would be ready for the next surprise and the one after that.

Michael and Bonnie were still learning just how un-romantic the wine business was at their size. It was about things like compliance, merchandising, production, category management, and the complicated game of sales.

And as they closed in on becoming a true national brand, they could see they were still too small. They had to grow to push their tiny profit margin ahead of the cost curve, and it looked like even 200,000 cases a year wasn't going to do it.

But to cover the country well, Barefoot needed more people, and to pay for them, they needed to sell more wine, which, of course, required more people, and the merry-go-round continued.

CONVERSATIONS WITH BONNIE AND MICHAEL

Rick: *Jennifer Wall was another person with the Barefoot Spirit pre-loaded. What did she mean to Barefoot's success?*

Michael: She was much more than a winemaker, she was a true entrepreneur. That means she took responsibility for whatever job needed to be done. If you're in charge, you can't make excuses, you get it done.

Bonnie: Jen was willing to pick up anything and she was always positive in her attitude. And she did get things done.

Michael: She used to bug me on a regular basis to do some task we needed. It was for my own good. She'd go, "Have you done it yet?" Then later, "We have to have it by 5." Then, "It's 4 o'clock, did you do it?" Eventually, I would.

Rick: *And then there was Jennifer the winemaker.*

Michael: She was an incredible match for Barefoot. I would write the back label describing the wine before she ever made it. That was the taste profile we wanted. Then she would produce it and win gold medals.

Bonnie: When Jen won a gold medal, I'd take her a rose and put it in a bottle from the wine that won. I'd say, "Here's your Gold Medal rose, you've done it again!"

Michael: It was actually called a Gold Medal Rose. It was a yellow rose from our garden.

Bonnie: Sometimes Jen would win multiple gold medals. I'd bring her a bunch of roses. But we only had one Gold Medal bush, so I'd have to cheat and take yellow roses from a different bush. We kept running out.

Michael: She made Bonnie strip the bush bare.

Bonnie: Finally, when she moved into a new house, we gave her two Gold Medal Rose bushes so she'd have her own supply.

Rick: *When you started learning about all the differences in state-by-state compliance, instead of your brick for the day, that must have felt like your brick for the minute.*

Michael: Oh, yeah, was that ever a new wake-up call. And they just kept coming.

Bonnie: We learned you had to go into every state with your eyes wide open. Each time, it was like we started with a blank slate. I know nothing about this state, then go from there.

Michael: One of the hardest things was when a chain would say they'll put us into five states, but it has to be $5.99 in all of them.

Bonnie: We'd have to learn the laws in each state to figure out all the variables.

Michael: We had no business saying, "Yeah, we can do that," but we didn't want to lose the opportunity.

Bonnie: We couldn't say, "Hold that thought 'til we get all the facts. We'll get back to you in a month."

Michael: Sometimes we lost money on those deals, but it got the product on the shelf.

Rick: *As you started to grow nationally, the difficulties got larger and more complicated. It must have really felt like your joke: All your success was killing you.*

Michael: The challenges became multi-dimensional. And they came from all sides.

Bonnie: With all those variations, we realized there was no one script for success. It was all ad lib. What got us through was the Barefoot Spirit. You have to believe there are answers out there or you won't look for them.

Michael: It's like the stories where you try to visit the wizard, but first you have to rescue the damsel, but first slay the dragon, but first find the magic sword.

Bonnie: And you don't get help. We were down to hammering out that sword.

Rick: *You learned you needed to grow, but at the right pace, and with kindred spirits like Skip Brennan. How hard was that lesson?*

Bonnie: We learned pretty quickly that the faster we sold, the faster we'd get discontinued. That's when we learned we wanted to grow in territories where we had a rep and were small enough that we could control them.

Michael: That's why we liked giving an exclusive to Brennan's! Skip was really good, and we only had to keep an eye on his supply instead of all of Wisconsin.

We started off thinking, we just need to get in somewhere. But we learned we needed an army to keep an eye out to get reorders. We used to say, it's not about placements, it's about replacements.

Bonnie: When you're new and you're a fast seller, you're in double jeopardy.

Michael: You not only have to prove it sells, you have to prove you can get reorders so the clerks and the distributors believe they can reorder on a regular basis.

Chapter Eight

Never Waste a Perfectly Good Mistake

In mid-spring 2000, Michael was in Chicago to show off some new Barefoot wines to major retailers including store owners, chain buyers, and restaurant wine people. New wines are called line extensions. They can be anything from a new varietal, like Barefoot Syrah, to a new style of Barefoot Bubbly.

Line extensions were a relatively straightforward sell. They first went to places already carrying Barefoot, and the extensions gave them something new to offer customers. From Barefoot's side, the more Barefoot wines a retailer carried, the more important Barefoot would be to them.

But line extensions were still risky. Even in 2000, Barefoot's financial margin of error was still zero. A new product had to take off quickly or it would create a cash flow sinkhole.

So Michael was staging a trade tasting at the historic Drake Hotel on Chicago's Magnificent Mile, but he was saving money by staying at a less expensive hotel a few blocks away. He checked into his hotel on a Tuesday morning—the tasting was that evening—and asked for the packages his Barefoot crew had sent him.

"I'm sorry, sir," the very polite desk clerk said. "We don't show any packages having arrived for you."

Alarm-bell time again. Michael took a breath and tried to sound patient. "Could you please check with your receiving dock," he said. "Have them look for a couple boxes of Barefoot wine."

Barefoot's staff had shipped the wine a few days earlier. It would have cost much more to have it fly with Michael and been somewhat risky, because the wine might have ended up sitting with the luggage on a hot runway. Plus FedEx had always been spot-on about getting things delivered on time. For this trip, it promised the wine would reach the hotel by Monday.

The clerk made a few calls and checked his computer. He found nothing.

"I'm sorry, sir," he said. "It was never delivered."

Michael went right to a phone and called Barefoot's office in Santa Rosa. They tracked it with FedEx. The wine was in a Midwest sorting facility about to return to California.

"FedEx said your hotel refused the delivery," a Barefoot staffer said. "The hotel told them on Monday there was no Michael Houlihan checked in. FedEx will have it back in Chicago by 10:30 tomorrow morning."

Michael took some calming breaths, reminded himself it's unprofessional to yell, and asked around the hotel to figure out what happened.

It turned out, the receiving guys got the delivery, called the front desk, and said, "Do we have a Michael Houlihan staying here?" Not, "Is there a Michael Houlihan checking in," or "Do we have a reservation for a Michael Houlihan," or even, "Is anyone named Michael Houlihan expecting any deliveries?" They just asked, is the man here right now?

The front desk botched it just as badly. It got a call from receiving asking about a guest. It shouldn't have taken much effort to deduce that an incoming guest shipped something to himself— the way hundreds of business travelers do. The desk clerk should have checked if "Michael Houlihan" was on the reservation list.

Now Michael had a problem he could only halfway fix. He ran out and bought a range of Barefoot wines, but the new wines weren't in Chicago stores yet, which was the whole point of the tasting. That night, Michael apologized early and often, and promised the biggest buyers he'd visit them Wednesday with his new wines. He promised the others he'd get them samples very soon.

When he got back to California, Michael sat with his team to work on a new procedure. Michael and Bonnie and the Barefoot crew were checklist fanatics on everything, but if there was one topic they attacked constantly, it was finding ways to avoid having things go haywire—the second time.

Blunders happen in business. Humans make errors. Some problems you just can't foresee. But if the same problem crops up repeatedly, and you don't change anything, that verges on the definition of insanity. So Barefoot operated under the principle most clearly defined by Randy Arnold: Never Waste a Perfectly Good Mistake.

They did that by brainstorming every mistake, even small ones. Those sessions weren't about who was to blame, but what went wrong—what communications failed, what was overlooked, what was ambiguous, what didn't Barefoot know. And they created procedures and lists so Barefoot could do everything possible from its end to try to keep that problem from happening again.

But there was more to this approach than just technical adjustments, it also involved Barefoot's internal attitudes and company culture—they celebrated mistakes, because without them, there was no learning lesson. And every mistake that happened was one more they could prevent.

That meant everyone at Barefoot had to resist the natural urge to just pick up the ball after a fumble and start running again. The point was to avoid new fumbles, not hide them. For that kind of thinking to work, it had to be cultural. Michael and Bonnie didn't want Barefoot employees to be scared to report mistakes, or for anyone to think they would advance because someone else messed up.

That's why Barefoot's approach was to say, basically, "Congratulations, you found a new way to screw up. We didn't know that could happen, but now we can keep it from happening again." (This was, of course, all about technical errors, not bad behavior or an inability to perform. It's different from, say, a winemaker telling salespeople to stop selling.)

After the Chicago hotel fiasco, they were satisfied with their new routine. It was still unfeasible for Michael to fly with the wine, especially when he was visiting a handful of cities on one trip. But after Chicago, every package of wine—or anything—shipped to a hotel had a wide strip of white tape on it with bold, black letters an inch high that said: **"DO NOT REFUSE THIS PACKAGE."**

Then there was another strip of tape and bold writing that said some version of: **"Hotel Manager Bill Smith is expecting this package. Call him at extension 700. If he's not there, call his assistant, Ann Jones, at extension 701."**

Underneath that, there was more tape. It said: **"Michael Houlihan is your guest registered to arrive on May 27, 2000. If you have any questions, call Barefoot Cellars in California"** and it included the office phone number.

At the bottom, there was one last strip that said once more:

"DO NOT REFUSE THIS PACKAGE."

*"Did you get a package that was all
gedunked up? That is for me."*

And there you go, problem solved. Everyone at Barefoot breathed a bit easier when Michael or anyone traveled to meet shipments of wine. That is, until mid-summer that year when Michael was checking into a hotel in New York. He asked for his package.

"I'm sorry, sir," the desk clerk told him. "We don't have any packages for you."

It happened again. The receiving dock and the front desk pulled the same trick, despite all the tape and the warnings. The problem this time: When the box of wine showed up, it came in tape side down. No one noticed it.

It was time to rewrite the procedure. After that, every box that got shipped to a hotel had the white tape and the bold writing on all six sides.

Michael didn't miss another shipment to his hotel. And lots of times when he checked in, he just said, "Did you get a package that was all gedunked up? That is for me."

It was a morning in 2002 and the commotion coming from behind the door to Michael's office was loud enough to echo down the halls of the Barefoot headquarters. Most people who heard it either smiled or rolled their eyes in recognition.

Inside the office, Michael, Aaron Fein, and Gary Arkoff were talking, mostly all at once, and at a decidedly above-polite-conversation decibel level. This happened a lot. The session began as they often did, at the start of the morning, with the guys sipping coffee, just chatting about the day behind and the day ahead.

Gary was the national account executive, Aaron was the sales manager who handled the national chains, and when the three got together, it tended to get loud, mostly because of Michael and Aaron. They were the excitable ones, Gary was the straight man. And they weren't loud at each other. Most times, they were, as Aaron put it, "in violent agreement." They were blowing off steam about the seemingly daily stack of difficulties and semi-disasters the company was running into because all companies run into difficulties and semi-disasters.

They'd come to call these sessions "Awfulizing." The mornings generally started calmly enough talking about some recent sales trip or meeting or just shooting the breeze. But they all had the same hot buttons that came from running a fast-growing national company with a spectacularly tight budget, a tiny crew. In 2002, Barefoot had 26 full-time people and no room for stumbles.

It usually didn't take long for the casual chats to devolve into semi-rants about the latest awful thing that happened, and to make predictions based on experience about the next awful turn of events that was coming.

These Awfulizing sessions had a direct link to the philosophy of Never Waste a Perfectly Good Mistake, and to its corollary, Get Smart About Stupid, which translated to this: Always expect somebody to botch some important step somewhere—maybe in getting Barefoot delivered, maybe in getting it reordered, maybe in getting wine delivered to a hotel—because no one is perfect.

So they didn't just complain, they tried to figure where the next blunders might happen, and tried to draw up procedures and lists to make it harder for someone else to mess up Barefoot's business. And after a few sessions, they even created a standard form to fill out during the Awfulizing.

It was a lesson Michael and Bonnie had learned over the years. They wanted to channel the energy that came from the Awfulizing, and they wanted to make it easy. So they produced that form and revised it over time. It asked the Awfulizers (or anyone in the company doing the same thing) to describe the problem, list the causes, propose solutions, and identify everything they needed to update—contracts, company policies, checklists, even job descriptions.

That made it simple to start fixing things. Gary was the unofficial stenographer for the group, and sometimes while Michael and Aaron were still in full Awfulizing mode, Gary would quietly reach into the drawer, pull out the form, and start writing down the thoughts bouncing around the room.

This morning they were talking about a pretty good-sized disaster that Barefoot had no part in causing. Michael was tossing out ideas for another procedure. Gary was less than optimistic. They weren't exactly coming to a consensus.

"I see what you're trying to do," Gary said, "you're trying to make the system idiot-proof."

"I'm not," Michael said. "I'm just trying to make it idiot-resistant."

"But Michael," Gary said, "right now, even as we're talking, they're building a better idiot."

It's something most businesses face. No matter your size or funding, someone else's inefficiency—or someone else's better idiot—will make a mistake that affects you, and it will cost you time and money. And Barefoot's solution applies to any business. Find ways to cut down the likelihood someone will make that mistake, and prepare for those errors so you can reduce the impact on your company.

For Barefoot, what came out of those sessions, and the company-wide brainstorming, stopped some problems cold. Sometimes they created solutions that were halfway there (see: Chicago hotel fiasco). Sometimes they led to more problems and goof-ups, then everyone would go back and Awfulize about those.

All of it, however, was progress. Or, as Bonnie said, "We're improving this company one mistake at a time."

During most Awfulizings, all three guys would claim they'd endured the worst horrible development. But on that day in 2002, Aaron was the clear winner.

His disaster involved a mid-sized chain of specialty stores that had carried Barefoot for nearly 10 years, and had sold the wine like crazy. The chain carried most of Barefoot's wines, and they'd always reordered regularly because everything sold quickly.

But the chain had hired a new buyer and he had not reordered in months. It made no sense to Aaron that after years of huge sales, suddenly they would screech to a stop through the entire chain.

It made even less sense, because Randy Arnold had passed along 800-number complaints saying stores from that chain were out of Barefoot.

Aaron sent some of his sales staff to search inside each of the chain's 30-plus California outlets. They looked on shelves and they went into back rooms to see if the wine just didn't make it to the floor for some reason. They found no signs of Barefoot at any store.

Aaron figured the problem had something to do with the new buyer, so he called and asked if he could take him to lunch. The buyer said, sure, but the problem was that Barefoot just wasn't selling. Aaron was sure something else was going on, but he let the comment go.

When Aaron got to the buyer's office a couple days later, the guy was ready for a confrontation. He had Barefoot's inventory up on his computer screen.

"Every store still has six bottles of each SKU," he told Aaron quickly.

"Every store has six?" Aaron said.

"Every store," the buyer said.

"Each SKU?"

"Each of them."

"How is that possible?" Aaron said as gently as he could. No point ticking the guy off.

"Look for yourself," the buyer said. He turned his computer screen toward Aaron with an air of satisfaction.

Aaron looked at the display, scrolling the page up and down for a moment. Then he saw it. He tried not to look as floored as he was.

The computer listed Barefoot as 750 ml bottles—which come 12 to a case. But Aaron knew they were actually the 1.5 liter magnums that shipped six to a case. The reason why the computer—and the buyer—thought there were still six bottles of every varietal in every store, was because they were counting six extra bottles per case that didn't exist. In truth, every store in the chain was sold out.

"Here's the problem," Aaron said almost sweetly. "It's just a computer glitch. I can see how that happened. The computer thinks you have 750s and we sell you magnums."

He was blaming the computer and trying to make it easy for the buyer. Aaron didn't want the guy to take it personally. That didn't help. The buyer just got more ticked. Aaron could see him trying to salvage his pride.

"Yeah, well, I think we're done with you guys," he said. "We're gonna discontinue Barefoot."

"Why?" Aaron said. "We've sold huge for you for years."

"I don't care," he said. "You're too much trouble. You're always complaining about stuff like this."

"We've never complained about anything before," Aaron said.

"Customers complain, too," the buyer said. "They're always saying Barefoot's out of stock."

What could Aaron say? Barefoot already marked the size of the bottles on boxes and order forms as clearly as they could. This error happened deep in the chain's offices when some clerk punched the shipments into the computer. But at this point, it wasn't about the mistake, it was about ego. Sometimes, the better idiot wins.

Those Awfulizing sessions and the principles of Never Waste a Perfectly Good Mistake and Get Smart About Stupid all came with the complete realization that Barefoot could make its own mistakes, too, thank you very much. But how they dealt with them was what mattered. Barefoot's internal culture of deconstructing gaffes also applied to the ways Barefoot dealt with its mess-ups that affected their business partners and customers.

That included the day in 1998 when Michael went back to visit Don Brown in the Lucky Stores' corporate offices. He waited on the hard chair in the hallway forever, of course, then went in to see Brown.

"What are you doing here, Houlihan?" Brown said. "You don't have an appointment."

"This is important, Don," Michael said.

"I got a busy day. This better be good."

"It isn't good," Michael said. "But it's right."

Michael put a cashier's check to Lucky for $6,000 on Brown's desk. The reason: Barefoot had shipped Lucky some 1.5 liter bottles of cabernet with 750 ml back labels, which meant Lucky's cash registers had rung up the 750's lower price.

Michael showed Brown his analysis. It detailed how many cases had the wrong back labels and what Lucky's loss was. The $6,000 covered that loss, plus the time and expense of dealing with the mistake. Don looked at Michael's numbers a while, then nodded that he agreed with them. He took the check and signed a release saying Barefoot had made good for the mistake.

But Michael went farther. "Here's how we're going to make it right, besides paying you back," he said. "We're going to make sure this never happens again."

Lucky might never have known about the bar code problem, but as any business will tell you, the cost of trying to hide a mistake is usually far worse than admitting it and making amends.

Just as much, trust matters in business, especially for a new business. That's why Barefoot overcorrected its mistakes. They made up any financial loss. They showed people like Don Brown step-by-step plans for undoing the gaffe, and they gave excruciatingly detailed explanations of the new routines to make sure the mistake wouldn't happened again.

Michael showed Brown a hurry-up schedule for swapping out the incorrectly labeled bottles from stores and the warehouse, and explained Barefoot's new procedures. They would confirm that bar codes were correct on the labels before they bottled, they were printing the bottle size in large type on Barefoot boxes and on every back label near the bar code, and they were creating signoff sheets, tightening the contracts with bottlers and printers, and changing internal checklists.

Michael told Brown he understood how mistakes like this create problems, and he wanted Brown and Lucky to know Barefoot would never hide something it messed up.

Brown looked at Michael for an extra moment or two. He almost smiled.

"You did the right thing, Houlihan," Brown said. "Now get out of my office."

New businesses make mistakes for all sorts of reasons, starting with the rather obvious one—they're new and still learning. And no matter how much documenting and planning you do, everyone still needs experience, especially when it comes to dealing with the variety of personalities you'll find. Sometimes, new companies just need to pay attention and learn.

Michael and his Barefoot team learned that when you are selling to a range of customers—whether it's a small store owner from New Delhi or New Jersey, the big markets across the country, or simply the general public—you'll only survive if you grasp all the customs, styles, and traditions you'll encounter.

When Barefoot was starting, Michael learned a lot about mom-and-pop owners and how hard they worked, spending sometimes 18-hour days in their stores. Often the owners were immigrants to America who opened stores in marginal neighborhoods because that's where they could afford the rent and because they believed their efforts really could turn their adopted country into a land of opportunity.

For Michael and all the Barefooters, that meant they had to pay attention and constantly be ready to learn about and adapt to cultures, operating styles, even regional differences in America. And, most importantly, they had to adapt their selling and customer service simply for people's personalities.

That point is an easy one to forget when new companies are creating business plans based on statistics and averages. The problem with averages is that they're rounded off compilations of individuality, and they make all that individuality disappear. But when you're selling, it's all about the individuals. It's a bit like entertaining; you have to read your audience and figure out what they respond to—and every audience is different.

There was, for example, the Southern California store owner who wanted people to think he was in charge, although his wife actually made the decisions. Michael learned to go in on days the wife was in the store. He would make his presentation to the guy, but in a way his wife could see and hear as she stood semi-nearby. Then Michael would casually look away, so the man could check with his wife, and get a nod saying, "go ahead and buy."

That same sensibility applied to thinking about shoppers buying Barefoot. The target customers were usually women, usually looking for a reliable wine, usually in a way they could buy it easily. The key word there was "usually." Each shopper made choices for different reasons.

That's why Barefoot tried to give people a range of reasons to buy—it had a popular flavor profile, was easy-to-spot, and had a friendly package. It was consistent, dependable, came with a sense of fun, and offered customers worthy causes, beach posters, purple feet on store floors, medals on the bottles, and, of course, the foot.

And the Barefoot team kept checking on their customers with research, questions at tastings, and 800-number feedback. Despite all that, there were times Michael and Bonnie messed up their read on customers about as completely as possible.

One of those times involved what they thought was a terrifically clever concept. It was called California Beau.

It all started January 1, 1990, when California lowered the blood alcohol level for drunk driving from .1 percent to .08 percent. (This was before it became the national standard.) News outlets across the state did story after story about the new level, stepped-up enforcement, and about how people, particularly smaller women, needed to be careful because just two glasses of wine could put them over the limit. Barefoot, like most wineries, restaurants, and bars, saw a drop in sales.

But Michael and Bonnie had an idea they thought was a slam dunk: lower-alcohol wine. It would have Barefoot's taste profile but just 6 percent alcohol instead of the usual 12 to 14 percent. People could have a second glass and stay under the limit, which seemed to match what they were hearing in the news stories— that folks usually had two glasses of wine or so.

The name California Beau was aimed at women because they appeared most at risk. "Beau" was supposed to signify a date of sorts for the women ordering wine.

Bonnie and Michel announced the new wine and got a ton of press. At the time, any new twist on the subject made the newscasts and papers across California. That press reaction encouraged Michael and Bonnie. A TV news crew from San Francisco came to Sonoma County for the first bottling. That encouraged them more.

They made 1,000 cases of California Beau and tested them in Marin County, a generally upscale region just across the Golden Gate Bridge from San Francisco.

Marin has a streak of activism, was home base for some of the lower-alcohol advocates, and generally welcomed the new limit. Marin, it turned out, was not typical, and Michael and Bonnie could not have picked a worse place for the test.

California Beau sold solidly in Marin, and Michael and Bonnie were even more convinced they'd come up with a terrific product. They bottled another 1,000 cases and distributed them around California. They waited to hear about the success.

Except, there was none. The wine just sat there. It didn't sell in stores, it didn't sell in restaurants, it didn't sell in bars. Michael and Bonnie had set up a separate 800 number for the Beau, and the calls they got explained everything.

"You're forcing me to drink twice as much," one said. "Now I have to pay for two glasses." "If you're giving us half the alcohol, then charge half the price," another caller said. Retailers told Michael and Bonnie they were getting the same complaints.

They bailed on California Beau pretty quickly. This was a case of reading the public wrong, but also of misreading the high volume of news stories as a public endorsement of the lower limit, and of listening to pundits who said people suddenly wanted their alcohol to be low alcohol.

The truth was simpler, if a little unromantic. It was also a lesson for Michael and Bonnie: People—and customers—don't suddenly change.

In 2001, Michael was on his knees in a supermarket in Florida putting the wine-colored Sticky Feet on the floor. While he was down there, a neatly dressed man in a nice suit cruised past followed by two more guys in suits. The man was pointing at wine displays, asking questions, sounding generally curious and occasionally concerned about something.

Michael had seen him before in other stores in other states. He would walk through, ask questions, talk to the people with him, ask more questions, chat with the store manager, then thank him cordially before he left.

Michael sometimes heard the gist of the questions. They were about displays, pricing, point-of-sale material, store traffic patterns. Clearly the man was in the wine business and knew his category management, but Michael didn't know who he was. So on this day he asked the store manager.

"I've seen that guy around," Michael said. "He was up in Georgia when I was there last week. What's he do?"

"That's Joe Gallo," the manager said. "Seems like a nice guy. He's been through here a couple times over the years. Says he wants to stay on top of things."

"Wow," Michael said.

Joe Gallo was the president and CEO of the E. & J. Gallo Winery. Michael was impressed, and surprised, that he was out walking stores around the country. But that also fit what he had learned.

There was no reason anyone at Gallo would have known it, but Bonnie and Michael had been admiring Gallo for years. They watched the big company's on-the-ground merchandising and its attention to detail, and tried to imitate it. As they learned more, Gallo had become a role model for Barefoot.

They also got ideas from Gallo's approach to what Michael and Bonnie called customer service. Barefoot considered everyone who bought or handled Barefoot to be a customer—distributors, brokers, retailers and more—just as much as they considered shoppers picking up a bottle customers. Barefoot tried to help them with speedy service, availability and more, because if dealing with Barefoot was easy and profitable, that meant sales and profits for Barefoot, too.

And here was the CEO of the biggest wine company on the planet working on that customer service face-to-face. He was making sure store managers were happy, walking through wine aisles, checking on things as small as shelf labels, because no matter how big your company is, you can never assume everything is always working smoothly.

Seeing Joe Gallo in the stores was validation for Michael. After all, Michael was a CEO, too, though of a decidedly smaller company, and he was also out in stores, keeping his hands on everything he could touch. He rarely saw other CEOs or company heads in stores. He did see marketing managers and top sales reps from wine companies, but Michael sometimes wondered if he was overreacting, or worrying too much.

But there was Joe Gallo hustling around the country, never taking anything for granted. Joe had a lifetime of experience, plus his family's experience, and if he believed he should be walking stores asking all those questions, that confirmed for Michael that he had read things right and he needed to be out there, too.

When Michael got home from that trip, he told Bonnie he was more convinced than ever that their hands-on, never-rest approach was what it took to be a successful national brand.

They talked about how they were seeing their choices validated, like the decision to focus their energy on sales and customer support and not to have a winery or tasting room to siphon off money and manpower. Being out in the stores, servicing buyers and managers, getting reorders, putting down purple Sticky Feet had to come first.

"We're going at this right," he told Bonnie. "Seeing Joe Gallo out there is proof we aren't crazy."

"We may be right," Bonnie said. "But he runs the world's biggest wine company and he's doing all that work. That means we have to keep working like that, too. What part of that sounds like we aren't crazy?"

CONVERSATIONS WITH BONNIE AND MICHAEL

Rick: *What was going on in your head when you realized the wine wasn't at your Chicago hotel?*

Michael: Oh, man, I wanted to throttle somebody. I lost it. I got pretty animated, I think is the polite word. I was on a tight schedule. I never dreamed, never possibly imagined, a shipment would be denied because I wasn't registered *that day*.

That was our brick. It's raining stupid out there. You really do have to prepare for the worst. In a calmer part of my head, I was thinking, how big does the note on the next package have to be to prevent this from happening again? Half-inch? No. One inch high, like the This Door Must Remain Open sign.

Bonnie: Some of the smart clerks who saw those packages with all the notes must have gotten a laugh out of it.

Michael: It was like shouting, HEY YOU, DON'T REFUSE THIS!

Rick: *How long were you having those morning sessions before you started calling it Awfulizing?*

Michael: A couple months. Every morning somebody was giving the worst-case scenario for the day. It was bad enough getting your brick for the day; we didn't want our own people predicting disaster.

Bonnie: But that was part of the solution. It changed when they started writing it down.

Michael: I told Gary, you know what you guys are doing, you're Awfulizing. Gary said, "Is that a word?" I said, "It is now." So we said, if we're going to Awfulize, we're only going to do it for 15 minutes. Then we'll write down how to prevent it.

Bonnie: Still, there was always something new that went wrong.

Michael: That's so true. Every time there was a bottling, every time we got a new test market from a chain, every time we'd go into a new store, something new went wrong. We kept writing it down and writing it down.

Rick: *The idea of not wasting a perfectly good mistake is so different from the way so many other companies think. Was it hard to convince people to operate that way?*

Michael: We'd hire new people, and they almost always would just correct a mistake they made and hope nobody noticed it.

Bonnie: We'd tell them, so a mistake was made, what gets better if we don't fix the reason for it, or if you start blaming each other?

Michael: We used to say, don't blame and complain, aim and gain. That meant aim at the cause of the problem, and we all are better off. Our company is permanently better.

Rick: *Then there was California Beau. Was that your biggest mistake?*

Michael: Well, we made a few good ones, but we completely misread that one. We thought we'd be the first to market with this hot, new, timely product.

Bonnie: What could go wrong?

Michael: We even test marketed it in a place where it did well, which turned out to be exactly the wrong place. But we thought we were leading the market. We were patting ourselves on the back. We thought it was a slam dunk.

Bonnie: It was just a slam.

Chapter Nine

A Smaller Slice of a Larger Pie

Michael was on the phone in his office, talking to Phil Aiello in Michigan. Phil was interviewing to be a Barefooter—a merchandising and sales guy, which, to Barefoot, really meant he'd be a customer service guy.

By the new century, Michael and Bonnie learned that, though their product was wine, they were really selling service. The sales business *was* the service business.

Also by the turn of the century, they had begun changing their company structure, adapting to the demands of being a national brand. But even before that, they had put their sales crews—their service people—at the top of the company heap. Everyone else at Barefoot worked to help sales.

So Phil was applying for a key job in Barefoot's system, especially because Michigan had potential to be a major market. Michigan had university towns like Ann Arbor and East Lansing, and more freshwater shoreline than any state in America—3,200 miles of it—with all the beach, boating, and vacation communities that were fertile ground for Barefoot.

Michael had interviewed a handful of people before Phil, and it wasn't going well. The main reason was that Barefoot had a somewhat radical pay structure. It could be far more lucrative than most straight commissions, but it started at a very modest base.

Bonnie and Michael created that pay system because Barefoot was a small company with large sales, and it couldn't afford unproductive people. Few companies can, but for start-ups and fast-growing businesses, productivity is an enormous concern. So Barefoot, basically, asked employees to bet on their own productivity. Or as Michael told job applicants, he was asking people to bet on themselves.

Michael and Bonnie understood that people want guarantees, but so did Barefoot. They wanted people who believed in themselves and who would work hard. But everyone he'd interviewed in Michigan so far didn't want to make the bet. They wanted a bigger base. By the time he got to Phil, he was pretty discouraged.

Michael asked Phil about his background, what he did in his free time, what ideas he had about the industry. Barefoot's usual procedure was to do a couple phone interviews with good prospects, then if they were impressed enough, bring them to California for a face-to-face and a final decision.

This was Phil's first round, and Michael liked Phil more and more as they talked. The interview turned into mostly a conversation. At one point, Phil asked Michael about pay. Michael said the base was low.

"What's the commission structure?" Phil asked.

"The more you sell, the more you make," Michael said. "There's no limit."

"Wow, no limit." Phil said. "Really?"

"Yup," Michael said. "Your percentage gets larger as you sell more, and there's no limit."

"Seriously? No limit?"

"Seriously," Michael said. He laughed a little. Michael liked Phil's enthusiasm and that he wasn't concerned about the base. Michael also liked that Phil seemed thrilled by the potential, although he also didn't seem to believe it.

"So I understand you have a lot of sales experience," Michael said.

"I was a merchandiser when I was still in college, then I was promoted to sales rep after just a few months," Phil said. "I was a rep for a number of years until I was promoted to district sales manager, and, uh, I want to be sure I have it right: There's no limit on commissions?"

It continued like that. Phil kept interrupting himself to be reassured the commissions had no limit. Michael had never talked to a guy like this, and after Phil asked one more time, he'd heard enough.

"I'm sure there's no limit," Michael said, "and Phil, you're hired."

Michael and Bonnie were sitting in the lobby of the Bellagio hotel in Las Vegas watching the crowd. They did that a lot, watched how people moved or talked or held themselves, and they'd both try to read who those people were and what their stories might be.

They were in Las Vegas for a National Wine & Spirits Wholesalers convention, and that afternoon they were waiting to meet

Eric Dorton, who Michael was interviewing for a merchandising and sales job for Texas. It was still early, so Bonnie and Michael were having fun watching the high-energy, chaotic scene in the Bellagio.

The lobby was filled with people moving at every speed in all sorts of moods and dress. Some were on the way to the pool, some were checking in, some had pretty much checked out. They wore beach shorts and T-shirts, or nice-but-casual clothes, or dressed-to-kill spike heels or suits.

First Bonnie, then Michael, noticed one man. He wore a business suit and dress cowboy boots, but still was not particularly tall. Yet he stood out. He had a walk—confident, deliberate, determined. He wasn't in a hurry. He wasn't hustling. He was just purposeful. The man was simply moving through a hotel lobby, but he broadcasted so much about himself.

"Look at that guy," Bonnie told Michael. "He looks like he's going to do something."

"Yes he does," Michael said.

The man came around a corner and headed toward the restaurant where Michael was planning to meet Eric Dorton.

"I hope that's Eric," Bonnie said. "That man means business. Michael, you should hire him."

"I haven't interviewed him yet," Michael said. "We don't even know who he is."

"That's Eric," Bonnie said. "Go hire him."

Hiring choices usually weren't so clear as bringing on Phil Aiello or Eric Dorton. Phil, for the record, turned out to be one of the best salesmen Michael ever met, and made the Michigan market—and his commissions—live up to everyone's expectations. And Eric, another extraordinary salesman, single-handedly built Barefoot's market in the huge and massively complicated state of Texas.

Hiring is so important to a new company, and new companies are precisely the ones who struggle with it, because, first, there's that irksome point that they're new and inexperienced, and second, they don't have time to focus on hiring when they're busy trying to stay alive.

Barefoot made some good hires because some great people were obvious, like Randy Arnold and Jennifer Wall. But Michael and Bonnie made mistakes too, because they were hiring for an industry they were still learning.

And sometimes they had to hire in a hurry. A supermarket chain would add Barefoot into stores in a new state, and Barefoot instantly needed a new person there to work on sales, reorders, merchandising, worthy cause events, and loads of other chores. Hiring fast is a dice toss—sometimes it works out, more often it's a bust.

By the 21st century, Barefoot still had a small staff, but its scope of business was large. The 235,000 cases it sold in 2000 made it one of the 40 biggest wine companies in America. By 2003, it made the top 25 with more than 370,000 cases annually and was one of the country's fastest growing wine brands. Being big was a very different challenge from getting started.

Barefoot was getting there, but it still needed to grow more—because of its perpetually thin profit margins and the escalating demands of being a national brand—but by then, there was also something to protect. There were chain store accounts across that vast and erratic national winescape, and there were relationships with distributors, brokers, bottlers, glassmakers and more. Michael and Bonnie had to learn a new trick: preserve what they had *and* grow.

So they changed Barefoot. In essence, they stopped hiring employees and started hiring entrepreneurs. They looked for people with drive, who wanted to build something, and who had the Barefoot Spirit themselves.

Michael and Bonnie thought a lot about how to motivate people—not push them, but seduce them to push themselves—so they would become invested in Barefoot's success and see it as their own success, and so they'd think of Barefoot as their team. They kept landing at the same starting point: so much is determined by pay. Not what you pay, how you pay.

It's human nature. If you pay by the hour, people will show up but some may not work hard. If you pay by the deadline, they'll meet the deadline, but may see no need for extra effort. If you pay straight commissions, some people ease off when they've earned a decent amount, or when it takes extra hard work for additional sales.

So Michael and Bonnie said, let's pay people for growth. Let's put in an increasing incentive, so each step—though harder— would be worth a lot more than the last. They wanted to give their people reasons to never give up.

Their new system was unique. It increased commissions almost exponentially. In simple terms, it worked like this:

If someone sold, say, 100 cases in April 2000, and 100 cases in April 2001 (these numbers are unrealistically small for simplicity), their commission would be the same in both years. But if they sold 10 percent more—110 cases—they would get $1 for every case over that 100, or $10 more.

If they sold 20 percent more in April 2001—120 cases—they would get $2 per case for every case over 100. Not just $1 for cases 101–110 and $2 for cases 111–120; they would make $2 for each case, or $40 more. They didn't just get higher pay for additional growth, they got the boost for *all* the growth. It kept multiplying. So, 30 percent more—130 cases—would earn $3 times 30 cases, or $90, and on up.

The point was, there was always a big incentive to keep selling and, as Phil Aiello knew, there was no limit to what he could earn. Michael and Bonnie were happy to take a smaller slice of a larger pie.

Michael and Bonnie wanted everyone at Barefoot to want that larger pie, and one way they got that was by tying everyone together.

It started with the company organization. They didn't divide Barefoot into conventional divisions like accounting, production, marketing and the like. They went with something far more fundamental. There were just two divisions: Sales and Sales Support.

Anyone not out in the stores selling and merchandising was in Sales Support—the receptionist, the marketing folks, even winemaker Jen Wall. Jen was, day in and day out, one of the pillars of Barefoot's success, but her division was still Sales Support.

And to help give everyone the same desire for Barefoot's pie to grow, Michael and Bonnie tied the pay for Sales Support to the performance of Sales, and to the performance of the company. The office was rooting for those people roaming the country, because their pay depended on them.

If Phil needed statistics to convince an Ann Arbor store owner to buy Barefoot, the office staff hustled out a report. If Randy needed signs and posters for an event in Seattle, the marketing crew jumped on it. If Barefoot won a gold medal in Orange County, staffers had shelf signs printed and in the hands of Southern California Barefooters the next day. Income was at stake for everyone.

Because the pay for Sales Support was also connected to profitability, they also had incentives to save money and time, to look for efficiencies, to maybe hold off using the color copier if they didn't really need it.

All of that together did more than create an efficient company, it created a team feel and a sense of camaraderie and equality. They were all in the same boat in the roiling ocean of the wine industry. Everyone had to row together. And the goals they were after felt reachable.

Michael and Bonnie started the changes in 1999 and 2000. By the end of 2001, they had created a very different Barefoot company, and that tone would continue over the next few years. They would keep attracting entrepreneurs and team players like Phil Aiello, Aaron Fein, Gary Arkoff and more. They were hiring people who came to the company with the Barefoot Spirit pre-loaded.

A decade later, when Michael was looking back at that challenge they threw out to employees to bet on themselves, he said the change in structure may have been one of the most important moves they made with Barefoot. "The people who took that bet," he said, "were the best people I worked with in my life."

It's rather obvious to say that Michael and Bonnie viewed their employees as assets. It's an approach that makes sense for any company, especially if it's a start-up like Barefoot was for a decade, or a fast-growing company playing on the national level, as Barefoot had become. But too many companies regard their workers as just another commodity, a budget line item, like printing or delivery service.

Simply from the financial standpoint, that made no sense for Barefoot. They wanted to hire good people, and they wanted to keep them. This was a company built on reliability and customer service. Everyone Barefoot dealt with, from the buyers to the worthy causes, all counted on the relationships they formed with people in the company. If someone like Phil left, some Michigan chain buyers might discontinue Barefoot just because they didn't want to break in a new Barefoot rep.

Plus it's expensive to replace people. You lose productivity when a job is empty. You spend time and money finding a replacement. You have to train the new guy, which usually means taking another staffer off her job to do it, and now you're down two people.

On top of that, Michael and Bonnie liked their employees; they wanted to keep them around. That's why they spent so much energy trying to create a satisfying and invigorating company culture. Pay was a foundation of that, but it was just one part. Just as important was Barefoot's internal behavior and its values.

The phrase "core values" has become almost cliché in a modern business world where many people are vocal about preferring to buy from, and do business with, companies that operate ethically and with honorable principles. But it was a concept that applied to Barefoot from the start.

Michael and Bonnie always believed their customers would be happier doing business with Barefoot if they saw what it stood for, but they also learned their values could make their own employees happy, too.

And if there was one concept at the center of those values and of the company's culture, it was the notion of permission.

You see it in the idea of the wine itself. People who drank Barefoot had permission not to be wine experts. The back label said, "Get Barefoot and have a great time."

You see it in their philosophy of Never Waste a Perfectly Good Mistake. People had permission to mess up, to try but fail. Just keep trying, just make mistakes right, was what Barefoot asked.

Much of the sales support and team building came from the culture of permission. A Barefoot sales rep in Florida didn't worry about getting blowback for asking for a sales report quickly. A receptionist didn't worry about getting blown off pitching an idea for a poster. Everyone was encouraged to take chances and suggest seemingly wacky ideas—when you get down to it, Barefoot itself was something of a wacky idea.

It was just as important to Bonnie and Michael that people felt they had permission to have fun. Barefoot's image was built on fun; the company needed to be a fun place to work—not unprofessional, but lighthearted, cheerful, and, sometimes, a little silly.

People could choose their own titles, if they wanted. Foot-related names were encouraged for obvious reasons. Michael's business card said Head Stomper. Bonnie was Original Foot. Randy was The Barefoot Guy. And Doug McCorkle, the company's chief financial officer, was "The Cork," partly because of his name but also because, as the money guy, when a bad idea picked up speed, he was the one who was expected to put the stopper on it. People had conventional titles, too. The point was, put anything on your business card, just make sales happen.

And they made games out of hard work. Michael's constant exhortation was that in sales, the answer is never "yes" or "no," it's "now" or "later"—later meaning eventually they'll make the sale. Bonnie turned that into the No Game.

The No Game was straightforward: Just keep trying until you get a yes. Lots of times, they cheerfully attacked getting told "no," as if it were a puzzle to solve. This came just as much from lessons Michael and Bonnie learned in their lives as from business experience.

There was, for instance, a dinner with Mabel in the early 1990s at a Mexican restaurant in Santa Rosa. Mabel couldn't get the server to let her order veggie fajitas. They only served beef, chicken, or shrimp. Mabel asked sweetly. No dice. She offered to pay extra. Nope. Fajitas, of course, are usually grilled meat, chicken, or seafood on a tortilla with loads of onions and peppers.

"OK," she said, "I'll have a chicken fajita, hold the chicken."

"No problem," the server said.

That's the No Game. Figure there's always an answer. Just keep playing. It was, in essence, how Michael and his crew dealt with the state-by-state mess of compliance. They kept asking, "How do we do this?"

At Barefoot, they would count the "nos." It was a morale booster. People would come back from sales calls and brag about who got the longest string of "nos" before they got a "yes." It wasn't even worth reporting until you got at least four.

On the other hand, Barefoot had to be careful that their fun culture and playful image didn't make the company appear frivolous or immature. That's one reason everyone at Barefoot dressed in business suits—which was sometimes a surprise to first-time visitors who assumed Barefoot's corporate office would be staffed with people wearing Hawaiian shirts and flip-flops and tossing a beach ball.

But Michael and Bonnie wanted vendors and buyers to have confidence in Barefoot, and to see they were serious business-people selling a fun product. Barefoot was a radical approach, but it was delivered with solid business principles. Plus the clothes were simply a gesture of respect to people outside the company and a message they were all in the same business.

Putting on serious clothes was also an act of solidarity by the office staff with the salespeople who had to wear business attire visiting stores. They were all players on the same team, they should all wear the same uniform.

There was one other benefit. Business clothes turned men and women into colleagues and put them on equal, respectful footing. Suits reminded everyone working at Barefoot that their co-workers were serious businesspeople, too. Michael and Bonnie operated on the theory that it's a lot harder to misbehave in a suit than it is in a bowling shirt.

The permission, the fun, the pay structure, even the clothes, all tied people together and it all merged to create a sense of inclusiveness that made the Barefoot crew feel safe about sharing goals, ideas and, of course, information.

That info sharing helped Jen and the Just in Time Wine program, and it was critical throughout a small, innovative company like Barefoot. But it was something of a pioneering idea, too.

Top-down, need-to-know management limits the source of potential solutions to just the few people who know what problems need to be solved. Still, few companies at the time embraced Barefoot's notion that everybody should know everything.

But Barefoot found it helped build a team connection if everyone understood where their pay and their commissions came from, and they saw that if everyone knew the company's needs, what stopgaps were in play, and what challenges they faced, then anyone could recognize a solution if they saw one.

Michael and Bonnie held quarterly briefings for all their crew to keep people informed. They weren't bland corporate meetings filled with platitudes and "go get 'em" slogans, they were real updates about everything from sales figures to what lucky breaks the company needed.

And that's how Barefoot got some lucky breaks. There were times when, as the saying goes, preparation met opportunity. Like the morning in 2002 when a well-dressed man casually wandered into Barefoot's office. He told the receptionist he was from the

Southwest, was just out in Sonoma County looking at wineries and had a question or two. He didn't say why.

She smiled at him. "Oh," she said, "are you a supermarket buyer?"

He mumbled an answer. She was already on her phone.

"Aaron, could you come out here," she said, "there's somebody you should talk to."

The visitor, it turned out, was from a major chain in Arizona and New Mexico, and was trying to get a read on Barefoot. What he got was the national sales manager talking with him in moments, and a read that this was a company on the ball. The buyer eventually brought Barefoot into all his stores.

Sharing information also meant everyone could share their skills. When Barefoot had sales meetings, everyone was invited, all the way to the people in accounting. And to the accountants, sales was an exciting world. They'd get energized. They'd throw out ideas, ask if more comparisons and better-detailed numbers would help the sales crew.

Sure, the salespeople would say. We'll get you those every Monday, the accountants would announce, suddenly more jazzed about their jobs and a little proud they could contribute.

On an early spring Sunday in 2003, Bonnie and Michael were hiking in the Armstrong Redwoods State Natural Reserve, a wondrous park near the Russian River filled with towering redwood trees that were once part of a medieval forest. It is an awe-inspiring world of filtered light, soft moss, full creeks, and impossibly huge, staggeringly old trees. The redwoods tower hundreds of feet straight up, like they were sketched with rulers, and some are more than 1,000 years old. The Armstrong Redwoods is one of Michael and Bonnie's favorite places.

Creating Barefoot wines, constantly traveling and selling and swimming upstream with the company on their backs, took its toll. Hiking was how they regrouped.

Bonnie and Michael were drawn to the calm of nature, the sense of the planet around them and the realization that there are things larger in life than any one worry. They hiked whenever they could and wherever they traveled.

And sometimes they hiked with their cats, which is not something you see all that often. They took their pair of friendly—and worldly—Abyssinians on serious, daylong hikes, and even camped with them now and then. They'd say hello to fellow hikers who often just had their mouths open watching the long, lean cats bop happily along the trail a step or two behind Bonnie and Michael.

One of their rules for hiking was, don't bring the darn cell phone, but on that Sunday, while they were coming down the side of a mountain, Michael's pocket started chiming. He was surprised his phone was in there, and surprised to see it was Randy who was calling. Then came the real shock.

"I'm going to have to quit," Randy told Michael.

By 2003, Randy was as much a flag bearer of the Barefoot Spirit as Michael and Bonnie. He was also their very trusted friend. Michael didn't know what to say. He asked why.

"I'm taking another job," Randy said. "It's not in the industry. I'm going to work for the Mono Lake Committee. It's a four-month birding internship, and I'm going to be a docent. It's the chance of a lifetime."

Mono Lake was a special place to Randy, his version of the Armstrong Redwoods. He first visited the mile-high lake on the eastern flank of the Sierra Nevadas when he was 14 years old. He fell for the haunting beauty there, the size and sheerness of the mountains to the west, the openness of the desert to the east, and the otherworldly grace of the stark and rocky landscape around the lake.

He also fell for the story of the Mono Lake Committee and how a then-small group of citizens—who had nothing at stake except preserving an extraordinary piece of nature—were fighting the Los Angeles Department of Water and Power, trying to stop the massive urban agency that had been diverting water from streams leading to the lake since 1941. Randy joined in the public support, and was thrilled, and surprised along with most of California, when the committee won its legal battles. The legal victories started with a 1983 state Supreme Court decision, then were made specific and real in 1994 with a follow-up and landmark ruling by the state Water Resources Control Board setting a minimum lake water level.

And now Randy was telling Michael he was in Lee Vining, the town on the lake's western end, and he was quitting Barefoot to go count birds and lead canoe tours. Randy said he believed that if people learned about their environment, they would do more to protect it. He'd always wanted to do something like this, and all the pieces came together.

"It's just too much time away from Barefoot," Randy said. "I think the right thing to do is resign."

"I know that place means a lot to you," Michael said. "Do me a favor, let us think about it for a day."

They didn't need to think long. Bonnie and Michael understood Randy, and they understood the hold Mono Lake had on him. Randy had carried the banner for Barefoot for more than a decade and had been a huge reason for its growth. He'd earned any breathing space he needed.

Michael called him on Monday. Take the job, he told Randy. Be a docent until September, and when the internship ended, his Barefoot job would be waiting, full benefits and right back to where he was.

"We won't fill it," Michael said. "Who are we gonna find who could replace you, anyway?"

"Are you sure?" Randy said.

"We're sure," Michael said. "We just want a few things."

"Name it."

"We want Barefoot in every store around Mono Lake," Michael said. "We want a tour. And we want to do a tasting at the lake to raise money for the Mono Lake Committee."

Getting the wine into stores in the area was what Randy did everyday, and he knew this area well. He had friends there. For years, when he was passing through, he'd stop at the Mono Lake Committee headquarters and drop off a case of Barefoot with a note, "Hope this helps the cause."

For Michael and Bonnie's tasting, Randy staged it in late summer and set up tables at the lake's edge in a remote spot more than a half-mile down gravel roads. He had white tablecloths, flowers, food, and elegant wine glasses all waiting.

It was late afternoon, which can be magnificent in the eastern high Sierra. The sun was moving toward the huge, dark mountaintops to the west, the sky was filled with puffy white clouds, and the clear, mile-high sky had streaks of reds and yellows and oranges. The sunlight put Randy's table settings and the textured rocks of the lake into sharp relief like a super-focused picture.

Randy and Michael and Bonnie stood by themselves. No one else was there. They didn't say anything for a few minutes, but Bonnie and Michael were starting to worry, and they were feeling bad for Randy. Had he struck out with this tasting?

"If you pour it, they will come."

"Is anyone going to show up?" Michael finally said.

Randy looked at his watch. It was a few minutes after 5 p.m. He pulled a cork from a bottle of Barefoot Bubbly.

"If you pour it," Randy said, "they will come."

Everything was quiet for a moment. Then there was a rumble. Off in the distance, down the road and behind one hill, they saw a growing dust cloud. A jeep filled with people rolled over the closest hill. Behind it came another, and in the distance, there was a line of more than two dozen cars.

Randy looked at Michael and Bonnie with a cheeky grin. "Everyone up here works 'til 5," he said.

Randy was, of course, a special case. He had become friend and family to Michael and Bonnie, and he was an elemental part of Barefoot. But in another way, his relationship with the company—back to when Michael hired him and said go sell where you'll be happy—was not unusual.

For Michael and Bonnie, all their dealings were personal. They treated customers, all their business connections, and everyone else as complete human beings—who responded best when they were treated well.

Most of all, they managed their employees that way. That got back to seeing their people as assets, and as they built Barefoot and its culture, they kept thinking about how they'd want to be treated, what would make them feel like part of a team, and what they'd want from a job.

They arrived at four big points. Although there had been whole books written about workers achieving goals, they decided that most people work for (1) pay, (2) recognition, (3) personal time, and (4) security. Not always in that order.

Their pay structure came from that. But their most out-of-the-box approach—and the tactic that would get attention from the business community and from academics—was something that seems so easy and obvious: Michael and Bonnie said good things about their employees. They applauded them in front of each other for good ideas, for growth, and even noble failures.

The concept came to them when they were researching company culture and asking job applicants, employees, and friends in other businesses why they left their old jobs. Two answers came up regularly.

First, in their unhappy jobs, people felt they overproduced but were underpaid, or that pay had little correlation to their performance. (At Barefoot, that would not be a complaint from people like Phil Aiello.)

The other big gripe was that hard workers often felt unappreciated by their companies.

That's a natural reaction. People want to feel useful and valued, and many people reflexively see their jobs as an extension of family, with the bosses in the role of parental figures. Which means, workers want to please their bosses, and they'd like to know when their bosses are pleased. Just like in a family.

So Michael and Bonnie would catch their people doing something right, and they'd brag about it—to the whole staff. They would sift through the year, looking for good deeds and they'd celebrate all of them. On every employee anniversary, they'd send a memo to the staff, praising, say, Debbie Johnson in accounts receivable, describing how she organized the department, or boosted income, or just made other people's jobs easier. It would say how she made Barefoot a better company.

And they would stand at a staff meeting and say it, too. They'd say, here's what Debbie did to save money for Barefoot and increase your bonus. This is why she's a good teammate. Then Michael and Bonnie would leave, and other employees would go, wow, we didn't know you did all that. It helped create a mutual respect in the company, plus gave everyone the chance to just talk together about their jobs.

Michael and Bonnie didn't know other companies that complimented their people the way Barefoot did, but they did hear warnings that if Barefoot praised employees too often, their workers might ask for a raise. And lawyers told then, if someone was fired, the ex-employee could use the praise and maybe sue, complaining the firing was not performance related.

Michael and Bonnie didn't worry about that. They were happy with their pay structure and so were their employees. And they figured if they were praising folks, they probably wouldn't be firing them anytime soon. The praise was about keeping good people, not making it easy to dump them.

That philosophy applied to how Barefoot handled the other two basic motivations behind job choices, time off and security. Giving people solid time off was usually less exotic than letting Randy lead canoe tours. It meant keeping people fresh with small vacations besides their big ones.

So they had Barefoot Days. Those were Fridays off with pay in any month that didn't have a three-day weekend in it. (Reminder: those are June, August, October, and either March or April, depending on when Easter falls.)

There were more Barefoot Days connected to national holidays that fell midweek. People got another day off on the shortest end of the week, which meant when a holiday broke on a Tuesday, they also got Monday off, or on a Thursday, then it was Friday off, too. If, say, the Fourth of July fell on a Wednesday, people also got both Thursday and Friday.

(The sales staff had a different formula, because holidays were their busy seasons. They got Barefoot Days to use when work demands were slower.)

And everyone got their birthday off with pay, or a day they could float. That's not unusual, but Barefoot also gave the birthday folks $100 to spend, and they were supposed to use it for themselves on something fun like a meal or gift, not for paying the electric bill. That $100 did come with one requirement. People had to tell everyone what they spent their money on. No receipts necessary, just bring back a story.

The Barefoot Days also got attention in the business world because it went against a common idea that days off cost productivity. Bonnie and Michael found it actually made people more productive.

For starters, employees never felt ground down by long work stretches. And people actually worked harder when they had time off ahead, partly to get their desks cleared, but also because no one in Barefoot's team culture wanted to leave chores hanging if someone was counting on them.

As for security, Barefoot did what many good companies do. They had a 401k plan (partly connected to the company's profitability, which was more incentive to work hard), and solid health insurance benefits. But they did something more.

It's normal for people to think about their futures and about what else they might do down the road, and Bonnie and Michael wanted Barefoot to be part of that. So they sent their folks to seminars, retreats, and trainings to learn new business skills. They found it made their employees feel valued, and it made them feel the company was filled with opportunities.

The thing was, Bonnie and Michael bought into the notion of workplace as family, and they took their roles as de facto parents seriously. They tried to be mentors and teach their people to be independent and creative thinkers, and to have confidence in themselves. It really was a bit like having kids. They wanted people to succeed no matter where they ended up.

Of course, they preferred to have their "kids" stay at home, so they tried to promote from within. Plus they let employees swap jobs when they wanted to try something different or learn a new skill. Often, those people surprised everyone, including themselves, with their affinity for the new role.

And now and then, someone would turn out like Debbie Johnson.

Debbie started as an intern in 2000 before getting hired full time. She was finishing up a marketing degree at Sonoma State University and was exactly the kind of person Bonnie and Michael looked for. Debbie was eager and bright, wanted to learn, and wasn't jaded by years in a bad job or a hard-edged industry. When she interviewed, she said, "I'll take any job. Put me anywhere and I'll just learn and absorb."

Debbie interned in marketing support, then was moved to the front desk when she came on full time so she could learn the company's rhythms and needs and get to know the players who did business with Barefoot. She was so good at it, she taught Michael and Bonnie how important reception could be. She was the gateway to the company, and she presented a polished first impression of Barefoot.

At the end of 2000, they told Debbie she was doing great, and asked what else would she like to try. She said, how about accounts receivable—the department that collected money owed to Barefoot, sometimes by people who, let's be honest, would prefer to stall.

"Really?" Michael said. "That's the most frustrating job in the company."

"My mom and dad owned an insurance company," Debbie said. "I understand the problems. I think I can help."

Debbie was not a forceful woman. She was slightly small and trim, and her most apparent qualities were that she was earnest and sincere. She wasn't the obvious choice as someone who could wrangle buyers who owed money.

But she was hyper-organized, understood people, and she was charming. Within months, accounts receivable was humming, and pretty much everyone who owed money seemed unusually good about paying up.

It wasn't long before Bonnie and Michael asked Debbie if she wanted to try something else new. She said, point of sale. That's a warehouse job. Moving crates and boxes, filling up other boxes and getting posters, shelf talkers, and handouts sent across the country in a hurry to Barefooters in places like Florida or Kansas.

"Are you sure?" Michael asked.

"I think I can handle it," Debbie said.

Yes she could. She had it reorganized in a week. In a couple weeks, she developed procedures for ordering, receiving, and shipping that made the entire operation as hyper-organized as she was. Before Debbie, Barefooters in the field often asked to get materials delivered more quickly. Those complaints stopped entirely. For years, Barefoot had hired part-timers for the job, but Debbie showed how much more the department could do, and how helpful it could be to sales.

Next came compliance. Debbie learned, translated, and tracked the nationwide tangle of laws regulating wine sales and shipping. One more time, her organization and energy produced another re-structured, well-thought-out department.

Michael and Bonnie were thrilled with Debbie. They were teaching her about business, but she was teaching them about their own company. Going into 2004, it was time to see what else she'd like to try.

Debbie suggested a job she said Barefoot needed but didn't have. She thought it would be a huge help. They asked what she was proposing.

"Logistics manager," Debbie said.

"We need that?" Michael said.

"You have no idea," Debbie said.

This was about trucking and scheduling and getting Barefoot out of the warehouse, on the road and into stores around the country before the stock ran out. Debbie had seen how this was a constant battle for Barefoot, ironically, because it sold so well, and how they could lose shelf space and even whole accounts when that happened.

Barefoot had fought that war for years with hustle and diligence, and with the Barefooters out around the country. But there were other problems, seemingly beyond Barefoot's control.

Debbie told them about a trucker who had driven out from Minnesota recently. When he got to Barefoot's warehouse in Sonoma County, he found that his company had not made an appointment so there was no load ready. The warehouse crew had their hands full staging wine for the other trucks lined up or on the way. It would have taken a day or two to get his load together. The trucker couldn't sit and wait. That would cost him even more money. So he drove home, back to Minnesota—without any Barefoot—and a few shelves there were left empty.

That was just one kind of problem, when trucking companies didn't make appointments, or got dates wrong, or didn't tell drivers to make their own appointments. Another class of flubs came when truckers used consolidators—third-party companies that arranged pickups of other wine or goods for truckers who didn't take on a full load of Barefoot. But sometimes truckers waited for more than a day at another warehouse and missed their Barefoot appointment. Or they'd pick up Barefoot then wait at those loading spots—with the wine sitting in the truck—and be late with deliveries.

Most wineries shipping less than about 1 million cases a year couldn't afford their own truckers, so Barefoot, like many companies, was at the mercy of the American trucking system. Debbie explained they were also at the mercy of the American agricultural system, because when something was in season that pays better, like Brussels sprouts, truckers might not take any Barefoot loads.

"Seriously?" Michael said.

"Seriously," Debbie said. "Maybe Gary should get our distributors to stock up before Brussels sprouts come in."

What Debbie proposed was that she'd coordinate the trucks herself. She'd contact distributors, truckers, and warehouses and make sure every truck had orders, appointments, and full loads.

"I would never have thought of this in a million years," Michael told Debbie. "I knew we had trucking issues, but never really knew why."

But, Michael warned, she'd be in a macho environment with guys who talk like sailors.

"They may not show a lot of respect for women," Michael said, "especially a woman who tells them what to do."

"I can handle it," Debbie said.

That's what she always said. "I can handle it." She had been right about every job so far.

A couple weeks later, Michael was walking past Debbie's office and heard her crying. He walked in.

"What's wrong?" he said gently.

"Nothing," Debbie said.

"Those guys pushing your buttons?"

"I can handle it," she said.

"You can swap out anytime. We already know how good you are," Michael said.

"I'll turn them around," Debbie said.

As 2004 went by, Barefoot began seeing serious sales growth in states where it had been battling run-outs for years. It was directly connected to the changed warehouse and trucking practices. Debbie got praise from Barefoot, but Michael and Bonnie still worried the rough-edged trucking world was taking a toll on her.

In mid-December, when the world was dressing up for Christmas, Michael walked past Debbie's office and saw piles of candy, boxes, and flowers decorated with red bows.

"What's with the flowers and candy?" he said.

Debbie smiled a bit shyly. "They're from the truckers," she said.

There it was, an office full of appreciation from a bunch of tough guys who don't do that sort of thing.

Despite their graceless resistance at first, Debbie made their jobs easier. She cut down turnaround times. She called around to other wineries and consolidated loads. Sometimes, when a truck was just short of full, Debbie would call distributors, get them to order two more Barefoot pallets, and get the driver on the road loaded up.

She was saving them time, reducing their stops, keeping them full, and making them money. And she was making money for Barefoot. That's how you get a win-win.

"Weren't those the guys who were calling you names?" Michael said.

"Yeah," Debbie said, "they were. They got over it."

In summer 2000, Bonnie and Michael had Europeans in their tree. There were a dozen of them, grown men in slacks, hard street shoes, and dress shirts. They were sitting in a Pacific Live Oak with branches reaching every which way. Michael and Bonnie called it the Octopus Tree, and it was in a small wood on the lush, calming country property around their home a dozen miles west of Santa Rosa.

The men were from Latvia, Lithuania, Estonia—guys in the rough-and-tumble wine and spirits distribution business in Eastern Europe. While Michael and Bonnie took pictures, they were smiling and giggling like kids on a playground.

If this was a tad out of the ordinary for men who once lived behind the Iron Curtain, it was pretty typical for west Sonoma County and for Michael and Bonnie.

There were layers to Barefoot's company culture and the Barefoot Spirit. They weren't just what happened at the office, they were about life, every day and everywhere. And what they were doing with their new Eastern European friends was connected equally to how they did business and how they lived.

Years before they stumbled into the wine industry, Bonnie and Michael fell in love with wine country. That's why they felt so at home in Sonoma County, and that's why they believed many other people loved wine country the way they did.

They also saw that almost everyone, from industry pros to regular folks who bought Barefoot in supermarkets, felt some link— sometimes subtle, sometimes powerful—between pouring a glass of wine and sitting somewhere green and peaceful in wine country. Michael and Bonnie's stone terrace was a place like that. It looked over a grassy meadow surrounded by trees, with a horse pasture off to one side, and in the distance, a rolling hillside vineyard.

So they gave people wine country. They brought their employees to their home, and they brought vendors, distributors, buyers, and allies like Skip Brennan from Wisconsin and Kel Becker from Pinkie's in Texas to their home and to spots all around Sonoma County.

They also figured industry people didn't need another tour of tanks and barrels and presses. Besides, those were about the grist of making wine. Michael and Bonnie wanted to remind them of wine's magic.

Instead, they took people on tours of the Armstrong Redwoods, or on canoe trips down the Russian River, or out to the Sonoma Coast, to maybe Goat Rock Beach or the little town of Jenner.

They'd bring truffles from a candy shop in Sebastopol to the beach to pair with a glass of Barefoot Merlot. Or they'd go on a short hike in the redwoods, come to a clearing, and find a picnic table Randy had set up, with Barefoot Bubbly, strawberries, bagels and cream cheese.

And they'd have barbeques at the house, wander the nature trails on the four acres surrounding it, pick herbs and vegetables from their garden, sit under trees and drink sauvignon blanc, and live on that one day the way everyone believed you're supposed to live in wine country.

With Michael and Bonnie, that really was how they lived, though usually without the truffles. They hiked, went to the beach, and wandered their own property almost daily. They ate from their garden and cooked with their homegrown herbs. They were telling their business partners, here's what we do, come join us for dinner.

Over the years, they saw how that became another key to Barefoot's success, but this was just as much personal as it was a business choice. They believed there was a right way to conduct business, just like there was a right way to treat people. That's why they bought that house, because it was a place to share with friends, and because it was everything a home in wine country should be.

The house is a large, single-story replica of a 1903 farmhouse with a great room and 20-foot peaked ceilings at one end, and a window-lined kitchen at the other. It seems to be all glass—huge windows, French doors, skylights—with greenery everywhere, and filtered light coming from every angle. Even being inside feels like you're out under the trees.

In the winter, they would entertain in the great room under the beamed ceilings and surrounded by windows. They'd pour a glass of wine, sit by the big fireplace, and tell stories. Sometimes Jen Wall would join in, because folks liked chatting up the winemaker. Some visitors became instant friends, and they would just talk about life and listen to the rain.

Woven into those winter nights and summer barbeques was Barefoot's full spirit, including the culture of permission—in this case, permission to relax, even on a business trip. They had permission to embrace California wine country.

It took a little urging with the Eastern Europeans, but only a little. They showed up in business clothes. Bonnie and Michael made them lose the coats and ties, told them they could roll up their sleeves, and even take off their shoes and socks and dangle their feet in the pool.

The guys were thrilled. Barefoot was already their image of California. They ended up running across the small grassy meadow, trying to throw and catch Frisbees for the first time in their lives. They toasted to California with Barefoot Bubbly, and later in the afternoon, Bonnie suggested they all climb onto the Octopus Tree for a picture to remind them of their time in wine country.

"Does everybody in California live like this?" a distributor from Latvia asked after their Kodak moment.

"Everybody who makes Barefoot wine," Bonnie said.

By 2004, the Barefoot team really was rowing together, and they were rowing well. All of that work—finding an approachable image, learning a wildly complex industry, establishing the brand, spreading the word, placing the wine nationwide, marketing through worthy causes, building a company culture, servicing the range of customers and more—was paying off. And it was all made better by the hustle of the Barefoot staff.

In 2004, the winery that was started in a laundry room by two people with zero experience in the business, sold close to 600,000 cases—a huge amount for any winery, especially one with an absurdly small staff of 40.

Barefoot was named an Impact Magazine Hot Brand for sales in 2003 and 2004, a rare award given by Marvin Shanken, the editor of Impact, Market Watch, and the Wine Spectator, for both fast and sustained growth over four years. Barefoot had been booming since 2000.

But Barefoot was doing more than just selling well. The Barefoot Spirit was spreading through American wine. It was helping give its own industry permission to have fun.

Barefoot was no longer the only wine with a friendly label and playful approach. There were critters and art and punny names on bottles, there were brand names poking fun at Old World stuffiness (though no one messed with Chateau Lafite), and there were Australian wines with shrimp-on-the-barbie themes. A growing food-and-wine enthusiasm in America not only made high-end wines more popular than ever, it also convinced more people that wine should be amicable and cheerful and an everyday part of life.

Meanwhile, Barefoot wines were winning medals across the country, more than any wine in its class. It was recognized over and over by judges and wine pros, some of them the same people who, a few years earlier, were aghast to find a wine with a foot on the bottle.

Barefoot's spirit sent out ripples beyond the wine industry. It helped hundreds of worthy causes nationwide, large non-profits and local groups that worked on the environment, children's issues, the arts, AIDS, education, civil rights, health care and more.

And it had become part of the culture. The foot, the slightly-tilted, surrealistic impression of Bonnie's right foot, defined the brand, inspired California dreaming, drew late-night phone calls, became a beacon to fans, and was by then one of the most recognizable wine labels in the country.

Plus, American business was recognizing Barefoot's style and success, too. Michael and Bonnie, once outsiders stumbling around the wine world, became welcomed friends in the industry and were asked regularly for advice and business wisdom.

Universities around the country did case studies of Barefoot's pioneering success as a completely outsourced winery—with no bricks and mortar, just rented space and contractors—and they studied its entrepreneurial ingenuity and grit.

The University of California, Davis—ground zero for American wine education—had Michael teach seminars that helped enology and viticulture students learn that the industry was far more complicated than simply growing and crushing grapes. (He told them, "Don't be the winemaker from the bankrupt winery—they'll blame you.")

"After 19 years," Bonnie said, "we're an overnight success."

But there was still one more act to come—and it was only 15 years late.

CONVERSATIONS WITH BONNIE AND MICHAEL

Rick: *By the millennium, doesn't the story change in a way? You were a successful company by then.*

Michael: We were becoming polished. The rough edges got knocked off by the bricks.

Bonnie: We really were a well-oiled machine. Not just Michael and Bonnie—the entire team. We were held together by our compensation system, the acknowledgment, the constant reinforcement, and all the fundamental good business practices that had kept us alive and created our culture. They all had a cumulative effect on our success.

Michael: We got good at the business of hiring. Personnel problems disappeared. Turnover disappeared. There was an air of excitement and enthusiasm. It was fun to come to work. We realized how much we had learned, and began to apply it to everyday business.

Rick: *You talked about being lucky that you were pushed so hard through your entire first decade just to survive. How did that affect the company's success later?*

Michael: If somebody had just taught us how the system worked, we wouldn't have survived because we wouldn't have tried so hard to learn about every tiny thing. Everything we learned, we learned on the street. Our business practices were fundamental good business practices, but they were also totally out of the box. We learned the hard way what worked and what didn't.

Bonnie: They were not the kind of things taught in classrooms. None of the college grads we hired brought that in.

We focused on customer service, but it wasn't the traditional definition. We saw everybody we dealt with as customers and everything we did as providing good service to them.

Michael: We developed the concept of the Barefooter—a person who represents the winery in the market who was specifically there to engage in Worthy Cause Marketing, merchandising, and supporting the distributor.

Bonnie: Most other wineries didn't even have someone who did that. They'd have winery ambassadors who'd pour and give talks. That's what a lot of our early hires wanted to be, but we needed people to do the nitty-gritty work and give customer service.

Rick: *The No Game sounds so sane. What was the effect in the company?*

Bonnie: It took the frustration out of situations. Challenges can be very tiring . . .

Michael: . . . and annoying. The thing about the Barefoot Spirit is, there was this air of fun that came with making games out of things, even when they're very serious.

Bonnie: And the lesson is, you keep looking for an answer. Sometimes you ask the question differently. Sometimes you say, oh, look, a puppy.

Michael: Bonnie actually came up with the average number of "nos" before we got a "yes."

Bonnie: It was seven.

Rick: *You said it helped the company that you saw yourselves as mentors. How did that work?*

Bonnie: We hired smart, creative, energetic people, then we encouraged them to do their best. We expected it from them so they expected it from themselves.

Michael: Bonnie and I never had kids, but we appreciated the fact that folks always look for validation from an authority figure, whether it's a parent or a boss. They want to know that they're doing the right thing.

Without that, people get frustrated. They're banging around in the dark. But once they know they're doing the right thing, it builds their confidence. That's good for them, and it's good for sales and productivity. The biggest part of mentoring is coaching your people in a way that says, look, you did it right, I knew you could do it.

Rick: *How much did it help that you entertained so many people, including your staff, at your home?*

Michael: We both moved to the wine country independently, but we didn't come for the wine, we came for the wine country life-style. We knew it was a tremendous selling point. We also knew we could make people feel comfortable and feel that they belonged here. That comfort made them want to do business with us.

Bonnie: But when we had visitors, even when we had our own staff over, it was all for fun. We didn't conduct business. We got to know people.

Michael: The best compliment we could get was when people told us they felt relaxed. That's why we steered them away from the industrial part of the industry. And people said, it's so nice not to stare at more tanks and barrels.

Bonnie: Of course, we didn't have any so we didn't have that option.

Rick: *When you got that call from Randy about the Mono Lake internship, what was your first reaction?*

Bonnie: We were sick. Randy's quitting? What are we going to do?

Michael: There goes all the fun.

Bonnie: He's The Barefoot Guy, he can't go.

Michael: Part of me is going, "Our national sales manager, a guy we love, is quitting to count birds? Really?"

Bonnie: Then we thought about it and we realized this was something he really wanted to do. And Randy had been working for us for more than 10 years. His job was extremely stressful because he gave so much of himself to each customer all over the country. He deserved a sabbatical.

Michael: When we asked him to put Barefoot into all the stores there and do a tasting, I also said, "I want you to think about me sitting in front of the computer, grinding out my email, while you're in one of the most beautiful places on Earth." A little guilt never hurts.

Chapter Ten

The Spirit Lives On

The weather turned warm for a November Sunday, into the low 80s, which was both a reminder of why so many people love California and an inconvenience for Michael and Bonnie.

They were hosting a fundraiser, and "friendraiser," at their home in west Sonoma County. This was 2010, and they were collecting money and supporters for a group named LandPaths and a concept called People Powered Parks.

California was dealing with another budget crisis, and parks up and down the state were among the casualties. LandPaths, a non-profit with a long history of working for Sonoma County parks and open space, was pushing one solution that could be spread statewide: getting park users—folks who hiked, biked, rode horses, and camped in the parks—involved in their upkeep, operation, and management. It was channeling volunteer muscle to replace lost public money, and LandPaths had been doing it well for ten years.

Michael and Bonnie, brand builders as always, came up with the name People Powered Parks and they were helping Land-Paths with marketing, branding, and financial sustainability. This day, they gathered more than 120 people at their home. Most were Sonoma County movers and shakers, including state and federal legislators and city and county officials.

The thing was, the bash had started out to be an indoor party. Then the weather turned too darn perfect to stay inside. So about 90 minutes before the guests were going to show, Michael, Bonnie, some LandPaths volunteers, and their caterer—Park Avenue Catering, which is owned by their friend Bruce Riezenman—were hustling to set up tables, chairs and decorations; reconfiguring the drink stations and food line; and generally doing a complete U-turn on the logistics of the afternoon and evening.

Michael was in full Michael mode, moving chairs about twice as fast as the volunteers, directing table locations, joking and pointing out unfinished tasks to anyone who crossed his path. Bonnie was in full Bonnie mode, working out details with the catering crew, moving flowers, warmly greeting early arriving friends—then sending them out to help.

By early evening, after hikes around the property, an elegant outdoor meal, and a toast with, of course, Barefoot Bubbly, the group gathered in the great room and Michael and Bonnie talked to LandPaths' friends.

"People want to know what they can do to save parks," Bonnie told the group. "This is an answer."

"LandPaths can be a model for the whole country," Michael said. "It's a way we can become engaged owners of the parks and wild places we all love."

This could have been an event backed by Barefoot. It could have been one of the hundreds of organizations Michael and

Bonnie had supported in their nearly two decades of connecting Barefoot Cellars to worthy causes and ideas.

That the wine company was not involved didn't much matter. Bonnie and Michael were still at it. They still had their enduring love for mountains, beaches and parks, and they still used their business tools and their never-say-die energy to motivate, organize, and strengthen groups they cared about. If Bonnie and Michael no longer owned Barefoot Wine, they still had every ounce of the Barefoot Spirit.

In January 2004, Barefoot got its first Hot Brand award—for sales in 2003—and it was clear within a few months that their 2004 sales would get them another in 2005. By June, they knew they'd sell close to 600,000 cases that year. The Hot Brand awards go to wine companies with fast and sustained growth, and they're given by Impact Magazine and the company that also owns Market Watch and the Wine Spectator. They are watched by the wine industry.

What the industry saw in Barefoot was a popular and consistent wine, an original approach that had carved out a distinct place in the market, an efficient and resourceful organization, and a brand that resonated around the country.

Industry folks who paid attention saw something else, too. Although Barefoot had spread across America, it wasn't spread all that thoroughly. Barefoot sold well wherever it was available, but it was available in only 18 percent of the U.S. market. It was selling nearly 600,000 cases but still wasn't in stores in more than four-fifths of the country. That screamed out a few messages, but the loudest was this: If people could buy Barefoot, they would.

Barefoot's success was an important chapter in American wine. It really did bring beer drinkers to wine, as Michael and

Bonnie had talked about years earlier, and it helped convince wine drinkers and the industry that wine could be fun and less than daunting. By the mid-2000s, there were still plenty of wineries with sophisticated tones to their marketing, but there were also lots of wineries—some of them making acclaimed, high-end wines—that had become as approachable and playful as Barefoot.

Barefoot's Worthy Cause Marketing also had a powerful legacy even beyond the support for all that charitable work. It showed wine companies and American business that you really can, as the saying goes, do well by doing good. Or, as Michael said, Barefoot stood as an example that you could play by the Golden Rule and still be profitable.

It was also an example of how companies can use all their tools to build their brand, because Worthy Cause Marketing was a cornerstone of Barefoot's success. They had, as Randy Arnold promised, used their wine to spread their brand and to build enduring relationships. By 2004, Barefoot had devoted fans in hundreds of organizations around the U.S. because of its early and unwavering support for them, starting with the Surfrider Foundation and a range of LGBT groups.

Even by 2004, Worthy Cause Marketing was Barefoot's *only* marketing. The wine might show up in ads when supermarkets ran specials, but those came from the stores. Here was a wine selling more than a half million cases without ever buying advertising.

That's what the industry saw in 2004—the numbers, the structure, the approach, the distinctive marketing, and that foot. And that's why it was time for one more step in the story of Bonnie and Michael and Barefoot Cellars.

It didn't take long after that Hot Brand attention for Michael and Bonnie to get an offer. It wasn't exactly a surprise. One of the very large wine companies asked about buying Barefoot.

For any entrepreneur, the term "acquisition" is never far from the business discussion. That was always true, but never more than into the 21st century. The era of venture capitalists rushing to invest in start-ups had ended. So had the days of frenzied initial public stock offerings. Getting acquired almost has to be the final target for many small and mid-sized companies in a grow-or-die business environment.

Michael and Bonnie had been in grow-or-die mode for most of their 19 years. With all their success, their national distribution, and their now-mainstream brand, Barefoot's survival may have been a bit less dicey, but it was getting harder than ever to grow.

By 2004, the wine industry was, in a way, shrinking. More precisely, it was consolidating. Big wine companies were buying smaller wineries, and big distributors were buying little ones. Once consolidation reaches a critical mass in any industry, that industry's biggest players get into something of a race to buy the smaller companies.

In the wine industry, with the biggest companies commanding increasingly large pieces of the market, their growing muscle was making it harder for everyone else to keep their places on the shelves, let alone grow. The wine business had become a game of musical chairs, and some companies were losing their seats. Barefoot wasn't so large that it didn't have to scramble for chairs like almost everyone else.

Even at nearly 600,000 cases, Barefoot was only in the top 25 in size nationally, and in many ways, that was where they were most vulnerable. That was yet another surprise for Michael and Bonnie—their very size could work against them.

They had hit a new level, and a new set of complications, in dealing with chain stores. On the one hand, Barefoot was popular and the chains wanted it in more stores and territories. That meant, of course, if Barefoot was going to continue the hands-on customer service that had built the brand, they needed to hire yet more Barefooters and take on new costs. That was the familiar challenge.

But now there was something else. Barefoot was big, but it wasn't mega-big. Chain buyers knew their accounts were vital to the wine company at that stage, and the buyers demanded larger and larger discounts.

So after all their growth and accomplishment, Barefoot was nearly back to Bonnie's description of their business model—they were losing money on each case but making it up in volume. "All this success is killing us," she told Michael after they priced out one chain expansion.

That was the business backdrop for Barefoot in 2004—great sales, changing industry, the tightrope continued. Michael and Bonnie were starting to see that their time running Barefoot could be ending. They might need to find a company with a larger reach, with more resources to help Barefoot grow in the reconfigured wine industry, and with a commitment to being stewards of everything Barefoot had become. The offers to buy the company were also set against that.

Michael and Bonnie saw one part of this coming. They had learned that 500,000 cases a year was a magic number in the wine business. That's when other companies start looking at you, nosing around, talking "hypothetically" about your interest in getting acquired.

As early as fall 2003, when they saw they were headed for 500,000 sales and a Hot Brand award, they had a good sense where it would lead, in part because Michael had some experience with acquisitions. Back in 1985, when he knew nothing about wine, his business consulting ranged into that field. (These days, he teaches college seminars about acquisitions and consults on the subject.)

So Bonnie and Michael talked to their own key people, and worked out "stay bonuses" for them, which were sizeable payouts if Barefoot actually was sold—but they had to still be working at Barefoot the day a sale went through. It was "must be present to win," as Michael called it.

The importance of making those deals would become clear within months. By mid-2004, Michael and Bonnie had gotten a couple more inquiries from other wine companies. One of them caused some problems.

The first companies came to Michael and Bonnie straight up and asked to chat about the future, or possible partnerships, or where they envisioned Barefoot heading. But one very large company tried to feel them out with a ham-handed, much-less-productive move: It started a rumor that it might buy Barefoot, just to see the reaction.

Michael and Bonnie heard about it through their big chain buyers, which was not good news. One buyer asked if he should discontinue Barefoot until things settled. Another hinted he might need a price cut if Barefoot wanted to avoid getting discontinued before a sale.

Barefoot's own people heard the talk, and one Barefooter asked Michael if he should quit and start looking for a new job.

That is the danger surrounding the sale of any business, and why talking about a potential acquisition—or recklessly starting rumors about a sale that doesn't exist—is a huge, often irreparable mistake. (There were plenty of wine industry examples in the mid-2000s, when some high-profile acquisitions dissolved after winery owners let the word out.)

For starters, employees parade to the personnel office to quit. They worry they won't survive the ownership change and want to be first to apply for whatever jobs are out there in the industry. You lose good people and you lose their relationships with vendors, buyers, and customers.

Plus, retail buyers know that a company is only as good as its accounts. So they demand deep discounts because they know the winery's sale price will plummet if it loses key stores and placements.

Michael needed to kill the rumors. He called the big wine company and connected with a top executive. He was blunt about it. "Stop spreading rumors about us," Michael said. "You're hurting the Barefoot brand."

The exec was all sweetness. He said he didn't know how Michael ever got the impression his company was telling people it might buy Barefoot.

"We wouldn't start a rumor like that," the executive said. "But, you know, as long as we're on the subject and I have you on the phone, what do you think about the idea?"

That convinced Michael he was right about them planting the rumor to hear Barefoot's response. He wanted to say, "We wouldn't sell to anyone as dumb as you guys." Instead he took a breath. Never burn a bridge. Michael gave a polite, "I don't think we're going to be selling Barefoot."

His next call was to his old friend Vic Motto. "I think we're going to end up selling Barefoot," he told Vic.

Vic Motto is a founding partner of Global Wine Partners and one of the top mergers and acquisition people in the wine business. He had known Michael and Bonnie for years, and he understood Barefoot. He watched it grow, saw it operate, knew its value.

And he'd heard Michael speak about the wine business at industry seminars, including on panels that Vic organized. (One panel also included Don Brown, who continued his gruff, yet oddly affectionate, relationship with Michael. "I hate to admit I'm agreeing with Houlihan on this one," Brown said a couple times during the session.)

Michael and Bonnie told Vic it might be time to hand off the baton to a company that could grow Barefoot to a size that would help it survive with its spirit intact.

And they said Barefoot would sell nearly 600,000 cases that year. They told him about the various inquiries and the bone-headed rumor. Vic was a dialed-in guy. He'd heard the rumor.

"We're not sure what's the best path right now," Michael told Vic. "But we are sure we need representation. We don't want the Barefoot brand to get destroyed."

Vic's sense of the situation was the same as Michael and Bonnie's. He agreed that a leap in growth would help Barefoot navigate the churning wine industry. He said their size, success, and uniqueness made Barefoot an inviting acquisition target. And he said once the industry saw Barefoot as a possible acquisition, more talk would circulate, creating more operational difficulties for the company.

"You need to get out in front of this," Vic told them.

His advice was, be prepared. He said put Barefoot's affairs in order. (That wasn't hard. Years of writing down policies and procedures and of documenting every move kept them in good shape.) He said do all the due diligence a buyer might want: Answer questions, corral trademarks, and supply the audits, costs, receivables, projections, and everything else that would paint a detailed financial picture. Make it easy if the right buyer gets interested.

Vic also told Michael and Bonnie to think about a profile of that right buyer.

This wasn't hard, either. They had thought about this. They came back and told Vic they wanted a buyer that didn't just swallow wineries but, instead, looked after a brand's uniqueness. They wanted a family-owned company that could make plans and stick with them, not a publicly traded one controlled by stockholders seeking quick returns. And they wanted someone adept at all the unromantic-but-crucial demands of the wine business and someone committed to the same staunch customer service up and down the line that was a hallmark of Barefoot.

Michael and Bonnie didn't say it, but they knew they were describing one preferred buyer. It was the wine company they had watched, and learned from, and tried to imitate. They were describing Gallo.

They asked Vic for something else that had nothing to do with the process or financials of a sale: They wanted Barefoot to keep being, well, Barefoot.

They wanted it to stay fun, approachable and inclusive, and to keep being California in a bottle. And most of all, they didn't want to abandon all those non-profits and worthy causes that had grown up with Barefoot.

"This is very important to us," Michael said. "We want to keep the Barefoot Spirit alive."

Vic told them he would begin to feel out potential buyers without naming Barefoot as his client. They would talk in numbers and generalities until near the end. He said he could not give them a timetable. The process could take months, it could take years. But if a buyer got interested enough to make a real offer, the end game would happen very fast.

"Be ready," Vic told them.

Vic was right about things happening fast. He had carefully tested the waters, then began working with the one buyer that fit Michael and Bonnie's profile, and that fit the brand. More quickly than Michael and Bonnie expected, Vic brought them a proposal. Gallo was going to make an offer.

On January 26, 2005, Bonnie and Michael told their board— Doug McCorkle and Jennifer Wall. That evening, they invited Randy over for dinner.

Randy ate dinner at Michael and Bonnie's house a lot. He wasn't just a key employee or even a good friend. By then, he was family. And Randy could tell something was different this time. There was an energy in the air, and Michael and Bonnie were bouncing around like excited kids, yet they seemed slightly off, maybe nervous, too.

They were all standing in the big, airy kitchen with the large island in the middle. Bonnie was cutting vegetables on a counter near the stove. Michael was putting together place settings on the island. They were making small talk but Randy figured he'd help them get to whatever it was that had made this evening so electric.

"So what's up?" he said.

Bonnie came over to him. Michael was on the far side of the island.

"We have some really exciting news to share with you," she said. "There's good news in it for you, too."

She paused for a bit.

"Sooo. . .?" Randy said.

Bonnie looked right at Randy.

"We've sold the brand," she said. "The largest family-owned winery in the world bought it."

Everyone was still for a moment. The room was almost kinetic. Randy's mouth dropped open.

If any person understood what this sale meant, in all its shades, it was Randy Arnold. He'd seen Barefoot when it was a newbie Northern California brand. He'd watched Bonnie juggle money and income and payments to keep the company alive. He'd spent nights on airplanes with Michael on the way to sales calls, or passed Michael in the skies miles above America when they were flying to different cities. He knew Michael and Bonnie had sunk nearly two decades of dedication and scrambling and sweat into Barefoot, and he knew their far-from-flush financial situation after all that. He saw them plow every cent they made back into the company, investing in growth because the only way to keep Barefoot healthy was to grow. He saw their tireless efforts to get big, to be stable, to become a player on the national scene and, he understood, to maybe attract the right buyer. He knew how long it had been, how hard they worked and what little they had to show for it. And because he was Randy, at that moment he was hardly thinking about what this meant for him. He only saw the long, long, finally triumphant, road to this moment.

So he just stood for a second. Then he reached out and hugged Bonnie, and he nearly fell into her arms and sobbed.

"I'm so happy for you both," he said clasping Bonnie like a buoy in the ocean. Bonnie started crying. Michael started crying, then came around the island and joined the hug. The three of them stood there in the kitchen, hugging and crying and giggling and crying again.

"You really, truly deserve this," Randy said.

When they stopped clutching each other, Michael told Randy that Gallo was going to keep the Barefoot Spirit alive, and that he wasn't supposed to say anything because nothing was certain, but Randy shouldn't worry about his job.

"You have a place in the next chapter of Barefoot," Michael said. "And we're going to take care of you, too."

"And you will always be our great, great friend," Bonnie said.

"Well, I knew that," Randy said.

The next day, they told their office staff.

"The brand has been bought by the Gallo family," Michael said. "They are committed to maintaining the Barefoot quality and spirit. They told us they were interested in the staff as well." Then Michael called each Barefoot salesperson.

On Friday, January 28, the news hit the papers. The Gallo family bought Barefoot Cellars.

Selling your company is a strange thing. It's a triumph, a business success of the top order, a huge validation of your work and ideas. There is relief from crossing a finish line and joy for the enormous accomplishment. In a way, for Michael and Bonnie, selling Barefoot was like raising a child, then sending a young adult out into the world with all the tools to succeed.

But it's also a loss. It's not your company anymore. They aren't your people either—a number of those people went on to stay with Barefoot, including Randy, Jennifer Wall, Eric Dorton, Phil Aiello, and Debbie Johnson (by then, Debbie Sherman). And, of course, your life changes.

For Michael and Bonnie, the speed of the change added to the impact. They lived with this project and this belief for two decades, back even before that thunderbolt of a moment when the foot—that now iconic, ubiquitous, happy symbol of the Barefoot Spirit—came tumbling into reality. Two decades. Then in a burst of tense action, the company was no longer theirs. It wasn't Michael and Bonnie and Barefoot as one reflexive thought. Now, it was Barefoot, standing solid with so much new potential, but it was just Barefoot.

When they were starting, when they were plotting with Mark Lyon, brainstorming a wine style for regular people, and hunkering down in a farmhouse laundry room, they had hoped maybe they could sell their little start-up in four years, give or take. When they told Mark that night after dinner they'd probably need four years, they thought they were guessing long, just to be safe. They were off by only a wee bit. It turned out, Bonnie said, "We had a get rich slow scheme."

They had stopped thinking about selling soon after they started, because they were too busy thinking about not failing. And now, Michael and Bonnie were exiting off the main highway of their lives since 1985. They were born businesspeople and this business had been all consuming. Barefoot was their existence. The Barefoot Spirit was who they were.

That's the other odd part about selling a company. If you invest in it, really give yourself to it, you give it a soul. That soul stays with you. The Barefoot Spirit never stopped being who they were.

But after the sale, Bonnie and Michael were in something of a daze. Almost a year earlier, they had planned a trip to Chile in February to visit some old friends and to celebrate Michael's birthday. The timing, it turned out, helped a lot.

Chile had a resonance for them. Beside its mountains and beautiful wine country, it was where they had gone a decade earlier when Jen helped save Barefoot from the grape shortage. They had built enduring friendships there through the years, and it was a good place for Michael and Bonnie to celebrate, to get their bearings, and maybe to cry a little.

They hiked in the Andes, they explored small towns, they tasted wine, and they sat with friends. Hugo Casanova, the owner of Hugo Casanova Wines, organized what amounted to a three-day party around Michael's birthday at his estate and two other wineries that also had long relationships with Michael and Bonnie and Barefoot—Viña Cremaschi Furlotti and Gillmore Winery and Vineyards.

It was approaching evening when Bonnie and Michael drove up the smooth dirt road to the third winery, the Gillmore estate in the Maule Valley. The light was turning the gold of a late Chilean summer day, and the tall, brick-and-earth-colored winery looked like a big lodge with trees behind it and a pair of three-story wine barrels sitting out front.

As their car got close, they saw winery owner Francisco Gillmore standing out in front of a group of people. All of them were holding wine glasses—and all of them were barefoot. When they got out, Francisco handed Bonnie and Michael their own glasses of wine. That's when everyone in the crowd took off their outer shirts or turned around to show they were all wearing Barefoot T-shirts.

Michael and Bonnie looked at each other, both with eyes a little moist.

"That," Bonnie said with a huge smile, "is the Barefoot Spirit."

After the sale, Michael and Bonnie stayed in the wine industry, working as consultants, teaching brand building and Worthy Cause Marketing, trying to help people avoid all those surprise daily bricks, and passing on the experience and lessons they'd learned the hard way about sales, company culture, motivating people and more. Their expertise in brand building has kept them in demand to a range of businesses and entrepreneurs outside the wine world, too.

They also stayed friends with many of the people who were part of the Barefoot adventure, particularly Randy, who is still a regular guest at their home, and they became proud friends with the man Michael so admired, Joe Gallo.

Without an ever-changing wine company and its daily demands strapped on their backs, they got to travel more, find more wild places, explore and hike—sometimes with their cats. One place that called to them, as it always has, is the Hawaiian island of Kauai.

Among the great charms of Kauai is that there are still so many isolated trails, beaches, and pieces of countryside, places of quiet beauty where you might see no one else for hours. One of Bonnie and Michael's favorites is Kauapea Beach on the north side of the island. It's actually a series of three beaches separated by rocks. All are narrow arches of sand with wooded cliffs surrounding them and with rocks at their ends. The beaches catch some big waves around storms, but when the Pacific is calm, the water just offshore is a bright explosion of tropical blues and greens.

It's also known as Secret Beach, in part because its steep and semi-rough trails keep most people away. On a recent trip to Kauai, that's where Michael and Bonnie were headed.

It was off-season and just after a storm. As they made their way over the craggy trail toward Beach Three—the most remote of the trio—Bonnie was getting excited about finding seashells. People who love beaches almost can't help themselves when it comes to seashells.

This was the first day of their vacation, and the weather was wonderful—mild, sunny, just enough of a breeze. They both had backpacks with lotion, water, towels, and books. They were ready for some serious do-nothing time. Michael was already in a slow-moving vacation gear on the hike toward their pristine beach. When they got to Beach Three, they were alone. This was perfect. Except for one thing.

There was garbage washed up from the storm and littering the sand the length of the 200-yard-long beach. There were juice cartons, candy wrappers, soap containers, soda cans, and a seeming endless number of plastic water bottles. Beach Three looked like an international dumpsite. The labels were in Chinese, English, German, Korean. Bonnie and Michael assumed they were looking at what happens when a cruise ship drops its garbage into the sea.

The garbage had clumped thickest near the cliffs. The beach was about 25 yards wide, so Michael, still in vacation gear, headed toward the water looking for a relatively clean spot to roll out the towels.

"How about over here?" he said to Bonnie.

She just looked at him. "We aren't laying out on a beach this dirty," she said.

"OK," Michael said, "let's find another beach."

Bonnie stood there. Then she put down her backpack and started walking toward the garbage.

"We're not leaving," she said. "We're going to clean this beach."

"Us?" Michael said.

"We're the only ones here," Bonnie said. "Who else is going to do it?"

Michael had seen Bonnie like this more than a few times. He didn't want to admit she was right. He was on vacation. He kept trying excuses.

"It will only take half as long if you help."

"When we come back here, it'll just be dirty again," he said.

"Maybe if people see a clean beach, they won't pollute it," she said.

"What are we going to put it in? We didn't bring any bags."

Bonnie walked a few steps and picked up a plastic bag that had washed ashore.

"Where there's garbage," she said, "there are bags."

Michael was running out of steam. He knew he sounded like a schoolboy who didn't want recess to end.

"But we're on vacation," he said. "It's going to take you all day."

By then, Bonnie had started picking up junk and stuffing it into the plastic bag.

"It'll only take half as long," she said over her shoulder, "if you help."

Michael watched her mowing through the garbage for a moment. By then, he was shaking his head and smiling. He bent down, picked up another stray plastic bag, and hustled after her.

CONVERSATIONS WITH BONNIE AND MICHAEL

Rick: *You have become pretty expert about how to build a brand. How else has the journey with Barefoot changed you?*

Bonnie: It's like biting from the apple of knowledge. There's no going back. You can't be ignorant about things anymore. We learned to treat people like you're standing beside them, to look at things through their eyes. You're not across the table trying to sell them, you're with them, helping them deal with their situation.

Once you stand beside them, it's what's you do with everyone, even if it's not business. You just do.

Michael: I became more humble. I realized I didn't know it all. At the start, I didn't know much. We learned to take the advice of people who knew better. To this day, that's how I deal with problems.

Sales is a humbling experience. I started off being someone who argued a case to convince the other person to do something. I tried to sell people on the merits—the price, the value, the medals. But they didn't care about that stuff. They wanted to know, are you interested in my business? Will you help me solve my problems? Will I ever see you again?

I also learned a lot about how to talk to people by listening to the sages, the guys who've done it before and for a long time.

Bonnie: We both realized you can help your community and all those worthy causes you care about, even if you don't have money.

Michael: That's the brand building we talk about. A lot of people have come to us over the years for help, including non-profits. We know we can help them. It's a good feeling.

Rick: *Barefoot started off as something new inside the wine world. But in the end, it actually helped change the wine world. Why did it resonate?*

Michael: We demonstrated financial success. And we demonstrated real, sustained growth. Everyone respects that. We earned awards that had been reserved for more staid wines. If they didn't respect us, they had to respect the awards.

That success gave the wine industry permission to have fun with wine and to popularize wine. They learned they could sell more wine doing that.

Bonnie: Our biggest frustration was that we knew people liked our wine and the label. At tastings, people would use the word "love" so often. They'd say, "I love the foot." But the retail buyers didn't believe it.

Michael: People wanted it, but the gatekeepers wouldn't give it to them. Finally, when they saw our success and, then, the Hot Brand Awards, they really saw what we were doing was working.

Bonnie: Randy says some people in the industry treat you in direct proportion to the retail price of your wine. So we had a lot to prove to some of them.

Rick: *You were also "accused" of using beer marketing. You must have found that funny, since that was exactly your model, right?*

Michael: Beer companies never really talked about how the beer was made. They told people, "You'll have fun with our product."

Bonnie: Well, they did talk about how it's made in a general way. They said, it's the water. But that was straightforward and clear.

Michael: And they had a cartoon bear saying it.

Bonnie: The bear was having fun, too. He went to a lot of parties.

Michael: The funny thing is that now a lot of wineries have fun, and a lot of beer companies are more serious.

Bonnie: I still like the bear.

Rick: *Your ideas and approach were original, and you used a lot of innovative techniques. What else did you do that was different?*

Bonnie: We had what we called Sell Cases. They were a Fuller Brush kind of case that our people carried into stores, and when you opened them up, they unfolded and showed buyers everything they wanted to see in 30 seconds. Really, we could do it in 10 seconds if we needed to.

Michael: There were wines lined up, all the medals, accolades from wine writers, pictures of stacks, point-of-sale materials, and they were this burst of color. We were confronted by buyer after buyer who said, "I don't have time for you." So we would say, "You have ten seconds?" Then we'd open the case. People were kicking me out the door and I opened it.

Bonnie: A lot of retail buyers got curious. They'd say, "I don't have time for you, wait, what's in the box?" We got a higher percentage of placements with the Sell Case than any other method.

Rick: *And your tables at tastings were different, right?*

Michael: They were a lot different. Besides all the color and playfulness, they were bar height.

Bonnie: We never knew why everyone else didn't do this. Everyone always had regular low tables. Ours were at the height you'd find in a bar. They made people more comfortable tasting wine.

Michael: The wines were at eye level. Tasters didn't have to look down at the wine, then back at our faces to talk with us. They were friendlier. People would lean an arm on the table like they were talking to their bartender. What we did was, we'd bring these four tubes and put them on the table legs to jack it up to the right height. It was easy.

Bonnie: They were good for another reason. No one had to reach for their wines looking below the belt of the person pouring it. They were staring at a smiling face instead.

Rick: *You ran into a lot of Catch 22s, like the way chains and distributors each wouldn't take you on until the other one took you first. What were some others?*

Bonnie: Stores would say, it needs to cost them less. Then when we dropped the price, they'd say, this can't be any good, it's too cheap.

Michael: Small and mid-size buyers wouldn't take us because they said we weren't established enough. Then when we got established, they said, "Oh, we don't support the big guys."

Bonnie: How about this one? Our employees could qualify for a mortgage because they had good jobs working for us, but the same banks would tell us, you can't qualify for a loan because you're self-employed.

Michael: That killed us. We finally had to make ourselves employees of our own company. We incorporated so we could buy a house.

Bonnie: Our accountant said if we incorporated, we were going to give back half our profits in taxes, and we said, we don't have any profits. He said, then incorporate.

Rick: *Do you still get the same feeling when you see a bottle of Barefoot in a store?*

Michael: We do. We feel the brand and the Barefoot Spirit is alive with the new owners. The spirit survived the acquisition. We didn't just sell a brand, we sold a movement and it's still going on.

Rick: *You both have a genuine attachment to that foot, the Barefoot, that seems to be something more than just having lived with it at the center of your life for two decades. What is it?*

Bonnie: For us, the Barefoot is the perfect symbol. It seems so innocent and human.

Michael: When you see a footprint on the beach, you don't know if it was made by a man or a woman, or someone who is gay or straight or black or white. You can't tell religion. It doesn't matter. It's just the impression a human makes when they walk on the earth. That's what matters. We're all on the beach together.

Michael Houlihan

Michael Houlihan is the co-founder of Barefoot Cellars along with partner Bonnie Harvey. Though his business card read "Head Stomper," he officially served as president and CEO for 19 years. Starting with no money and no knowledge of the wine industry, he and Bonnie used out-of-the-box thinking coupled with solid business principles to build a leading national brand. They relied on "Worthy Cause Marketing" instead of conventional advertising to grow a loyal following and promote their favorite causes.

Barefoot Wines went on to win the industry's top sales awards. They were selling well over a half a million cases annually when the E. & J. Gallo family purchased the brand in 2005. Since then, Michael has been a valued advisor to large and small corporations and start-ups, improving their profitability, culture, and brand with real world experience. Sales, marketing, and performance-based compensation are his sweet spots. He also donates professional time to non-profits to help them improve their image, and achieve financial sustainability.

Michael is a funny, informative, and inspiring speaker who delivers keynotes for conventions, corporations and national conferences. (Audiences love the quirky Barefoot stories he weaves in with how-to advice.) He is a seminar and webinar leader, guest lecturer at business and entrepreneurial schools, active blogger, and contributor to a variety of publications.

Bonnie Harvey

Bonnie Harvey is the co-founder of Barefoot Cellars, where she was Vice President for 19 years. While Michael's role was "big picture visionary," Bonnie translated his ideas into workable processes and displayed a genius for managing the millions of details that come with a start-up. She proved to possess a rare combination of creativity and business savvy that served Barefoot well.

In the early days, Bonnie was responsible for bottling oversight, supply inventory and label design—in fact, the famous footprint is actually hers! Later, she focused on overview and direction of the business, company goals, and board matters. She managed all financial aspects of the business, oversaw legal relations and compliance, and edited countless press materials, presentations, official manuals and other documents.

Bonnie also donates professional time to non-profits to help them improve their image, increase donations, and achieve financial sustainability. With Michael, she coauthors weekly business blogs at *www.thebarefootspirit.com* and *www.thebrandauthority.net*, and consults with several clients.

Bonnie has a passion for helping young entrepreneurs choose the right path. With her varied "hard-knocks" experience, she offers practical solutions for all aspects of starting a business. She loves showing others how to avoid painful and costly mistakes, and directing them toward profitability.

Get more of

Have Michael and Bonnie speak to your group or company

Sign up for webinars and seminars

Read weekly blogs on business, entrepreneurship, and branding

Sign up for future publications

www.barefootwinefounders.com
www.thebrandauthority.net